GOOSE FEVER

GOOSE FEVER

The Diaries of an
Amateur Wildfowler

1933 — 1975

By

DOUGLAS McDOUGALL

I.S.B.M.O. 903731.00.2

First Printed September 1972

2nd Impression February 1973

3rd Impression (Enlarged) July 1975

Published by Wildfowl Publications, Chestnut House, Old Buckenham, Norfolk

Printed by Creaseys Ltd., Beccles, Suffolk.

"There is a peculiar aura that surrounds in my mind anything and everything to do with wild geese. That I am not alone in this strange madness, I am sure; indeed, it is a catching complaint, and I hardly know any who have been able to resist its ravages, when once they have been exposed to infection".

Peter Scott.
("Morning Flight")

ACKNOWLEDGMENTS

I am grateful to Peter Scott for agreeing to my use of some words of his as my "introductory text", and to his publishers, the Hamlyn Publishing Group Ltd., for permission to reprint this quotation which is taken from "Morning Flight".

I am similarly indebted to "BB" for allowing me to include several extracts from his own writings. These cover three of our early expeditions together, of which I unfortunately kept no diary records myself. Chapter 6 is largely taken from "Dark Estuary", and the rest of this Chapter, together with Chapters 3 and 4, is taken from articles that appeared in "The Field", the Editor of which has kindly given me permission to reprint. This permission also covers several of my own contributions to "The Field" — material in Chapters 13 and 23, and the letter on the hanging of game in Chapter 33.

Some variety from the interminable pursuit of wildgeese is provided by three short articles that have already appeared in our daily paper, the "Eastern Daily Press", and I am grateful to the Editor for permission to reprint these articles — two by my eldest son Colin (Chapters 8 and 17) and one by myself (Chapter 16).

If there are any other parts of this volume which have already appeared in print elsewhere and I have overlooked them in my acknowledgments, I hope I may be excused and forgiven.

My younger son Keith, who has taken part in so many of these expeditions, has added his own special contribution by providing the numerous black and white sketches throughout the book.

Finally, this accumulation of over 30 years' scribblings could not have achieved the status of print without secretarial assistance, and I acknowledge with thanks and admiration the achievements of a long succession of secretaries who have converted my scrawling manuscript into legible and impeccable typescript. I hesitate to name all of them, for fear of overlooking some of the earlier ones, but in recent years the main burden has been borne by Alison Peeling, Beryl Livock and Ann Reekie.

DOUGLAS McDOUGALL.

Catfield Hall
April 1972.

ILLUSTRATIONS

The ordinary run of wildfowling does not provide much scope for outstanding or dramatic illustrations. Vast expanses of mudflats and huge fields of grass or stubble hardly make interesting backgrounds. Even the quarry itself is not easily recorded on film, except en masse in the distance, or laid out in lifeless ranks at the end of the day.

So there remain the "dramatis personae", and many of the illustrations are simply snapshots which I have taken at the conclusion of a morning's flighting — often on a dull winter's morning of those who happened to be with me.

But this volume would not be complete — for me at any rate — without these visual reminders of my companions and of the various expeditions which we have shared together.

CONTENTS

FOREWORD

For many years now I have made a practice of taking a short holiday in the middle of winter; not to escape from these islands and go winter-sporting on the Continent, nor to flee further south in search of the sun; but to enjoy one of the finest sports that this country can offer — wildfowling.

Shooting has always been my favourite form of recreation, from the time I was given my first shotgun — a 16 bore — while still at school. But it was not till I was over 30 years of age that I went on my first fowling trip — a weekend on the Wash — and suddenly realised the tremendous fascination of this type of shooting, particularly the pursuit of wildgeese.

For a few years these weekend trips to the Wash were the only opportunities I had. We seldom came home empty handed, but it was usually only a few duck or a couple of curlews in the bag, and more often than not we were unsuccessful so far as geese were concerned. But geese were always the main objective and the provocative challenge. We saw them in thousands, and during those first few seasons on the Wash we watched and studied them and acquired our skill the best of all ways — by a long practical apprenticeship.

Later we began to venture further afield. A few visits to the Solway and an occasional day on other Scottish estuaries broadened our experience and produced an occasional red-letter day, such as the 8 geese with 9 shots after a long stalk on the far N.E. coast, and the 11 geese shot by three of us over Bob McGuffie's decoys.

In the close season there were pictures and writings to stir the imagination and keep one's interest alive. Peter Scott was then producing his paintings, which have always seemed to me to capture the atmosphere of wildfowling better than those of any other bird artist. And his two books "Morning Flight" and "Wild Chorus" could be relied upon to produce severe attacks of goose-fever after reading — or re-reading — a chapter or two.

Came the war, and the opportunities for wildfowling were not so frequent or easy. I still managed to sneak a few odd days in Scotland, but the more frequent chances came in weekends on the Severn where an added interest was the change in species — Whitefronts instead of the Pink-feet and Greylags of the Wash and Scotland. The last time I was at the Wildfowl Trust at Slimbridge (1969) it was amusing to think that nearly 30 years ago I had carried a gun after the Whitefronts on some of the land that is now part of the Trust.

But the most significant event in my own search for more and better wildfowling was the lucky chance that put me in touch with "BB". I had long known his writings; his book "Manka, the Sky Gipsy" is a classic of wildfowl stories, and now and again articles on goose-hunting would appear from him in "The Field" and other journals. It must have been in 1943 that an article in "The Field" particularly appealed to me. It described one of his annual trips to Scotland, and clearly indicated that he had discovered a most attractive and productive centre for wildfowling with suitable lodgings in a small village near the estuary. I wrote to him "out of the blue"; what I said I cannot remember, but it all led up to the suggestion that he might let me join him on one of his expeditions. "BB" — bless his heart — replied sympathetically, and asked me to join him on his next trip, in January 1944. And so, in due course, we met for the first time in the upstairs sitting room over a small village shop which he had established as his H.Q. Thus began a partnership and friendship which has continued ever since, and which opened up for me a wonderful new district that has provided fascinating sport in a long series of wildfowling holidays. After a few seasons I even copied "BB's" habit of making diary notes of our activities and wrote them up into fairly full accounts of each trip.

And that is what this book mainly consists of — a series of descriptions of wildfowling holidays from 1933 to the present day, but with a few chapters on other allied subjects to introduce a little variety into what may otherwise seem rather repetitive. "BB" has kindly allowed me to include some of his own articles where these describe our earlier joint expeditions, while much more of our adventures together is to be found in his own two books "Tides Ending" and "Dark Estuary".

5

INTRODUCTION
TO ADDITIONAL CHAPTERS

(Third printing)

Since this book was first published in November 1972 another three wildfowling seasons have come and gone: and three more expeditions have been mounted and disbanded. The usual brief notes were made at the time, and on my return home were written up into the usual "diary" records. These further diaries thus account for three of the additional chapters.

At the same time another chapter has been added from earlier diaries — our fortnight in December 1953. This had been omitted from the original text simply because it seemed rather too repetitive of other similar trips of that time. But it had been a good holiday, with considerable variety in it, and it was one that I could fairly describe as "Tom's Year". Tom had been one of our party on so many occasions, but often in company with a "new boy" who naturally became associated in my mind with the whole expedition and his introduction to wildfowling. But no-one could be keener or more enthusiastic than Tom. On several occasions he brought his spaniels with him, and though they caused some caustic comments when he took them out to the fields for dawn ambushes, they were invaluable down on the coast where they did some spectacular retrieves in the dense reed beds or out on the mud.

There is also included a chapter which attempts to take a fresh look at the problem of shots taken at extreme range. In recent years I have been forced to question my own practice in such matters — not so much from the moral point of view, but rather from the practical problem of choosing the right ammunition for the special conditions under which wildfowling takes place. What had served me so well with a double 8-bore on the coast, was not so convincing when translated to inland shooting with a 12-bore. It was probably our trip in December 1971 which finally convinced me that I must make a study in greater depth of the ballistics, patterns and range limitations of the various loads available — particularly for 12-bore guns. The result has been a slight shift in my views, and to that extent this chapter should be read as modifying in some respects the opinions expressed in the earlier chapter on "Guns and Gear".

Chapter 40 is not new. It was written as the concluding chapter of the original book, and is now moved to its corresponding — and proper — place as the last chapter of the present enlarged edition.

Finally, in venturing to close this record of over forty years' experience with an Epilogue in verse, I must acknowledge the inspiration derived from the well-known Rubaiyat of Omar Khayyam. So many of the quatrains — after suitable revision! — seem to provide an attractive medium for expressing the spirit of wildfowling.

Catfield Hall   D. S. A. McD
May 1975

CHAPTER 1
THE FIRST GOOSE
(1933)

It is interesting to realise how important and significant some "first occasions" can be, though not always appreciated at the time. I can well remember the first time I went out wild-fowling and came home with a wild goose. The curious thing is that I had not given such a venture any serious thought before. Both my younger brothers had tried their hand at it: Michael had been out on the Solway with friends, and Tony had started exploring the Wash when he was at Cambridge. I never heard much about these expeditions and I have no idea what success they had — precious little I suspect.

Anyhow, it was in November 1933 that Tony asked me if I would care to join him on an expedition to the Wash, and that first trip established the pattern of several we were to make together over the next few years, and was responsible for other more lasting and deeper results.

On that first occasion, as on others that followed, we got away from our office jobs as early as we could on Friday evening — having got leave to miss Saturday morning — and rushed home to change and collect our gear. We then drove the 100 odd miles to the Wash and then had the whole of Saturday on the saltings, including both morning and evening flights, and then had the Sunday morning flight before driving home after lunch. If the moon was right we might also have a few hours under the moon.

This first time Tony had fixed up rooms at a pub in Dersingham, and on the Saturday morning directed me down to the coast at Snettisham where we proceeded to get the car well and truly bogged down in the loose shingle at the head of the beach.

I do not remember much about the morning flight, but we had some shots at duck and curlew, and then when it was light we saw two large skeins of geese moving inland well to the north of us, clearly heading for feeding grounds on the uplands of North Norfolk. These must have been the first wild geese I had ever seen, and the chance of coming to terms with them seemed pretty remote.

In the afternoon we were still wandering up and down the beach, waiting for fowl to start moving again at evening flight; and with no sign of any geese feeding on that stretch of the coast, and then suddenly Tony called out "geese coming", and we both rushed to the top of the beach and flung ourselves against the crest of the seawall. Sure enough a long low line of geese were heading back to the Wash from the Sandringham marshes. They must have been feeding within a mile of the coast all day, and we had never seen or heard a sign of them. They were flying quite low, but of course rising all the time, and most marvellous of all they were heading straight for us. On they came, a skein of perhaps a score of geese, while Tony and I remained frozen to the ground, hardly daring to look at them, and then of course as they crossed the seawall we sprang to our feet and let fly.

A single goose fell out of the skein and landed on the beach behind us with a dull thump — stone dead. At the very moment of excitement and success I remember being disappointed, and even surprised, that we had not done better. The geese had seemed in easy range, appeared to be flying quite slowly, and I could not think why we were not collecting 2, 3 or even 4 of them. But of course, as one came to realise so well with more experience, geese are nearly always further away than they seem, and they never fly slowly!

My next impression was one of mild anti-climax that the goose was such a comparatively small bird. I suppose I had half expected to see a large fat creature like a farmyard goose tumble out of the sky, yet here was a small inconspicuous bird, not much larger than an Aylesbury duck. Dull in colour, grey with a brownish tinge to its neck, a feminine little head with a "black neb" and those wonderful pink feet and legs; a streamlined bundle of muscle capable of migrating between Iceland and the Wash each year, and weighing only about 6½ lbs. It was of course a "Pink-foot", and with every expedition and every contact one developed an increasing admiration and respect for these tough and wary fowl, surely the most truly wild of all wildfowl.

Later on we added a mallard to our bag, and on Sunday Tony shot a scoter, and that was the total for the weekend.

But there is no doubt that this first expedition opened up a whole new world to me, and a new branch of shooting which appealed to me enormously. In fact, on that Saturday afternoon on 11th November, 1933, I got well and truly infected with the virus of goose fever, which has remained in my system ever since, and flares up each winter as regularly as the firths and estuaries of these islands fill up with the wild geese.

It was not long before I realised that my armoury needed overhauling. Game guns with 2½" chambers were clearly hardly adequate for geese at the usual extreme ranges. So within a year I had equipped myself with a double-barrelled 8-bore — bought second-hand for £26 I think in 1934. This was not nitro-proved and so had to fire black powder cartridges. But the performance was as impressive as the mere spectacle, with a great cloud of blue smoke billowing up at each "woomph!" After the war it was difficult to get cartridges specially loaded and I risked having the gun proofed. It stood the test, and is now nitro-proof for 2½ oz. shot. Unfortunately the standard I.C.I. cartridge for 8-bores is only loaded with 2 oz. of shot in a 3¼" case, whereas my gun will take a 3¾" case — and hence the 2½ oz. of shot.

We had many enjoyable weekends on the Wash; usually with Tony and also very often Tom Nicholson. Curiously enough, I cannot recall the actual details of any successful shot at geese, though I can remember some glaring misses. We usually came home with something: two or three duck, a curlew, some waders — and occasionally a goose or two. One weekend we collected a couple of pheasants! There was a small shooting party on the Sandringham lands (keepers or tenants I would think), and no doubt some of the birds fled to the saltings for safety. There we flushed them out of the little broken gullies crossing the marsh. Where we shot one of these cock pheasants there was a length of brickwork strengthening the seawall, and we stuffed the pheasant into a hole in the bricks, leaving it to be picked up on our way homeward. But by the time we came back the tide had risen and the base of the brick wall was under several feet of water. So an acrobatic act had to be mounted with someone being lowered by his heels from the top of the wall to reach the pheasant in the hole.

On another occasion we collected a hare by running it down in our headlights on our way down to the coast before dawn. And yet again we once did the same with a partridge, accelerating into a covey that was just starting to cross the road, and catching the last bird in the radiator as it rose in front of us.

Sometimes there would be large flocks of waders over the Wash, flying in dense clouds and swooping low over the water in wonderful aerobatic formation. One day I found them flying close to the shore when the tide was in, and by wading out in the shallow water I found I could get almost out to them. I could not resist the temptation of trying a shot "into the brown" and let off both barrels. The gun was a 12-bore this time, with 3" cartridges and no doubt with nothing smaller than No. 3 shot (or possibly No. 4 for duck). The result was 22 to be picked up and subsequently to be eaten in a pie (breasts only).

But of all my recollections of those pre-war years on the Wash some of the most outstanding are of our quarters. After that first stay at Dersingham I think we always made our H.Q. at The Chequers in Holbeach. This was then a free house, owned — or at least run — by a family of father, mother and daughter. We usually had the place to ourselves, though there might be one or two more tables occupied at lunch time. Whatever time we came in after morning flight there would be a splendid "brunch" laid on, starting with porridge and probably ending with a pudding or cheese and biscuits. Then there would be an equally satisfying supper when we came in from evening flight. After that we would stay up with the family in the bar, after the locals had drifted away, until it was time to turn in. Father was by then comfortably mellow and he would lead us up to our rooms and ask us when we wanted to be called. Sure enough, in a few hours time, and promptly to the minute, father would shuffle into each room in turn, apparently just as mellow as when we said goodnight, and still dressed exactly as we had last seen him. We really wondered whether he ever went to bed at all!

But his office was the gem of the establishment. A small room, just large enough to hold a desk and chair, and papers everywhere. On the desk, on the floor, in trays, in folders, and perhaps most of all just filed on the simplest of all filing systems — a metal spike standing up on a wooden base. Bills, invoices, receipts, circulars, price lists — all were distributed with apparent complete impartiality over the various lodgement areas. I once ventured to pick up a few loose papers off the floor — they turned out to be bills, 2 or 3 years old, and with no sign of having received any attention. I fear that all this may not be entirely unconnected with the fact that the hotel was soon afterwards taken over by a brewery. It then advertised itself as providing "quarters for fowlers", the place was smartened up; and when I called for a meal sometime after the war, there were several tables occupied by obvious fowling parties. Similarly, when I drove down to the seawall at Shep White's Cottage there were a score of cars parked at the end of the track. In earlier days there **might** be another car as well as ours, and if there were **two** we began to grumble and complain about the place becoming overcrowded! But The Chequers proved a most suitable and homely base to work from; I know my usual bill for accommodation and all meals for the weekend used to work out at about 25/-d.

After the war we hardly ever went back to the Wash; conditions had changed; the place was overcrowded and overshot, and by then we had ventured further afield to explore the Solway, the Severn, Holkham and eventually most of the principal goose areas of Scotland.

But I shall always remember that first goose shot on the Wash in 1933 — it was largely responsible for much that followed.

CHAPTER 2
JUST IN CASE
(1937-1938)

A convenient mixture of business and personal affairs took Tony and myself up to Scotland recently, Tony being my younger brother. Seeing that we should have to spend several days in the North-East of the country, we both decided to take our duck guns with us and an optimistic supply of 3-inch cartridges — "just in case".

After a few days it became apparent that our affairs would take us to a certain small town near a firth that we knew to be a good centre for wildfowl. From that beginning it was easy to plan the opportunity for which we had been hoping; we would arrive at our little town on Tuesday evening, get the evening flight and the following morning flight down on the coast, and have the rest of Wednesday free for whatever the district offered in other directions. Our other affairs would only take us an hour or two and could be squeezed in some time on Wednesday.

A message sent on ahead of us produced our friend Sandy, a local wildfowler, awaiting us at the hotel on our arrival at Blanktown — for we did not know the district well and had never actually shot on this firth before. Sandy, in turn, had a friend Jock, who would like to join the party, and who — in hopeful anticipation — was already waiting discreetly round the corner. So immediately our party became a foursome, and remained so for the following twenty-four hours.

Of the evening flight down on the estuary there is little to record, and still less of the following morning. From the latter we came in at 9 a.m. after two and a half hours of wind and rain, very little shooting, and nothing in the bag. But Jock reported that he had been making enquiries over-night and it was said that there were plenty of geese on the firth, and that they were feeding on the usual inland haunts during the daytime. Neither Sandy nor Jock had yet been out after them that season, as it so happened, but they knew both the geese and their haunts of old, and were itching to get on terms with them again.

This was cheering news, and quickly restored our spirits from the setback which they had suffered from an unsuccessful evening and morning, while a piping hot breakfast on generous Scotch lines did equally good work in dispelling the influence of wet and cold.

By 9.30 we were off again, all four packed into the car, and heading for the stretch of country which the geese were known to frequent. By this time the wind had lost some of its early morning strength, though it was still quite fresh, and the rain had ceased entirely. The clouds were higher and no longer entirely covered the heavens, so that small patches of pale blue showed up in the East, over the sea. In the distance the mountains showed white with a light covering of snow, but down by the coast there was still no sign of frost, and the day might almost have been one of early spring, were it not for the fallen — and still falling — leaves.

We had gone many miles before Sandy and Jock began to take any interest in the proceedings. By now we had reached a stretch of open rolling country, with large square fields, many of them pasture but with a fair proportion of roots, old stubbles, and stubbles recently ploughed and sown. Large areas of this country consisted of low-lying "flats" with the fields divided by drainage ditches; between and around these "flats" the ground rose to slight undulating hills.

Where the road slipped over the shoulder of one of these hillocks Jock at last gave the word to stop, and we all tumbled out to study the surrounding countryside. Sandy at once proved himself to be the possessor of eyes like a hawk; "Look, what's that in the green field to the left of those trees?" But a careful examination with the glasses revealed nothing beyond some tussocks of rough grass. "There they are — in the field beyond the sheep — in line with the house!" But again it was a false alarm, and after a little while, after we had all had a turn with glasses, Jock announced with conviction and finality that there were no geese in sight. On we went again, until the road brought us to another good vantage point, and again the same careful search took place, with again the same results, in spite of several exclamations from Sandy. In fact, we were beginning to suspect that Sandy was not so much blessed with exceptional sight as with imagination and optimism.

At the third stop I let the other three do all the spying, while I took it easy in the driver's seat, but with the windows down and engine turned off, in the hope that my ears might bring me a clue where eyesight failed. Waiting thus, looking idly out to sea, I suddenly noticed a thin black line against the distant sky — a line so sharp and precise that there was never a second's doubt as to what it was. "Look! there they are!", and even as the others turned to follow my eyes, someone else called out, "And there are some more — further to the right!" Sure enough, nearer than the first lot, and in a longer line, appeared a second skein, beating their way inland against the wind to their feeding grounds.

"Listen!" — the sound of them, calling to each other as they flew, at last reached us. What an extraordinary thing is the sound of wild geese — impossible to describe and yet quite unmistakable; entirely unmusical and yet sheer music to a wildfowler's ears. I suppose the enthusiast in every branch of sport knows some particular sound which never fails to give him a thrill, and set his nerves tingling. To the partridge shooter it may be the whirr of a covey getting up in front of him; to a pheasant enthusiast it is probably the tap-tap-tap of the beaters' sticks ringing through a wood on a still crisp November morning. To the wildfowler it is most certainly the call of wild geese.

And all the time they were flying nearer and nearer towards us.

"Look out — they're coming straight for us" — "They look as if they want to drop into those fields on our right — they're beginning to break formation!" — "No, they're too high — they're going on". And go on they did — at a tremendous height, probably 500 feet, recovering their perfect V formation after the one sign of hesitation. As they passed almost over us we could count twenty geese in the first lot, while there must have been fifty to sixty in the larger skein.

Steadily they flew on; we watched them disappearing into the dull light of the distance; one, two miles they must have left behind them and between us; with the glasses we followed them another mile or more, and then they melted into the grey background of cloud. We could only hope that they would come down somewhere within reasonable distance. But for the time being we decided to leave them behind and push on towards the mouth of the firth, in the hope of finding other lots. Another half-hour sufficed to cover most of the remaining likely districts, but in spite of many spyings and several enquiries, no trace of geese could be found — neither sight nor sound. So the only thing left to do was to follow the direction taken by the two skeins, and hope for the best.

Every half mile or so we stopped and scanned the countryside, our hopes repeatedly raised by the irrepressible Sandy and as regularly killed by the evidence of the glasses, though in fairness to Sandy it must be admitted that at one point he worked us all up to believing we could see a lot of geese rising from the fields about two miles away. Yes, there they were — I could see them against a patch of light cloud — "They're just over those trees now — now they're over the edge of that hill — look, they're quite clear — Oh hell! they're rooks!" By this time they certainly were rooks, but I still believe they started as geese, and that my eye changed over from a skein of geese to a nearer bunch of rooks. Anyhow, we all had sufficient confidence to follow this one possible clue, and we made off at full speed for that distant hillside against which we had seen the geese (or rooks !).

The road ran conveniently along the side of the hill, giving us an excellent view of the low ground below on our right. Twice we stopped to inspect, and drew blank, and the third time Sandy again raised our overworked hopes with his usual "There they are !" But even as he said it we realised there was a ring in his voice which carried conviction, and we all grabbed together for the glasses. But no glasses were necessary — the geese were only three fields away!

Picture the view, if you can. From the narrow country road a grass field runs down to the flat land below. The next field is a large square field of roots, looking very green against the rest of the landscape. Beyond the turnip field, on its North side, is another grass field, and as our eyes get used to the focus we can see that all those greyish blobs scattered all over the field are — not boulders, not molehills — but geese! There seem dozens of them! Scores of them! Why, good heavens, there are hundreds of them! "And there are more in that field to the left!" Sure enough, the grass field to the left (i.e. West) of the turnip field is also full of geese — hundreds of them. In those two fields there must be over a thousand pink-footed geese. How to get at them? We take stock of the position and debate alternative plans; in the main there are only two choices — either to stalk up to within shot of the geese where they are, or else to take up positions as near as we can get to them and leave one of the party to put them up over us. The first (North) field looks the more promising — the geese are spread all over it, and it looks through the glasses as if some of them may be within range of the right-hand (East) boundary. As far as we can make out this seems to be a fairly deep ditch with an occasional tree or bush growing along it. Half-way along this ditch another fence runs up to it at right angles, but we cannot see if there is any ditch along this fence or not. However, running eastward this fence soon joins up with a long, narrow spinney of young fir trees, which in turn extends several hundred yards further east. There should be no difficulty in making the cover of the spinney — but shall we find sufficient cover to creep unobserved along the intervening fence to the boundary ditch, and if we reach the latter will that in turn provide sufficient cover to creep along into position opposite the nearest geese? We can only try and see. Jock propounds a still more ambitious scheme — of making the boundary ditch, of working along to the corner of the turnip field, and then creeping along the ditch between the turnips and the geese until we reach the North-West corner of the turnips where all three fields meet — the two grass fields of geese and the turnip field! His idea is that if we ever reach that point we shall be right between two big lots of geese, and if one lot isn't then in range we are almost sure to get a shot if and when they get up. But the original plan looks difficult enough and carries Sandy's backing, and we eventually decide on it. In case the geese prove to be out of range from the ditch, Sandy nobly volunteers to stay behind and act as "beater" if required. He is to allow us half an hour for our stalk, and if nothing happens by then he is to stroll across the fields in such a direction as should put the geese up over us. Our plan of action settled, we park the car and set off — agreeing the time with Sandy as 11.20 a.m. Jock boasts a quaint looking single-barrelled repeater which fires five cartridges, and I'm afraid Tony and I both regard it with a certain amount of suspicion and that usual hint of disapproval with which all British sportsmen view any departure from the orthodox.

We soon reach the spinney, and I find with a feeling of shame that I am disgracefully out of breath — but so are the other two, and we realise with relief that it is only the effect of increasing excitement and anticipation. Progress through the spinney is easy — the young trees are close together and fairly bare up to six feet or so, so we can walk upright, and only need to place our feet carefully to avoid crackling twigs. Some cattle in the field on our left give us some anxious moments ; they see us amongst the trees and start a foolish sort of mild stampede round the field — and towards us. Stupid beasts! Haven't they seen men enough in their time? Why must they show such unnecessary and quite unjustifiable excitement! However, they calm down and the geese seem to have suspected no danger.

To our great joy we find that the fence joining the spinney to the boundary ditch is in fact a fence-cum-ditch, and that it continues along the edge of the spinney. So, well before we get to the end of the spinney we climb through the fence and slither down into the ditch. There is only about one or two feet of water in it and this together with the depth of the ditch itself gives us sufficient cover for our purpose. Slowly we creep along in single file, bent double, Jock leading. The other two have thigh waders, but I have only rubber knee-boots, and in the deeper pockets of the ditch the water soon comes over them and fills them up. At length, after what seems an age, we reach the cross ditch — the one bounding the field where the geese are. Our luck holds — and improves. This ditch is still deeper than the last one and we can stand up in the bottom of it and take a welcome breather.

So far we have not seen the geese since leaving the car, nor have we heard them as they are feeding in silence. Presumably they are still there. Jock volunteers to take a peep over the top. While the two of us watch in anxious suspense he crawls up the bank and slowly raises his head — and as slowly lowers it again. A consultation follows in the bottom of the ditch — the geese, it appears, are straight ahead of us, but a long way out — sixty to eighty yards; what on earth are we to do? It is now 11.40; in ten minutes Sandy will start making himself conspicuous; is it better to risk a long range volley at the grazing geese, or rely on Sandy putting them right over our heads? While we are debating the position in the lowest whispers my brother's face lights up with an enormous grin of delight, and his raised forefinger suggests that he has heard something really encouraging. He has, he whispers, caught the sound of geese "gabbling" as they feed, more to the right, and closer.

This time I offer to inspect, first creeping along the ditch some twenty yards or so to the right. The ditch is overgrown with brambles and the sound of them scraping past my leather jacket sounds like rending cloth to my anxious ears, while the noise of our feet shuffling along the muddy bottom of the ditch seems to be exaggerated to a tremendous splashing that cannot fail to give the alarm to the geese. But all is well; choosing a convenient bush on the top of the bank, I crawl up behind it and take a look over the top. There they are. My first sight at really close quarters of geese feeding. Just in front of me the edge of the flock is perhaps thirty to forty yards out, but still further along to the right they are within fifteen to twenty yards of the bank and ditch. Back into the ditch bottom again to report: "The nearest ones are still twenty yards further along" — "Call it forty" whispers Jock, with obvious reflection on my ability to estimate distances. On we crawl again. After a while Jock stops, then after another few yards, Tony, and finally, after a further interval, myself. We had agreed to crawl up into position, and on a given signal to jump up and open fire on the geese. What the signal was to be, and how it was to be given, we did not stop to think. I was the last to clamber up the bank, which was almost vertical opposite me, but I had chosen this particular spot for the sake of a handy bush of broom growing on the top. Half-way up I felt I was going to slip backwards into the ditch (that would make a glorious splash!), but my handful of grass held, and I at last wriggled up behind the clump of broom. There was a convenient gap in the bush, and through it I could just see three geese within easy range in the field in front of me: one was grazing, another was having a rest sitting down, while in front was a large old codger standing with his head well up — very alert. I kept my eye on the old codger, and it seemed to me that his piercing little eye was looking straight through the hole in the broom back at me. Out of the corner of my own eye I had an impression of more geese to the right — and I could only hope that there were plenty in front of my companions on my left.

I pushed off the safety catch on my gun (what a noise it makes in the presence of geese) and quietly rested the muzzle in the gap in front of me. Now for the signal —?

A glance to my left showed me my brother — or rather just his face with an expression of enquiry all over it. Jock was out of sight — presumably flattened to the bank further along.

I raised my eyebrows back at Tony, but it was no use two of us playing at that game. I took another glance at Old Codger — to make sure he was still there — glanced back at Tony, gave him a nod, he nodded back to me — and then —?

In the next fraction of a second two thoughts flashed through my mind. Firstly, I was not going to fire until one of two things happened; either I heard the guns on my left go off, or the geese took to flight. I have spoilt sport for others before by firing too soon, and was determined not to wreck the present occasion in that way. Secondly, I was not going to take my eye off the ball again (the ball being Old Codger).

As it was, everything seemed to happen instantaneously: there was a report on my left, Old Codger spread his wings and started to "take off", and my own gun went off. The first report developed into a regular cannonade as I leaped up for my second barrel. How quickly geese get away! They were well up in the air and yards further off by the time I could pick out my second bird. He banked over on his left wing as I fired and fell sprawling back to the field again.

And now we were all scrambling down the bank, over the wire fence and into the field, Tony and Jock dashing out to right and left after two wounded birds, while I collected Old Codger and some others.

In all we had eight geese; with nine shots, for Jock had got off all five of his cartridges.

We pulled Jock's leg unmercifully for having missed one of his shots and spoilt a 100 per cent result, but he pleaded that with five shots one must allow a "sighter"!

And so, back across the fields and up the slope to the waiting Sandy, who had witnessed the climax to our stalk just a couple of minutes before he was due to advance on the geese from the far side.

"Man", said Jock, "it was the best stalk I've ever known". With which Tony and I both agreed.

CHAPTER 3
NEVER A BLANK DAY
(1943-1944 JOHN'S YEAR)

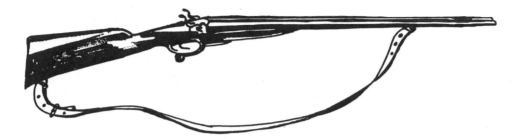

John and I stood on Rugby platform waiting for the train which was to take up to our "goose grounds" in the north. Our luggage having been sent off some time before Christmas, we were travelling light, an absolute necessity these days. Glumly we regarded the seething crowds and wondered if we should ever get a seat, especially as our bicycles had to go with us; for we had a long, long ride at the end of the journey.

The first train in was crammed to the last inch, but with the next train we were more fortunate. When the train came to a squeaking stop, we found an almost empty carriage in front of us; we climbed in and found corner seats, and, after all, we were only an hour late into the terminus. What a relief it was to get into the clean-smelling northern air and to hear on all sides the rich brogue of the north. Brilliant stars shone from a cloudless sky, it was mild, with no moon. Soon we were bumping over the cobbles between the street lights, which were rapidly left behind, and we were out on the straight road, with a gentle westerly wind at our backs; and wasn't that good! Wasn't it good to smell the hills and the pinewoods and the rotted bracken! Wasn't it good to know that ahead we had a clear fortnight of goose hunting!

"BB"
The author of this Chapter
and of the following one

We did not reach our G.H.Q. until after midnight, but, nevertheless, we were up for the flight the following morning. A ride of three miles or so brought us to the estuary, and in the half-darkness we recognised old familiar landmarks, the haystacks, the rows of outbuildings by the farm; and the soft glow of a lantern gleamed under a stable door. The lane was just the same as of old, rutty and full of puddles, and soon we heard the clamour of geese ahead. Hearing it we stopped to take bearings and counsel. Where were they? Was it the Leaning Buoy marsh, Bight Point, Smith's Post, or Curlew Bay? I made my plan. I sent John to the Long Breakwater, a deadly place to kill a goose when there is no moon, giving him minute instructions as to where to go and what to look out for. I decided on Leaning Buoy, an old love of mine.

I knew the way like a hunted fox knows his country, the same gap in the wire, the same opening in the bushes. Dawn was now breaking over the hills, golden plover and peewits rose from the field ahead as I stumbled over rough plough (they plough very deep in this part of the world)- and in a short while I was sliding down the bank under the brambles, ripping my nose with a briar as I did so.

For the first time in memory the path through the reeds was unfrozen and squelchy. Geese sounded on all sides, but, as the dawn broke, most went to sea or flew off up the estuary. I did have one shot, however, with the single eight-bore (I had only four cartridges for this gun, and those were old cases reloaded). Just as I came off the bank at the end of flight two geese passed overhead, but they were behind a tree, and I failed to connect.

When I met John he told me that he found the Long Breakwater a difficult place in the darkness. He had, however, got out along it and, as the light grew, observed many birds, which he took to be ducks, among the short reeds not 40 yards distant, but he held his fire, as he knew geese were about. He thought that they were "big ducks", but when they all flew off he saw they were geese! Had he taken a chance he would probably have had a goose with his first shot.

On this estuary the full moon is very unproductive, and our first week was our best in the way of chances. There must have been some hoodoo on me, because during the whole fortnight I never had a fair chance of a goose. John was more lucky: he shot his first before the week was up. That was when "Mac" joined us. Mac is six-foot-two and of dynamic energy where geese are concerned. He joined us on the second day, armed with a monstrous fowling-piece, which only such a giant could lift. But, my goodness, what a gun! It fired three and three-quarter eight-bore cases loaded with BB shot and black powder.

It was wonderful how the geese made for Mac. I accused him of exercising some form of radio-location. The astonishing fact was that, if there were geese about, they made a bee line over him. On the first evening flight a skein of pinks flew over him from the sea. I saw they were very high (I should never have shot) and I hoped Mac would not fire. I saw those geese in a straggling black bundle head right for his post (he was at Leaning Buoy), and, to my mystification, I saw one speck detach itself and fall reedwards. Then a mushroom of blue smoke rose up from below, and a shattering explosion followed. Mac had got a goose with his first shot on his first flight! Each day Mac went out he brought back a goose; he never had a single day blank! He finished up his last morning by dropping a single goose into the reeds, which bird he could not find, and by stalking the grand army of greys at the Goose's Graveyard, killing a magnificent gander greylag His luck was astounding. All fishermen know how sometimes one man gets all the luck, whilst others not a foot or so away, never have an offer. So it was with Mac. The geese could not keep away from him.

John shot his greylag on Reed Island, a small pear-shaped mud wallow out in the estuary, a nasty place to lie up if you are squeamish about mud and wet and trapping tides. A bunch flew over him just as the moon rose, and a long case of AA felled the best goose of the whole trip, a grand eight-pounder. My own goose is hardly worth mentioning, for I believe it was a pricked bird. The facts are these: at high tide I went out on the Long Breakwater and as I picked my way among the slimy stones I saw a large and fat goose walk unconcernedly out from behind a rock 60 yards away; it had not seen me; I fired with No. 3 shot and knocked it over; then it made for the sea, and I tried to follow; but the mud was too deep. It swam out some way, turned, and regained the breakwater. I stalked it again, and it rose into the air, coming over my head and offering an easy chance. It seemed in good condition and fat. It may have been a pensioner from Mac's elephant gun.

Misfortune seemed to dog me wherever I went. I tried the Harrier Haunt, a stretch of marsh which, in the past, has provided many a goose and where the gaggles used to come to feed. But there I found an old rascal in a ragged coat cutting reeds. He was a picturesque figure enough, and his flat-bottomed reed-boat might have come out of a Rembrandt etching. But, of course, no goose was near. I tried Curlew Bay and, in company with John, essayed to stalk some greylags. A spot of brown afar off drew John's attention. "A bull", said he. "A cow", said I, after a brief inspection. But John had a good pair of binoculars. The sex was soon beyond dispute. It seemed peaceful enough, and I have no great fear of bulls. But after a while a dull booming roar came faintly on the ear. The bull was on the move towards us and he seemed put out. We fled for the fence, and the bull quickened his pace. He was not a pretty sight. He knelt upon the ground and made uncouth sounds; he attacked a bush of broom and reduced it to trampled rags of green. We crossed a burn before we felt safe, and even then he tried to get at us.

The trouble was that Curlew Bay is good for wader shooting, and the larder was low. We ambushed the curlew near the burn, but they flew over the whins on "Ferdinand's" domain. So I suggested to John that he should ambush the curlew on the north end of Ferdinand's country whilst I drew the latter away to the southward, taking care that a respectable fence was between us. This was duly done, John bagging five curlew, whilst I acted as a decoy. We later learnt that the bull was owned by a man whose father had been killed by a bull on that very marsh.

When the moon came to the full the geese went away. I had two nice mallard one night at Leaning Buoy, but no more shots at geese. And so ended my worst season so far on that particular estuary.

CHAPTER 4
NEW TACTICS
(1944-1945 ANGUS' YEAR)

"Jam yesterday, jam tomorrow, but never jam today", a familiar saying and one which applies to goose-chasing more than to any other sport. Yet, amazing as it may seem, I am now able to say that for once in a while it has been definitely "Jam today". Indeed, in the dozen or more successive expeditions that I have made in years prior to and during the war, this fortnight of January 1945 has been the best. The reason? Partly the weather and mostly the luck of the game. Even the long journey up was the best since days of peace, with the train only ten minutes late at its destination. There was the familiar ride down the familiar road with a wind at our backs; a mild moist night, with the moon in its last quarter veiled by flying cloud.

I felt almost like an old wild goose myself returning to his old well-loved grounds. My companion was, as usual, one of the "young entry", a boy who had never done any goose-chasing, but was of the right breed, tough, keen, fit after a winter term of Rugger, and, though his parents denied it, a good shot. So I come to the first morning flight, always an auspicious occasion to the fowler who can only spare a short time every winter. It was January 3rd, the morning mild and windy after a gale during the night, the moon still bright and high in the sky.

When we reached the head of the lane we stopped to listen. In the uneasy gloom ahead we heard the chiming of the geese, a sound which is as sweet to the fowler's ears as is the chiming of hounds in kennel to the foxhunter. I guessed pretty shrewdly where they were — by Reed Island; if I were lucky, they would be ashore, resting after the wild night. I had my 8-bore, a single gun, one of the old "bank" guns which must have shot scores of geese on the desolate wastes around the Humber. I sent Angus off to my right, where I heard more geese. He was armed with a 12-bore and BB shot.

I pushed my way along the bank, the thorns tearing at my coat and thigh waders, and soon saw the gleam of the sea framed by dark hills. The geese were at Reed Island, sure enough, and so I began my stalk. The wind rustled, drowning my footsteps, and I was glad of that. Soon I was down on all fours, gloves off, my naked hands deep in the icy mud. I had smeared some of this mud on my cheeks and forehead, for it is the finest camouflage and good for the complexion! Soon I was going like the humble worm, flat among the mud and herbage; for I saw that the grand army of the greylags were indeed right inshore. Inches at a time I crept nearer; the gabbling and croaking was deafening. Surely I was well within range!

But the moon was now hidden, and the dawn was only just beginning to break over the hills. Indistinctly I saw the geese massed in front of me. I was surely within range, and I dare not risk another inch forward. Rising on one knee I lifted the massive gun, and at the action some sharp-sighted sentry must have seen me. With a truly awesome sound the whole marsh spouted geese, not only to my front, but on all sides of me, and even, I believe, behind me. I had crawled right among the grand army, it was the chance of a lifetime! By luck and influence I had secured twenty-five pre-war 8-bore cases, loaded by Bland with black powder. There was a sheet of flame and a recoil that sent me backwards, but the gun had done deadly work. As I stumbled forwards three geese lay dead out in front, each bird killed instantly.

Never before had I started the season by killing three geese with one shot. This gun has, however, killed two geese at a shot, on the Wash, many years ago, as a skein came over the bank. I gathered the birds and retired to the reeds to await the coming of day. Just as the sun topped the hills two more greys passed me, high left, a shot I like, and the leader fell at my feet. This made four geese in one morning. I could scarcely struggle back up the bank with so heavy a load, where I found Angus awaiting me ; he had had no luck, but his was to come.

January 4th was a blank, the weather still mild. On the 5th I got my fifth goose, again by Reed Island, the only goose which came in over our part of the coast, though geese were moving up on the tide. On the 8th, Angus made his kill. I saw it. First, a skein heading for Reed Island (I had given him my place) was seen by me to waver and rise, and one small blob hurtled earthwards. Ten minutes later, another skein came on the same line. The same thing happened, another blob slumped downwards. Angus was doing well for a beginner! The 8th brought the great cold, the frost and snow. It was a memorable flight, one of the best I have ever witnessed on this northern water. All down the coast straggling parties of pinks and greys came tacking in, the snow in their eyes. But neither I nor Angus had a successful shot, the skeins just missed us, passing in too far on either side.

"Mac" — with his double eight

As we cycled home to our wildfowling G.H.Q. in the little fishing village, we saw geese dropping down on to a stubble field by Castle Doone. We went there and found it was a barley field which had been cut by a combine. Just the place for flighting duck! And that night, as we lay on our backs on the darkling field and saw one high turret of Castle Doone light up a single window, the duck came streaming in, circling and quacking. Never have I seen so many duck in all my life, and yet the farmer had told us there were few duck in the district! I shot and shot again, and missed and missed. I had yet to get my "night eyes". Angus, however, killed his first duck. "Mac" had joined us, making a third gun, Mac of the mighty double eight, who last year slew a goose every time he went forth.

NEW TACTICS

On the 9th, Angus again distinguished himself by getting a pink in the darkness as they flighted in over the snowy fields, and another grey by Reed Island. My lead was diminishing; but neither Mac nor Angus were destined to equalise, my lucky star was burning ever more brightly. The geese were now flocking to the stubble below the Castle walls. We built a hide-out in the field, and Mac put out two decoys which he had brought all the way from England in a large wooden coffin. The geese ceased to flock, they circled, cackling wisely, well out of range of even Mac's terrifying gun.

New methods had to be tried, and it was then that I hit upon an entirely new scheme, one so deadly that I am not going to put it in writing. I can only say it entailed the employment of two men. No pit was dug, no hide was built, more I cannot say. I was the first to shoot (we took it in turns), and I bagged another grey. Next morning I had three geese, one after the other. Mac had two, a right and a left, and should have had two more out of a later bunch. Angus had another, and then the geese grew wise. For geese grow wise in a very short time. But I can honestly say that we deceived even their sharp eyes.

Towards the end of our stay I got my "night eyes" and, on this same field, slew three mallard in four shots in the half-darkness: Mac had one, and Angus another. I have never decided in my mind which flight I like the better, the morning or the evening. I think on the whole the evening flight is preferable. The chances for geese are nil, but, for all that, there is a peace and sense of excitement which is perhaps lacking in the dawn. Punctually at six o'clock, when the sun had long gone, I lay on my back among the stubble, head pillowed on a mound of straw, eyes on the sky. Soon came the stuttering quacks, and the wheeling teams of duck appeared, some pitching almost within shot, others coming right over out of range. I like shooting when lying on my back, a good swing is easy if the birds pass directly over, but side shots are almost always missed.

We finished up with an exciting ambush on the shore. By the 15th the moon had, of course, gone, and, as Angus and I lay in the whin bushes and the red fire of the sunset died, we saw and heard the greys swimming in to us on the full tide. Inch by inch they came, but yet kept their distance until at last, when the light had almost gone, they were the faintest dim blobs upon the water: it was hard to tell whether they were ten or forty yards away. I think that they were probably well in range, but I would not fire at them because they would have been lost on the tide which would soon be on the ebb, and I had left my magnificent Labrador at home.

When at last darkness fell we were surrounded by goose-talk, that comfortable, gosling-like murmur of geese at feed and feeling well secure. It was a fitting end to our trip. I hear that murmur still and shall continue to do so, off and on, for many weeks to come. Only those who have suffered from "goose fever" will understand that last remark. For me the wild grey geese will ever be the most fascinating birds that fly, and the hunting and watching of them the finest sport on earth.

CHAPTER 5
THE DOUBLE STALK
(1949-1950 BILL'S YEAR)

Our party of three assembled at Grantham on the morning of Saturday, January 14th, and after stowing all our gear in the car we set off along the Great North Road for our distant fowling grounds in the North. At Scotch Corner we struck off westwards and crossed over to Carlisle, eventually stopping for the night at a comfortable little hotel a few miles over the border.

An easy day's driving on the morrow brought us to our first quarters, a small village inn lying a mile or two inland from the coast. As we arrived well before dusk it was unanimously agreed to cruise round the usual goose grounds for a while, to see what the district held in store for us. Very soon we found a large party of greys on a field close to the coast, so we waited in the car to watch their flight out at dusk. Sure enough at about 4.30 p.m. they lifted and swung out to the estuary. At the same time other larger skeins of geese could be seen against the sunset sky, streaming out in long lines to their sleeping quarters from more distant feeding grounds. So there were plenty of geese awaiting us, and using the same old flight lines.

Next morning — Monday — we settled down to our normal routine; up at 6 to 6.30 a.m., straight down to the coast (or the fields) for the morning flight, and back again when it was all over. We had a rule that if we were back by 10 we had breakfast, but if not we waited for lunch. If we had breakfast we usually went out again before lunch, and invariably we went out again about 3 p.m. and stayed out till after the evening flight.

Monday morning yielded nothing; there was quite a good flight in off the mud flats, but the geese mostly came too wide or high; we all tried a few long shots, and Bill even started off with a stalk — towards a lot of greys who were resting close in on the mud. But his stalk, like our long shots, was unsuccessful. After breakfast we did a "recco" by car and spied a large number of geese on a field of winter wheat. We found the farmer and got his permission to go on his land, but decided to wait till the next morning when we would lie up for the geese at dawn.

Evening flight down by the coast was uneventful and unproductive.

Next morning we thought we were up and out in good time, but even as we were choosing our positions in a deep ditch bordering the wheat field we heard a small party of geese land in the middle of the field — though dawn was hardly beginning to show. In about ten minutes I could just make them out, and in another ten minutes I could see they were pinks. So there was nothing to do but keep down in the ditch and await developments. Gradually the geese moved nearer to Bill and me, and we were just making signals to each other that we had better bob up and risk a long shot at them when they suddenly took off — and came almost straight for us. As they crossed our ditch I picked two birds bunched together for my first barrel and a single bird for my second; all three dropped dead !

After that greys began arriving, but kept landing in the field behind us. "BB" got a nice high one before long, and then I crept round and put a big lot back over the ditch and over Bill — he got one. Then "BB" got another, and the flight was all over. A very nice beginning — six geese in a morning.

In the afternoon we found the greys were back on the same field where we had seen them our first evening. So again we sought out the farmer, got the necessary permission, and proceeded to attempt a pincer movement. The field was flat and large, but at one corner a farm track led out into the field and appeared to be raised about 18'' above field level. So a belly-crawl seemed possible, with a few outlying geese just in range of the end of this track. Bill started off on the stalk, "BB" took up position on the road between the field and the coast, while I edged my way round to the third side of the field. If the stalk was successful the geese should give either me or "BB" a chance as they swung out to sea, but if Bill couldn't get within range I would try and flush them over him. I gave him about half an hour but as there was still no sign of a shot I guessed he couldn't approach within range; this seemed to be confirmed by the changed position of the geese seen through glasses. So I continued edging nearer to the geese until at last they rose with a roar — and made off towards Bill. I could see a figure leap up from the apparent bare ground and before the sound of his shots reached me I saw a blob detach itself from the departing skein and hurtle to the ground.

After that we went down to the coast for the evening flight but no geese came near our positions.

On Wednesday we had planned to move further North for a few days in a new district, but before departing we slipped down to the coast for the dawn flight. It was fine and calm and the geese tended to come in rather high but we all had a few shots. One lot of about a dozen pinks came straight for me; I was well hidden near the edge of the mud and they never saw me for they came on a straight course till I stood up and took the leader of the V well forward. He fell as dead as mutton a few yards behind me, but I missed by second shot.

After that a hasty breakfast and the high road again.

We reached our new quarters in daylight and at once contacted the two farmers over whose land we had obtained permission to roam. Their reports were not encouraging; few geese were about, they had been badly beaten up by local gunners over the New Year, and they had not been seen feeding much on these particular farms recently. Our reception at the local hotel was also discouraging; our unusual hours for coming and going, and our strange meal requirements seemed to worry the management, and although the hotel was admittedly empty there was some curious reluctance to give us a room of our own where we could keep our gear, clean our guns and generally relax. A long morning by the sea wall next day soon convinced us we were wasting our time. Although we heard a few geese in the estuary, not one took wing, and we never saw a goose in the air (or on land) all day. In the evening we saw a few near the shore, and later on Bill passed the time by making a detailed study of the local goose population through his telescope. He assured us there were exactly 263 geese in the estuary, but it was clear they had no intention of making any contact with us. So we sent off wires announcing our immediate return to our old haunts and spent the rest of the day waiting for the evening flight of wigeon to some flood water they had obviously been visiting. We had a few shots but no luck.

Next day we left the far North — more in sorrow than in anger — and returned whence we came. A quick recce before dusk yielded a gaggle of about 30 geese on a grass field bordering the railway. They were quite unapproachable, but the railway lay between them and the coast, and the actual railway track was about 2 - 3 feet above the level of the fields. So after the usual formalities we decided to crawl up to the railway and wait for the geese to fly over us at dusk when they would return to the mud. All went well, and to save ourselves a long, laborious crawl, we took advantage of every passing train and gained many yards in a sprint as each train roared past between us and the geese. After that it was just a question of crouching under the slight embankment and hoping we had chosen the right line for the flight. And then suddenly the geese were over us, with hardly a honk of warning. But they had climbed faster than we had expected, and though we all let fly at them in the dusk not a bird fell.

We packed up for the night with two blank days behind us and no very clear idea as to how or where we could hope to get a goose on the morrow.

Saturday morning flight on the coast was uneventful, so after breakfast we set out on another recce to find the geese. We soon found them; 3 - 4 miles inland, under the hill, and feeding on a grass field. The farmer in question refused us permission to shoot on his land as the shooting was let, but the field was a boundary one, and between it and his neighbour's field was a small open drainage ditch — which might or might not provide sufficient cover for a stalk. We had already got the neighbour's permission to shoot, so we decided that as the geese appeared to be within range of the ditch we would attempt a stalk and if necessary face any consequences.

"BB" had a bad ankle and couldn't manage the full programme, so Bill and I started off on the stalk together. We dropped into the ditch a quarter of a mile or so lower down (at A) and set out on our long slow approach. "BB" got as far as B, and waited there. The ditch was about 2 - 3 feet deep to water level, with another 2 - 2½ feet of water and mud in the botton, so we could just manage it in waders and only needed to crouch to keep out of sight of the geese. Between B. and C. the surface of the water was often frozen, so Bill — who was leading — gently broke up the thin ice with his hand and so avoided the crackle that we should have made by forcing our feet through it. At C, we allowed ourselves our one and only peep at the geese throughout the stalk. I slowly raised my head and peered through a small bush; a glimpse of the first few geese told me everything — first that they were still there and unsuspecting, second that they were still within range, and third that we should have to move another forty yards or so before we were opposite the first geese. All this I tried to convey by signs and whispers to Bill, and thus we pushed further on — ever more carefully, more slowly, and now bent nearly double, for the ditch was getting smaller, narrower and shallower. At last I reckoned we were far enough — still no alarm from the geese — and I signalled to Bill to get ready. We cocked our hammers, slowly straightened ourselves up, pushed our muzzles over the bank in front — and then bedlam was let loose. The geese took wing, our four shots rang out, and the immediate impression was of slain geese filling the view. In actual fact we got our four geese with the four shots, and one could scarcely hope for more!

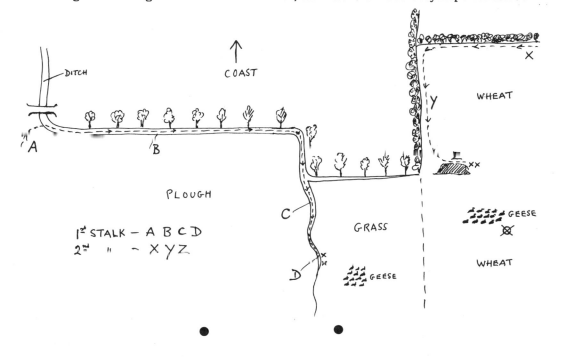

Even "BB" had a shot as the geese swung back over him, but they were then too high and no more fell.

We returned to lunch full of glee and went over it all again with "BB" — he told us we had taken just an hour for the stalk from the time we dropped into the ditch.

In the afternoon we took the car out again and happened to pass along the same road as we took in the morning. To our great surprise the geese were already back again — not in the same field but in the next one, under winter wheat. By this time we had found out that the friendly neighbour was the shooting tenant of the farmer who had refused us, so we could now plan a renewed attack on the geese with clear consciences. This time it appeared there was a possible stalk if we could reach a lump of rubbish at Z, so Bill and I again set out, this time taking the line XYZ. X was about 500 yards from the geese, so we openly walked along this hedge. Along Y we found we were largely in dead ground and could continue at a crouch. But later on we came in-full view of the distant geese at ⊠ and had to resort to hands and knees, while the last 30 yards or so had to be covered ventre-a-terre. I found it far more exhausting than the morning's stalk: there was a hard frost and the ground was like concrete, and we were wrapped up in thick clothes. By the time I had dragged myself behind the heap of bean straw I was sweating all over. I waited for Bill to come up and take his place beside me, and meanwhile took one cautious peep round the side of the lump. All was well, and no further movement was necessary. Bill and I exchanged the same signals and whispers and then brought the stalk to the same tingling climax. The same pandemonium broke out in front, the same four reports — and again four pinks left behind on the ground. Eight geese with eight consecutive shots! It will be a long time before either Bill or I do that again. The departing skeins swung round and actually gave us another chance as they passed to our left, but though we had time to re-load and fire we added no more to the score — except a few feathers floating down.

With Bill after the second stalk

It was of course too much to expect anything more that day and the usual evening flight on the coast was fruitless.

In fact, the whole of the next shooting day (Monday) was a blank for all of us, and I myself never even fired a shot.

But on Tuesday our luck returned. We had found that the greys were still using — intermittently — the field where we had found them on the evening of our first arrival, so we decided to wait for them at dawn and to use my two decoys. Two of us in turn were to wait in the hedge on one side of the field — with the decoys about 40 yards out — but as the field was such a large one and the geese might settle on the other side of it (300 yards away) the third man was to wait in a spinney on the far side and put up any geese that settled on that side, in the hope that they would come back over the two hidden guns.

Again we thought we were up in good time but even as I was setting up the decoys at first light a small party of pinks came in and obviously intended to settle in the field. Later the greys began to come and we all had chances. "BB" brought off a lovely high shot at a single goose, which I — waiting in the spinney — had to chase nearly into the next parish as it only had a broken wing. Then, when it was my turn in one of the hides, a party of six greys actually landed by the decoys and I got a couple as they took off again. Soon after I bagged another as it flew over the decoys, and Bill hit one hard that appeared to come down about a mile away but it was hopeless to think of looking for it. Certainly the decoys had worked well, and had converted remote possibilities into actual probabilities. It particularly pleased — and surprised — me that greylags should respond to pink-foot decoys

24

THE DOUBLE STALK

In the evening we went down to the shore for the evening flight as usual. We were all optimistic, as a mist offered hope that the geese would fly out low, and later on tide and moon conditions suggested that geese might come close in shore while there was still light enough to shoot. I made my way down a deep creek which opened out on to the mud banks and waited for the flight. Skeins came out to right and left, but none over us, but presently I could hear the geese on the water moving in towards the shore. They sounded only 50 yards out, but were no doubt 200 yards or more. Anyhow I crept further out on the mud as the light went and hoped the geese would either swim ashore in front of me or possibly float up my creek on the rising tide. And then quite a different chance occurred. It all happened in a few moments: one second a small skein of half a dozen geese loomed up out of the murk, the next second my gun was up, and the next a greylag had fallen with a thump in the mud beside me. But it was a near thing: all evening I had been warning myself not to shoot at anything that would fall the other side of the creek, as to retrieve it would have been impossible, or at least exceedingly unpleasant, with the creek full of water; but these geese were coming from the other side of the creek and I had only to wait till they were safely over. But my inclination to take my first shot well in front nearly overcame my thought of the creek: the goose fell on the near edge of the creek — fortunately dead! A yard sooner or a wounded bird and I should have lost it.

Wednesday morning produced the best morning flight of the whole trip. "BB" and Bill each got a goose, but it was my turn to draw blank, though I had three shots.

After breakfast we could find no geese on the usual fields, so we set out to tour fresh ground, and eventually found a large number of pinks feeding on a new field. A stalk looked possible but difficult so we left Bill to take it alone, while "BB" and I hid ourselves behind a post and wire fence (!) to intercept the geese when they lifted. By the time Bill got into position the nearest geese were barely in range and when they eventually came over "BB" and me they were still less in range, so we were probably not justified in firing the ineffectual shots that we did.

In the evening we hoped for another promising evening flight on the coast, but we had no luck — and few chances.

And so we came to our last day — Thursday. Bill had to catch the 10.50 a.m. train homewards but was determined to have a last crack before he left, so some elaborate plans had to be made.

We decided to repeat Tuesday morning's procedure — morning flight with decoys; so Bill's urgent luggage was left in the car at the farmyard, and as Bill had no watch, three blasts on the whistle were to warn him that it was 10 a.m. and that he must then leave the field of battle, drive himself to the station, change in the car, repack his luggage, and leave the car there to be collected by one of us later. The decoys did their stuff well again. The morning was misty and the ground covered with a thin coating of snow. Several small lots of geese came to the decoys; "BB" got one very high one, and then a couple of greys swished in from behind me — without sound or warning — and landed by the decoys. I got one and hit the other hard, but the latter, after landing in the next field, took off again and disappeared in the mist. A little later another half dozen came in low over me and gave me an easy shot.

For our final sortie "BB" and I went down to our favourite stretch of coast for the evening flight. The mist had got quite thick, there was still a heavy frost, but no wind so that all the rushes and reeds were plumed in white. There was not a sound at first and the shore had a wild, eerie feeling about it. And then the geese started coming out from the fields, and the sky was full of sound. They came low — as we had hoped and expected. A big skein of pinks came straight over me and I hit one bird hard. Unfortunately he glided down to the mud on a broken wing and to go out after him was out of the question. "BB" had better luck and finished up with a clean kill with his last shot of the trip.

Next morning we were on our respective ways home, after an early breakfast. "BB" and I agreed that it was the best wild fowling holiday either of us had ever had — 27 geese in a fortnight of eight shooting days, and every sort of shooting — morning flight, evening flight, waiting for the dawn feed (with and without decoys), stalking and even driving.

CHAPTER 6
PUDDY TAT HILL
(1950-1951 TONY'S YEAR)

For some reason which I cannot explain I did not keep a record of my trip with "BB" and Tony Wilson in January 1951. But fortunately "BB" kept his usual diary notes and later wrote a brief article for "The Field" and also described parts of the trip in his book "Dark Estuary".

These two extracts, here combined, provide the story of the whole trip, to be told in "BB's" own words.

"It is a fallacy that hard weather is good for wildfowling. Snow and frost drive geese away from their winter haunts, though exactly where they go to is rather a mystery. On the coast the duck are perhaps easier to come by, but when you are on the long trail of the grey geese, duck are ignored, even when they spring up in front of you within easy range. Chances which at home would be eagerly taken are disdained, for when, in the dimness of the dawn, you hear the far cackling of geese, no other game will do.

In January last the Arctic conditions coincided with our prearranged trip to a far northern Firth.

I was to go with Bill on the 4th of January, meeting Mac with the shooting brake at Grantham on the morning of that day, and going on north with him.

But two unforeseen circumstances occurred to upset our plans. First Bill, ever a reckless driver, took a corner too fast and woke up in Rugby Cottage Hospital. On the 2nd and 3rd, snowstorms swept the Midlands and made travel by road a hazardous undertaking. Frantic 'phoning to the A.A. for road reports gave no cause for optimism: The same intelligence was always forthcoming "roads over the Pennines unsuitable for motor traffic . . . ice, snow and drifts at Carter Bar".

At the eleventh hour my cousin, Tony Wilson, took Bill's place, and as Mac and I could not pick him up at Grantham he came to me my train and I met him at the station.

I got on the 'phone to Mac in Norfolk and, to my astonishment, he told me he intended to start in the shooting brake whatever the weather. Hang the road reports! Snow was not lying deep in Norfolk and he thought he could get through. When on the trail of the grey geese, nothing can stop Mac; he is that sort of person. But conditions were different in the Midlands, and Tony and I decided to go by train. On the 4th it snowed harder than ever, and soon after breakfast the 'phone rang. It was Mac. He had reached Holbeach and was pushing on, with conditions getting worse. On the following day Tony and I settled ourselves comfortably in our carriage, and we were soon watching the white landscape with its leaden sky pass in a procession before the steamy windows. Discussing a very excellent roast goose in the dining-car (most appropriate dish for wildfowlers), we speculated where Mac was. Tony, draining his Worthington, surmised he was probably at that moment upside down in a snow drift.

Now I had actually started, the old excitement was rising in me, every bump of the rails was taking me to the land I loved, to the call of the geese along the dawn tide. The sight of the snow-blanketed Pennines, already half visible in the gathering gloom of the winter afternoon, added a spice of anticipation.

When Tony and I disembarked from the train at the little wayside station, the wan light from the single platform-lamp shone on glistening, hard-caked snow. It also illuminated the broad shoulders of Mac who was waiting to greet us. His journey had been an eventful one. He had made it, but only just. And as we drove away down the road, ice hissing and crackling under the wheels, he told us the latest goose news. He had that evening been down on the shore and had never seen so few geese. Just as I feared, the continued hard weather had driven them away. The prospects were far from cheerful.

Looking again just now at my diary of this trip I see the same monotonous entries, "Dawn flight at Leaning Buoy . . . hardly a goose on the Firth . . . Evening flight Curlew Bay . . . three pinks came in fairly early, nothing else moving, more frost last night and the flooded fields are frozen solid".

These frozen, flooded fields presented a unique sight and one which I had never seen before in that locality. During the daytime when the sun shone — and we had much clear, glittering weather for most of our time — miles of flooded land was visible from the high hills to the north of the firth. The dazzle of the sun formed a wide, glittering path on the icy skin which locked plough and pasture alike.

Geese breaking formation as they spiral down to their feeding grounds

It was our regular procedure each day, after morning flight was over and we had had breakfast, to make a tour of the high ground, scanning the low-lying pastures next to the firth for feeding geese. It made me realise how difficult it is for anyone without some means of transport to carry out this routine spying for fowl. If we had confined our attentions and energies to the shore alone, our bag would have been very meagre, apart from much wasted time during the daylight hours.

I would say that no matter what the weather, the daily tour with the telescope is essential if you really wish to get the most out of a wildfowling holiday. We had many farmer friends on those flat lands bordering the firth who were only too pleased to let us have a try at the geese if they happened to be using their pastures.

Though all this glittering icy expanse of flood and the white crisp grass was attractive to the artist's eye, we saw no sign of geese, only numberless crows, rooks, partridges and pheasants, and an occasional hare which looked as big as a well-grown dog against the snow.

In normal times, when the weather is open, all this ground is real "goose country", and a tour by "scouting" car will discover for you many hundreds, sometimes thousands, of geese feeding on their favourite fields. Pinks seem to prefer barley stubble to fresh grass; greylags eat a good deal more grass than pinks. It is strange that the two species do not seem to mix, though I have frequently seen both species feeding on the same field. Usually, however, you will find greys in one field and pinks in another.

The best time for watching the big lots is in the early part of the year, just when they have arrived in late October and November. After that time the big gaggles break up and scatter, though in an open winter on the firth I have in mind one may count on 1,500 to 2,000 geese, pinks and greys mixed, which make up a resident population. The greys are far less apt to wander and do not appear to change their feeding grounds as frequently as pinks. The latter may be here today and gone tomorrow and you cannot count on them with any degree of certainty.

On referring to my note-book, I see that our first morning flight, after a frosty night, was quite mild and a temporary thaw occurred. There was very little moving at morning flight, though I missed a single chance at a greylag which came in to the sea over my head. As I was of course, looking the other way, I never had a chance to get the gun up until the goose was well out over the muds.

But that afternoon we had our first exciting moment (date, January 7th). From a mild morning the weather had changed again; the hard times were coming back. A cold mist gathering soon after midday was its advance guard. We were scouting in the van and, drawing a blank at all our favourite fields, we went higher up the firth to hitherto unexplored country. Soon I noticed a small conical hill of stubble on which the snow still lay in patches away to our right. We stopped the van and Mac took a spy through the glass.

I had noticed, with the naked eye, some dark spots ranged along the hillside, and thought they were feeding rooks, but Mac soon exclaimed, ''There they are!''

I should say that thirty geese — whether pinks or greys we could not see from where we were — appeared to be busily feeding on the south slope of the hill, and we at once made our way to the farm.

Personally I hate asking for permission from strangers, nor is Tony good at this delicate business. So Mac had to go, as he always does, and after a long interval he returned with a rather dazed expression.

Apparently the door had been opened by a quite ravishing blonde, and a few moments later this lovely lady appeared, driving a large car down the lane. Neither Tony nor I could blame Mac for having a far-away look in his eyes. She had been most gracious and told us we could certainly try for the geese. So it was we were introduced to Puddy Tat Hill, and this locality was to provide us with some exciting times for the rest of our trip.

We left the van in the farmyard where sparrows chirped and the smell of far-off summer still seemed to linger, and walked past the house to spy the land. We found that a narrow and very rutty lane led directly towards the swelling hill, passing a little to its left. This was the obvious course to take and, as we were about to return to the van, a large party of pinks came cackling from the sea. After wheeling several times round the hill, they settled on some flat fields on the left of the lane, about a hundred yards from the hill where the other geese were feeding (or at least we imagined and hoped they were).

These newcomers rather upset our plans and we held a council of war. We decided on the only course open to us. If we walked boldly down the lane, we should at once be seen by the pinks who were now chattering and feeding in the flat, unapproachable field. These geese would rise and give the alarm and take the others with them from the hill.

The only course was to drive the van slowly down the lane and bring it to a standstill behind some straw stacks which were on the left — between the geese and the hill. This we did and, as we drew up behind the stacks, the pinks all lifted with a great clamour and made off. We were sure that the birds on the blind side of Puddy Tat Hill had lifted too, though we hadn't seen them do so. The only thing was to have a spy. We tossed for the chance. Mac won.

We were still a little way from the foot of the hill, so we decided to take the van farther and disembark Mac at the foot of the fence. We slowly moved off. Than a rather surprising thing happened. Over the fence and not thirty yards from the lane I suddenly caught sight of five long necks sticking up like umbrella handles. They were greylags. They had seen and heard the van and were on the point of flight. Mac, with great presence of mind, immediately reversed the van and we gained the shelter of the stacks again without the geese lifting. Greylags will sometimes allow one to do the most outrageous things and they (like big game in a national park) had evidently not connected the van with their deadly enemy.

Mac now got out with his Magnum 12 and, with BB in both barrels, began to squirm back along the lane, keeping close to the fence which was the usual "goose country" type, post and wire. A fringe of dead grass grew all along the bottom of this fence and the road was slightly below the level of the field. Even so, he had no more than an inch of "freeboard" and had to keep well down in the melting slush.

In about twenty minutes Mac had wormed a dolorous sixty yards and was almost up to the geese. It was watching him creeping along the fence which gave us the obvious title to the hill. Mac was, without any doubt, Sylvester, the wicked Puddy Tat of the song.

At last there came the moment when we saw Mac's booted legs spidering crabwise into the lane. He was pivoting on his elbows for a shot which he took through the wire, one on the ground and one as they rose. Bang! Bang! Mac was up battling with the wire.

One jump and he was over and vanished out of sight over the rim of the stubble. I did not know whether he had scored or not, for I had seen no geese rise. We walked down the lane and Mac's head came bobbing over the hill. Two greylags hung from his left hand, their snow-white sterns together and broad wings flapping wide. It was a good start to the trip and it had been a good stalk too.

It is not easy to pick out the best moments of the trip. There was that foggy morning when visibility was less than 10 yards and, luckily for us, the pinks were in the firth. As it grew light we could hear them calling in the murk. Suddenly a skein appeared out of the fog directly overhead, and the leader thumped the mud within 3 ft. of me.

"BB" waiting in a ditch near Puddy Tat Hill

There was that sunny afternoon when Tony and I lay in wait on the steep side of a burn while Mac went round a mile off to walk some pinks over us. I lay on the snow watching and listening to a fieldfare on a dead thorn bush close by; a hare hopped miserably along, sniffing at the snowy crust, within a few feet of me. Then the hard white rim of the field in front of me spouted geese. They swept down as big as bustards, but turned 60 yards out and headed for the firth. I downed the nearest bird with BB shot.

But it was not always like this. Tony spent all one afternoon bellying along a fence in the snow to where four greys were grazing in a grass meadow. The geese were working up the fence, eating the grass which showed under the wire, the only visible herbage the poor birds could find. When Tony was almost in position a Spitfire zoomed over the hill and the greys arose heavily and departed for the sea.

Our total bag for 10 days was 12 geese. I contributed three with my magnum (in all fairness be it said that I had only four chances, so I cannot grumble) and Tony one. Mac with his double eight-bore, grim persistence, and utter disregard for bodily comfort (internal or external) well deserved his eight. These included a right and left. We lost only two birds and we should have had one of those if we had taken a dog with us".

CHAPTER 7
THE FLIGHT OF FLIGHTS
(1951-1952 CHARLES' YEAR)

The start of our trip followed the familiar pattern of our expedition in January, 1950. We met at Grantham on November 3rd, and reached the same little hotel over the border that evening. Next day we reached our H.Q. on the Scottish coast just before 4 p.m., and went straight down to the seabank to see what prospects were like.

As we had passed through the Central Lowlands, the weather had become wild and stormy, and we eventually arrived with a full gale blowing and driving rain coming in off the sea.

A small lot of greys lifted off a nearby field and battled out to the river just as we reached the seabank, and then for perhaps half-an-hour we never saw another goose. But just as the light began to fade, the sky suddenly filled with skein after skein of geese dropping down from over the northern hills, and beating out to sea against the rain and wind. For perhaps a quarter of an hour the sky over a 5-mile stretch of coast was streaked with the weaving, waving lines of the skeins, many of which crossed the coastline within reasonable range.

Never have I seen such an evening flight of geese, though I am not sure that it was so much a true "flight" as a mass arrival of new geese from further north. Several thousand must have dropped into the river that evening, and our hopes and excitement ran high.

I think we all slept fitfully that night, with one ear on the raging gale outside. But it held, and it was just as wild when we got up at 5.45 a.m. next morning and set out to meet the morning flight on the coast. I chose my favourite spot where I knew I could get out through the reed beds to the edge of the mud without having to cross any deep creeks that might cut me off on a rising tide. But I could find no beaten track and had to force my way through a dense stand of reeds, bent nearly flat with the wind. Twice I almost gave up the struggle and began contemplating alternative plans, for it would be hopeless to be caught in the middle of the reed bed at the height of the flight. But in the end I got through and reached a good vantage point — but soaked through from the knees upwards, for where the rain hadn't penetrated from outside, the perspiration had from within!

And then began the most wonderful morning flight we had ever seen — a continuous stream of geese in large and small skeins coming in off the mud banks, and mostly at a reasonable height. Of course, with a 5-mile stretch of coast, the number of geese over any individual gunner must be limited, but we all had several shots and all got geese.

I had a couple, "BB" got 3, while Charles on the right of the line had no less than 6 down, 2 of which he retrieved at once, 3 dropped across a stream but were found later when we went out again after breakfast, and 1 was lost. Altogether, 10 geese in the bag, all pinks except one of mine which was a grey.

During the middle of the day we did the usual "recce" by car of all the likely feeding grounds, and in the evening we went back to the coast for the return evening flight. But the wind had now dropped somewhat and there was nothing like the flight of the previous evening. Of the few lots that came out low, I was lucky to get one, and I also managed to pull down a mallard and a teal (with the 8-bore).

The next day was a good deal calmer and the morning flight, though still impressive, was not so good. We had moved to a new stretch of coast, and the only goose we got was a pink which I dropped in the reeds with the first shot of the morning. As on several other occasions, the chance of a left-and-right had to be sacrificed to the need for absolutely accurate marking of the first bird. Otherwise the chance of a retrieve from the dense reeds was extremely remote. In these dense and tall reed beds, the visible horizon is often only a few yards away, and the only practical method of "marking" that we have discovered is to note carefully the most distant but clearly identifiable reed — perhaps ten yards away — on the line of the fall, go straight to it and tie a small white rag to it. Then, if conditions permit, walk out on this line and tie another piece of rag to a reed at the distance at which you thought the goose fell. You can now go back and await the end of the flight, and leave the actual search till later. A goose can lie half-buried in the tangled undergrowth of reeds, and be invisible within a couple of paces, so that a methodical search, yard by yard, is often necessary. Later in the morning, I shot another goose which carried on and suddenly dropped out of the skein a quarter of a mile away — but still in the reeds. This was one of the few shot birds we never found.

The geese came in alright — but at a great height

I also managed to get a mallard out of a small party flying back to the river. It dropped out in the water, but the incoming tide and wind took it along the coast and past the mouth of a small (but uncrossable) creek. I guessed it would be floated up into the short reeds and left there when the tide ebbed. Sure enough, in the afternoon I went down to the other side of the creek and found my mallard caught up in the reed stubble, but already showing signs of a carrion crow's attentions.

The evening flight was uneventful, though quite a number of geese came out very high.

On our third morning we decided to wait for the geese inland, on a stubble field they were using. But the morning was too calm; the geese came in alright, but at a great height, circled the field and in most cases obviously suspected that there was a catch somewhere. We had two decoys out, but as it was a large field, we reckoned we should have few chances from the hedges and ditches. So we arranged to lie out in the centre of the field; two of us at a time, with the third man to cover us with loose straw and then signal the approach of geese with a whistle — from the cover of the hedge. "BB" managed to get one goose, but though Charles and I both had chances, we messed them up. We made two mistakes and found them out the hard way. Firstly, we had lain down so that we could watch the distant coastline from which we knew the geese would first appear. But the wind was also blowing off the coast, which meant that the birds swung round behind the prostrate gunners and came in to land from behind them. This made it almost impossible to judge the instant for sitting up and getting into action. We soon learned that it is essential to lie facing the final glide-in of the geese, or rather facing slightly to the right of that line so that one can follow the birds round to either the right rear or the left rear. The second difficulty was to get rid of the loose straw on one's face and gun before trying to shoot. It is impossible to aim with a small straw stack lying along one's barrels! But in the excitement of the moment it requires no small effort to devote the extra couple of seconds to clearing away the straw.

The fourth day produced a fair morning flight, but we only got one grey, which I shot at my favourite spot near "Goose's Graveyard". But after breakfast, a "recce" yielded a party of six pinks feeding on a barley stubble, two fields away from a main road. A drainage ditch separated the second field from the first, and then turned at right angles and ran through a bridge under the road. The geese seemed to be within range of this ditch, and it was therefore a straightforward stalk along the ditch. I even thought at first it was going to be a dry stalk, as I could just walk along the bottom of the ditch in my long waders. But there were several deeper holes and before long I was well over the tops. When I reached the point which I calculated should be opposite the geese, I clambered carefully up the bank and peeped over, but at first could see nothing. Then, as I raised my head higher above the convex surface of the field, I saw the geese a long way out. Apparently the stationary car on the road had worried them and they had been walking quietly away the whole time I was working towards them. There was nothing to do but try an immediate shot with the 8-bore. I fired at the six umbrella handles and let off the second barrel at one of the departing bunch. I was somewhat surprised to see one goose left dead on the field and a second one drop out of the skein at the far end of the field.

As on the previous day, the evening flight was uneventful.

The following morning we were back on the coast for the morning flight, and I got well out on to the mud along the remnants of a stone breakwater. The flight as such was one of the most impressive I have ever seen, skein after skein lifting off the river between about 7.30 a.m. and 8.30 a.m. But very few offered shots; one small lot of greys tried to slip in between me and the land — quite low, and I dropped one on the mud; neither of the other two guns had a fair chance. In the evening not one of us even had a shot.

The next day exceeded all early promise. We had decided to try again the field we had worked on our third morning — the geese had already started using it again. At first light it was a dull grey morning, with little wind, but by the time the geese began to arrive, it was blowing half a gale, with driving rain. Geese kept trying to come in with half their usual caution, and at half their normal height, and moreover we profited from past experience and improved our technique. The result was ten more geese in the bag — 4 to Charles (who got a L. and R.), 3 to "BB" and 3 to myself. Even when we thought it was all over at about 10 a.m. and were shivering in the ditch eating our sandwich breakfast, a skein came beating in low against the wind, and "BB" and I got 3 with our 4 shots from the ditch.

The following day was Sunday, and during the day it became clear that a field in sight of our quarters, which we had been watching for the last few days, must be dealt with first thing

Charles with "BB" — and Jock, the tame village Greylag

on Monday. Over the past four days, the geese feeding on this field had worked up from a mere handful to about 500, and by Sunday midday they had obviously nearly cleaned up the grain on the stubble. They then began moving to two neighbouring stubbles. So that afternoon was spent in tracing the farmers of the fields in question, and getting their permission to shoot on their land. Late on Sunday night we went out and pegged sheets of newspaper all over the two new stubble fields in the hope of discouraging the geese from flying straight to those fields in the morning.

Our plans worked fairly well, but the calm weather was against us — and possibly the geese were growing increasingly suspicious of lumps of loose straw lying about their favourite fields. But we managed to bag 5 — Charles and I two each and "BB" one.

In the afternoon, some greys were back in one of these fields and offered a possible stalk. Charles set out and got to the point where the geese should have been. In the meantime the geese had moved towards him, and they must have passed a few yards apart with a fringe of reeds between them! When he saw the geese they had already seen him and were away.

By now the geese were no doubt getting harried and very few were to be seen at the next morning flight. I flushed and shot a grey from the reeds as I made my way out at first light, but he was no doubt a pricked bird. Later, when coming in from the mud I spotted a goose lying out in the open, which proved to be a freshly expired pink, and in the reeds I almost walked on to another pricked bird. There is little doubt these were all "our" birds, as no other gunners had been out recently.

That night Charles and I went out under the full moon, in the hope that geese would be moving up and down the coast, but there was very little sign of any geese on the wing. We nearly got up to a party of greys just beyond the limit of the reeds, but the night was too still, and with so many geese already accounted for, we did not feel inclined to get down to a serious stalk on our hands and knees in the mud. We stayed out a couple of hours and then gave it up.

Our last day hardly seemed hopeful; the weather remained calm, the geese were obviously both avoiding our immediate stretch of coast and also going further afield to feed. Our usual flight lines and feeding grounds were almost deserted. It seems that this district can only stand about ten days of intensive goose hunting — and incidentally, that is about as much as the hunters can stand. Yet our last morning flight was quite a fair one. Most of the geese could be seen departing up-river for new feeding grounds, but a few skeins proved faithful, and I had two lots right over me. The first — a large group of several skeins — came over rather too high, and passed unscathed. The second was a small skein of about a dozen that came straight for me, within comfortable range. I kept right down till the last second, then took the leader well in front — he dropped dead with a crash a few yards behind me. That night, as the others had packed ready for an early departure next day, I went out alone to a stubble field and hoped for a final shoot under the moon. Elaborate disguise was out of the question, but I took the two decoys — put them out between me and the moon and sat on an apple box in the middle of the field. It was barley stubble that had been combined, and there was plenty of loose straw to throw over my legs, shoulders and cap. There was much astir — mallard were chattering, teal whistling and even an occasional "whee-oo" from a wigeon, and then soon after 11 p.m. I heard pinks on the move. Altogether I had three lots down in the field — but all in far corners, and I had to put them off to prevent them decoying others to them. I saw two more lots pass right overhead — but out of range, and I heard several other parties flying about. It was all very thrilling, but I never had a shot, and at 1.30 a.m. I gave it up and crept back to bed. Next morning came the day of departure — the checking of the bag and the dividing of the spoils. The final score was 36 geese, 2 mallard and 1 teal in nine shooting days, and never a blank day nor a dull one.

CHAPTER 8
FAMILY SHOOT
(1952)

The family were all together again so my father suggested the customary shoot — en famille. It is a day always for a pocketful of cartridges, gum boots, a dog or two, a nonchalance for getting wet and a sense of humour. Thus it was at 10.30 the four of us started off across Church Field with a small but enthusiastic army of beaters.

The morning was clear and crisp with an horizon which only comes from proximity to the sea, and a wind which chilled the gun barrels and kept one moving. We pushed what birds there were into that oddity of acres, Roundabouts — Roundabouts with the trees on three sides and water beyond : a boundary field and wet. When after game the only effective method is to walk round it as its name implies. On this occasion I stood forward of the rest of the party, in a small clearing, and waited for what should come. On my right stretched the main dyke, dark and clear, and to the left lay the field visible past the hazels. First came the rats, two of them, swimming into the reeds, leaving their V track behind them. Then as the deep Ho-Ho of the small army grew louder and their sticks whacking the briars came keener to the ear, the pheasants broke for the marshes and streamed over to the west. A hare flickered by, gauche and obviously out of place ; and then the rabbits.

How soon one gets to know men's voices. Young Eddie was on the left (I caught traces of his favourite song), and Andrews, with the piping whistle and long tread rummaging among the thorns, was obviously by him.

After Roundabouts, Jack Kemp, and then on to the willows and a beat through Church Wood. Alan and Keith went forward here to the footpath, while we took the wood in one sweep towards them. Being low ground on the fen there is little chance for that classic shot, the high curling pheasant, unless one is lucky in choice of stand. Alan was. Standing in the ride with a bare twelve feet of clear sky above him, he tumbled his first cock bird into the reeds as it clattered past over the firs. The splash sounded back seconds afterwards with a plop of reassurance. It was a shot of merit, combining quick eye and swing, and to those of us who are merely adequate shots, such occasions come perhaps once or twice a season. This was just such a time, and we shall doubtless remember it till next autumn. Further back, at Fuller's Folly, Keith did the same thing though prompted and piqued by a solitary teal which had pirouetted virtually unscathed over his head a second previously.

After lunch we tried Goose Marsh for rabbits, and took two and a rat from a bramble thicket. Beyond them we felled an old cock pheasant. He was quite the oldest bird I have ever seen and a fitting reward for the weary splash through the Heronry with its twenty-five dykes all brimming deep. Fallen trees make deceptive bridges when, with considerable skill, one has balanced precariously down the length of a trunk only to find that beyond the vertical roots lies a bigger and deeper pool than has yet been met.

FAMILY SHOOT

With the failing light we pushed out in the grey punt to the hides on the broad. I waded ashore at Heronry Point to my barrel knee deep in water, Keith was dropped off at The Island, Alan at Mamba Point, and my father took the punt to his own post on Long Island. It was a moonless winter's evening with a thick bank of cloud hiding the sunset and a sharp freezing wind driving through the trees to move the mist off the water. By no stretch of imagination could the flight be termed a battue; the teal were very wary, the mallard none too plentiful, but we all got good shooting at fast birds. In the shallows of Rose Fen the call duck continued to quack indignantly and sallied forth during each lull across the water, only to turn helter-skelter back for the reeds after each shot — a bobbing and complaining motley. It is their nightly ritual. Once they have crossed those first few dark yards of clear water they are in the main farm dyke, and may swim undaunted for a mile if need be to the bare staithe at Woodend. But on flighting evenings, their courage fails them.

As the night grew darker and the dropping wings loomed large and then blurred completely with that queer trick of the half light, there was strong shooting from all of us though the bag never promised to be heavy. One lone mallard, dropping in against the dark alders, met Keith with mutual surprise and scrambled off through the islands before the latter could collect himself and turn round in his barrel. A faint cackle from across the water told me that the incident had not gone unnoticed by others. Almost towards the end of the day came a tantalising swirl of teal over our heads. Once, twice, five times they swept round, and then as they dropped in for the last time, that uncanny instinct sent their necks arching back and their feet pulled in as they crabbed away into the frost and loneliness of the December night, towards Hickling perhaps, or the river under the hill at Wayford.

The pick-up was lengthy, the dog tired and the torch weak. Those of us who had gone "over the top" enjoyed the anticipation of warm socks and a fire, the retriever waited for clean straw and a bone, and the four of us to a post-mortem in the Oak Room with the game book.

CHAPTER 9
RETURN TO THE WASH
(NOVEMBER, 1952)

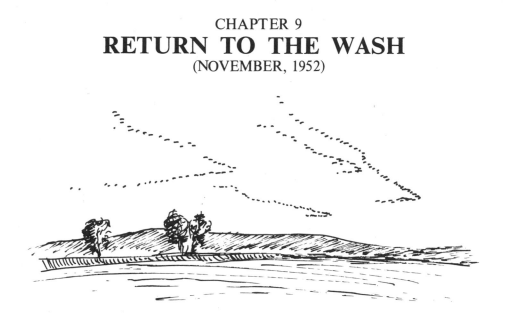

I have just got home from a brief goose-hunting expedition to the Wash. A fellow enthusiast rang me up a few days ago and suggested we should go off together this weekend. I tried to get Colin for a third, but he couldn't get away, and so I got Peter Wilson to come instead. It's always thrilling to go out after wild geese, and the first foray of the season is especially exciting. "BB" and I always tell each other we have chronic goose fever, and the first sight or sound of wild geese in the autumn always brings on a severe attack of the disease which can only be assuaged by packing our guns and kit and heading for one of our fowling haunts. A few days ago Andrews told me he had seen a large skein of wild geese flying over Catfield, so I was in a susceptible condition to receive my friend's invitation.

We drove up the coast on Sunday, collecting my friend halfway, and arrived at the Wash in the late afternoon. This friend — I will call him Henry — has an old single-decker 'bus which he has converted into a self-propelled caravan. In the summer he lets it as holiday accommodation on the Norfolk coast: in the winter he drives it up to the Wash and leaves it there as his wild-fowling H.Q. for weekend trips with two or three friends. It is parked at the end of a road leading up to the sea-wall — right in the heart of the goose country, and thus makes an ideal base for fowling trips.

That evening Peter and I just had time to walk out on the marshes to see what prospects were like and heard a few lots of geese moving out to the mud after their day's feeding inland.

Next morning we were to get up early and take up position as far out on the mud as we could get to intercept the morning flight, but a disaster occurred. Henry had forgotten the alarm clock, and in spite of all our resolutions we all overslept in the morning: instead of getting up at 5.30 a.m. it was 6.30 before the first of us awoke. Half the trouble was that in the middle of the night we had been woken — and tormented — by the cries of geese moving in to the fields under the moon (it was the last quarter rising at about 11 p.m.), and after that we eventually fell into deep but late sleep that carried us an hour past our planned hour. So we tumbled into our clothes and dashed out across the marsh. But even as we hurried out the geese were flying in — high and wide, and we never had a shot though we saw several hundred.

After a late breakfast back in the bus we took a walk along the sea-wall to spy out the land but saw no geese, though we marked several likely potato fields. At 3 p.m. we set out again, striking out across the saltmarsh and mud to where a deep creek gave us good cover — about a mile out from the land. We hardly expected to get any chances at the geese but were hopeful of seeing some duck.

We did in fact see several lots of geese come out to the mudbanks, and quite a few duck came beating in from the open sea for their nightly feed. Only one pair of mallard gave me a chance, flying low over the mud the other side of the creek. I gave them a crack with the 8-bore, and hit both birds; but it was the rear one (the drake as usual) which crumpled up; the front one also came down but recovered and flew off again.

I sent Laddie across the creek for the drake but he arrived just to windward of the bird and continued to quest up wind. After some minutes he came back empty-mouthed and I had to send him across again, this time further down wind. He soon picked up the scent, found the bird, and swam back across the creek with it. By this time it was nearly dark, the flight was over and a sudden squall of driving rain broke over us. It was a long, wet tramp home, in the teeth of the wind and rain, and we were tired, wet and hungry by the time we reached our caravan.

Next morning we organised a human alarm clock in the person of one of the R.A.F. cooks from the nearby bombing camp. At 5.30 he banged on our windows and we were out in good time. I took Peter further up the coast and intended to get right out on to the mud again, but before we left the saltmarsh, and when it was just beginning to get fairly light, I stopped and examined the mud banks in front of us, through my glasses. And there — straight in front of us, and perhaps 500 yards ahead — were 60-70 geese sitting on the mud. They were too close — and it was too light — to risk going any further out, so we both got down into the nearest creeks and awaited developments. At 6.40 a.m. the first skeins appeared in the sky, from both further up and down the coast, and most of these geese seemed to be making for one of the potato fields we had spotted yesterday. Several hundred geese were soon circling over this field, and presently many more — probably 500 — rose from it and joined those circling above. No doubt the latter had moved in under the moon and stayed in the field till dawn.

Eventually there was a nearer outburst of clamour and the party of geese in front of us rose and headed for the land. They came straight for Peter and myself, but climbing fast. Peter fired first and of course they shot up still higher, and by the time they reached me they were barely in range. Anyhow no goose fell to our fusillade, though two were obviously hit and lagged behind the rest of the skein for a long while.

After another quarter of an hour the flight was clearly over — the glasses showed no geese left on the mud and we tramped home again. Meanwhile Henry had got one down from the sea wall, and though it fell on a bare ploughed field, by the time he went after it it had struggled to the edge of the field and disappeared. No doubt it had got into the boundary ditch and made off along that: we never found it. And that was the end of the trip: we made our usual breakfast, sorted out our gear, packed our bags, loaded up the van and left the caravan locked up but ready for the next visiting party.

Curious that one should travel 90 miles (each way) and put up with quite considerable discomfort and hardship for a couple of days — and have 1 mallard to show for it (and sometimes not even that), when I can stroll down to my own marshes at home any evening and shoot several mallard in perfect comfort. But of course there is something about real wild-fowling, and goose-hunting in particular that "gets" you, and if you are susceptible to goose fever you are beyond hope.

It is just 19 years since I shot my first goose on the Wash, and though I now know of better places and get better bags, I am quite sure that of the many times I have been to the Wash I have come away without a goose more often than with one — and still the old magic works!

CHAPTER 10
THE FLIGHT IN A SNOWSTORM
(1952-1953 Alan's Year)

The general pattern of this wildfowling holiday followed very closely that of previous ones that I have described. This year, however, there were four of us; myself and my second son Alan, "BB" and his friend Tom. Also, we had two vans which increased our powers of reconnaissance, and Tom and I each took a dog.

Alan and I left Catfield on Saturday, December 6th, and got over the border that night, where we met "BB" and Tom at our usual rendezvous.

Next day we reached our fowling headquarters and, as usual, timed our journey so that we arrived just before dusk and were able to go straight down to the coast to see what was moving. It was then full tide and there seemed to be a good number of greylags swimming in the water close to the edge of the reedbeds. A bit later, as the light was failing, several large skeins of pinkfoots came swinging out to the centre of the estuary, filling the sky with their clamour, but only just visible high up in the dusk.

The weather was mild and cloudy, but in no way stormy, and "BB" and I warned each other that we could not expect a repetition of last season's marvellous first-morning flight.

In the morning we were up at six with the usual feelings of excitement and speculation as to what the day would bring. We went down to the coast and crept out as near as possible to the edge of the mud to await the morning flight. "BB" found geese close in where he was and stalked up to within shot of them in the darkness, but he missed with his shot and at the report all the geese close in rose with a roar of wings and moved far out into the river. Where they went after that I cannot say; Alan and I only saw a few distant skeins moving inland and never had a chance of a shot ourselves. It was a very disappointing start.

Our usual recce after breakfast was almost as bad; we only spotted three small parties of geese feeding inland; one big lot on a potato stubble, one on a stubble near the railway, and a gaggle of about 60 greys on a stubble next to the main road. Later we went round to see the various farmers and get permission to go on their land.

By that time there was nothing left but to go back to the coast for the evening flight. On the way we spotted a single goose on a stubble next to the seawall, so the other three slipped round to get on the seaward side of him while I waited to put him up. But he flew rather wide and passed unscathed. While this was going on another five geese dropped into another field close by, so now I had to stalk round to the landward side of these newcomers, to try and put them over the waiting guns on the foreshore. But again the geese gained the estuary untouched, and though we all waited for any further lots to flight out, we had no more chances and returned to our quarters somewhat dispirited after a blank day.

Next day things began to go better. We had decided to wait for the geese on the potato stubble at dawn, with decoys out. At first few geese came near, probably largely due to a team of men who turned up on the far side of the field and started baling a stack of hay. A shepherd with his two dogs wandering round a flock of sheep on an adjoining corn stubble also tended to make the geese wary. But at about nine, the men went off for a breakfast break and the geese began arriving more frequently and more boldly. "BB" got three with two shots out of one lot, and Tom got another.

Later, as one of the last skeins came over, the others got in a volley of three shots and I noticed one goose obviously hit. It failed to keep up with the others and lagged further and further behind. Such a bird very often collapses before long, and this one I followed with my glasses after it was beyond normal sight. Sure enough, it finally packed up and fell to earth. It must have been quite half a mile away where I eventually found it — dead on a ploughed field. So our bag for the morning was five and we went home for lunch in better spirits.

Incidentally, at one point in the morning a single barnacle goose landed in a field behind us with a small party of greys — it was the only goose other than greys and pinks that we saw during the whole trip.

With Tom after a morning flight

In the afternoon we continued searching the countryside for further feeding grounds — with no luck, but towards flighting time we suddenly heard geese on the wing and spotted a skein heading out for the sea. They were coming straight for our little convoy of two vans and quite low, so there was a wild scramble for guns and cartridges. Three of us were ready for them in time — crouching behind the vans — and gave them a volley as they crossed the road. My second barrel brought down one, which toppled into the field behind me. But it regained control before hitting the ground, glided to a stop and by the time we had sent the dogs after it, had recovered sufficiently to take off again, and make for the river, which it appeared to reach.

THE FLIGHT IN A SNOWSTORM

The evening flight on the coast was also profitless. We saw several big lots of pinks coming out very high, and opposite me on the mud a small party of 30 greys had settled on the mud quite close to the shore. As the light failed I tried walking out quietly towards them, but when I was only 100 yards out and still only halfway to them, they became aware of me and took off.

Next morning we considered our best chance was to try the corn stubble by the main road. This was a very large field and it seemed doubtful whether the geese would come near the one boundary ditch that afforded any cover. So we put the decoys well out in the field and took it in turns to lie down flat in the field covered with loose straw. We did this two at a time while the other two hid up in the ditch and gave warning of approaching skeins by giving a blast on a whistle. The two gunners had then to gauge the moment when they should leap into action and deal with the approaching geese. But it is a tricky business and none of us did very well. "BB", Tom and I each got one in turn, and then "BB" and I had a skein right over us on our last turn in the field. "BB" fired first, and then as they swung still higher over me, I managed to get clear of the straw and bring my gun up. My second shot hit a bird which dropped out of the skein and fell dead close behind me. It was a lucky shot — one of the highest I have ever seen — as the bird had stopped a single BB pellet in its neck.

When the geese stopped coming in, we gathered together for our sandwich breakfast and then spent the rest of the morning doing the usual recce. We located several small lots of geese, but nothing that held out much hope.

In the afternoon we repaired to the coast, Alan and I going out beyond "Goose's Graveyard". We found a gaggle of greys close in and began to plan a stalk, but the geese had clearly seen us as soon as we had seen them and moved off up river. So we waited there for the evening flight — one eye on the land for geese coming out, and the other on the estuary for duck coming in. Before long four mallard came along, and I managed to down one. It dropped out on the mud across a creek and I couldn't have retrieved it without Laddie. Then as Laddie and I got back to our patch of cover, a skein of a dozen greys came planing down silently to the mud — exactly where we had been collecting the duck five minutes earlier! That was the nearest we had to a chance, though we saw and heard the usual big lots of pinks coming out high up. No doubt they had been feeding far inland and had had to climb high to clear the hills.

Thursday broke still and clear with a bright, waning moon. We were down to the shore before dawn as usual, though it all looked pretty hopeless. Alan on my left had several shots at high skeins, and I thought I heard a distant thump after one of his shots. The only skeins that came my way were either very wide or very high and I never even fired. On the right, "BB" and Tom seemed to be having a few shots half a mile away. It was a wonderful sunrise — the geese showed up black and sharp against the pale green of dawn, then a few clouds tinged with flame showed that the sun was about to rise. At nine it was all over, and I went to collect Alan who, sure enough, had a goose down in the reeds. Back at our quarters we found "BB" and Tom had got four — to our great surprise; two skeins of greys had come in low over them and they had downed five, though one was never found in the dense reed beds.

After lunch, "BB" and Tom set out by van to try and find the more distant feeding grounds over the hills, while Alan and I explored further stretches of the coast. Eventually we returned to our favourite spot for evening flight, but as we were walking down to the shore I spotted three lone geese on the last field. So Alan went off in a wide arc to get on the seaward side of the geese. I gave him a quarter of an hour and then started off across the open fields towards the geese. As I got near this last field I could see four more geese on it, and before long all seven lifted and swung out to sea. This time the drive was successful; the nearest birds passed within range of Alan, who got one. It dropped in a dense patch of reeds, but Laddie soon found it for us.

We stayed on for the usual dusk flight, but nothing came near us, though large skeins of pinks again came streaming out with the last of the light — all bands playing.

When we got back to the village we found "BB" and Tom with wonderful reports of having found tremendous concentrations of geese over the hills; 1,800 - 2,000 pinks in one field alone, and 600 greys in another. Then and there they got permission to go after the pinks, and Tom bagged two after a comparatively short stalk. So the day's total came to 8, though when I awoke I would have bet even money we wouldn't get a goose all day.

Next morning again looked disappointing — still and clear, but we faithfully went down to the shore as usual. I had nothing at all near me, but Alan had several shots and dropped another grey in the reeds, and "BB" and Tom also had a few chances and shot a grey which turned back to the sea and dropped far out on the mud, 200 yards out. Tom's springer made a spectacular retrieve, going across a **creek** to bring the goose back.

Tremendous concentrations of geese over the hills

After breakfast we took a sandwich lunch and set out inland for the farms "BB" and Tom had found yesterday. There were plenty of geese on two farms on either side of a country road, but not so many as the day before. We got permission to go after the geese on the lefthand farm at dawn on the morrow, and decided to leave them undisturbed for the time being. We than approached the other farmer and got permission to go after the other lot of geese — which we did at once.

A large party of greys were on a potato field and meadow bordering a small burn — and within gunshot of the burn. So we attempted a stalk — all four of us together down the burn! It was hard going for a quarter of a mile, moving slowly and as quietly as possible, and bent double all the time. At last we got nearly opposite to the geese, when suddenly they rose. We leaped into action and let off all our eight barrels between us, but only 1 goose fell at once (to my first shot) though another dropped out on to the next field but one. There is nothing like wildfowling to reduce one's opinion of one's marksmanship! But the difficulties of an exhausting stalk, a slippery stance in a burn and aiming through thorn bushes and a post and wire fence — to say nothing of the general tense excitement — all offer some excuse.

Walking back to the van for lunch, two pinks came straight for us. We "froze" against the posts of the nearest fence, and as they passed high overhead, we let fly; one fell but the other passed on.

After lunch we waited in the burn for geese to come back, but though a few skeins came over high, they would not return to the same fields though we had set up a couple of the dead geese as decoys. No doubt they could see one or other of us, as the cover was poor. Four gunners together load the dice very much in the geese's favour. However, 5 for the day exceeded our early expectations.

Saturday was to be our last day's shooting before returning south, and we had planned to deal with the pinks on the other farm over the hill. It proved a grand climax to our week's trip. We calculated that our usual routine would get us to the distant field in time to be ready for the pinks as they arrived from the mudbanks for their morning feed. So we rose at six and left our quarters at 6.30 a.m. with flasks and sandwiches for breakfast. It was a cold, frosty morning with a slight powdering of snow. As we struck up the winding road over the hills, the snow get deeper and after

THE FLIGHT IN A SNOWSTORM

Tom — down on the coast

we had left the last cottages behind, we found ourselves driving over a smooth unbroken covering of snow with no marks except the occasional tracks of rabbits and hares.

Arrived at the farmyard, we struck out across the fields, laken with guns and decoys, and found our way in the dark to a potato stubble and a grass field lying on either side of a small narrow burn. These fields had been covered with geese the day before, and we felt confident they would come again. To the south lay the hills over which we had just come, and over which the geese should soon be following us. The countryside lay cold and white, with a slight N.W. breeze and heavy clouds building up in the north. We put the decoys out in both fields; two greys behind us on the potato stubble, and two pinks in front of us on the grass field, and took up our own positions along the burn — crouching in clumps of rushes or behind thorn bushes. Just before eight the first sound of geese reached us and skeins began arriving — so did the snow. For a couple of hours there was hardly a moment when there was not a skein in the sky, or at least the sound of a skein approaching through the curtain of snow. As the light improved, our cover became inadequate and it was difficult to keep concealed. I tried crouching in the centre of the burn and merging with the rushes, but the water came over my waders and I was soon wet through. Also, not expecting snow, I had foolishly left my waterproof overjacket at home and was soon wet through more or less all over. Worse still, my cartridges began to get damp in my pockets and I had to borrow from the others.

We kept changing our positions as the line of flight became more clearly established, but on the whole most of the geese responded to the decoys and came straight for them. One lot even landed by the decoys in front of "BB" — who hadn't seen them arrive and I had to make frantic signals to him to take appropriate action. He crept up the bank of the burn and bagged one as they took off!

We all had several shots but it was amazing how difficult it seemed to be to bring the birds down; many carried on for several fields before dropping out of the skein and then were found to be dead when later retrieved.

Our final bag was 10 — two to each of us, an extra one to "BB" and one shared. They were all pinks except one grey shot by Alan.

About 9.30 a.m. we collected together by the burn and tried to eat our breakfast, but were continually interrupted by the sound or sight of geese and a wild scramble for cover.

Eventually the flight eased off — the geese had settled in distant fields, and we started to collect our gear and make our way back to the cars. Several long searches took place for birds seen to drop out of departing skeins and all were finally retrieved except for two.

We got home to our quarters for lunch and a change of clothes. I can't remember when I was last so cold and wet.

We were all too tired to do anything energetic in the afternoon. "BB" and Tom went off to the nearest town for some cartridges and other errands. Alan and I lazed in front of a fire and thawed out. Later, Alan went off by himself to our old potato stubble in search of a duck. Several came in at dusk and he managed to bring back a fine drake mallard.

Tomorrow, or on Monday, Alan and I will have to start our homeward journey.

It has been a grand week and though it looked far from promising at first, with very few geese using the fields near our H.Q., we were fortunate in finding two such fields in use and two farms over the hills where the geese had moved to and where we were able to follow them up.

Our total bag for the six days shooting was 32 geese and 2 mallard, and only the first day was a blank one.

POSTSCRIPT

I had intended to rest and recuperate on Sunday and start homewards first thing on Monday morning, but events turned out otherwise.

On Sunday afternoon we went for a drive over the hills, and as we came out into the clear winter air, I saw a skein of geese — probably 60 to 70 strong — lift from the potato stubble a mile away where we had shot over decoys on Tuesday morning. So it seemed that the geese were already back on that field in some strength and that another morning shoot over decoys might well produce results.

So I decided to stay for the morrow's morning flight and have one final encounter with the geese.

Meanwhile, our Sunday afternoon drive took us first to the scene of yesterday's expedition, to see if the geese were back again on the same two inland farms. But both farms were devoid of geese; the stalk on Friday and their reception on Saturday had driven them elsewhere, so we set off to see if we could find their new feeding grounds. Sure enough we soon located one large party on a stubble half a mile away and then we toured some dozen miles of that open countryside beyond the hills — up and down the small river that flows along the bottom of that broad valley. And geese we found in hundreds; on potato stubbles, on corn stubbles and on grass fields geese were feeding in gaggles of a score or more up to several hundred at a time. And there was hardly a moment when skeins were not visible in the clear afternoon sky, moving from one field to another. Altogether we must have seen quite 1,000 geese — mostly, if not all, greylags, and we added greatly to our knowledge of these more distant feeding grounds of the geese which leave our estuary every dawn.

That evening Alan and I packed our gear and stowed everything in the van ready for a quick departure in the morning after the flight.

Monday morning broke cold and clear. Saturday's snow had gone but the ground was now as hard as rock, and on such a cold still morning I did not think that many geese could be so mis-guided as to try and find food on a frozen potato stubble. But our decoys worked wonders, and we were soon enjoying one of the most successful morning flights I have ever seen. When it was hardly light the first four greys slipped quietly in to the decoys, but I had luckily spotted them against the first gleam of light and got one of them with the first shot of the morning. After that a regular succession of skeins appeared out of the distance, and though many headed straight for the hills and the farms beyond, a fair number set their wings half a mile away and came straight for us.

THE FLIGHT IN A SNOWSTORM

We all had chances, though Alan and I in the centre of our line along the ditch had most shooting — for the simple reason that it was our turn to be nearest to the decoys, some 40 yards out in the field.

By 9 o'clock the flight was virtually over and we collected the spoils. Two distant birds were retrieved from fields where they had dropped far away, and the total score came to 12 — all greys.

It was a wonderful finale to our week, especially for myself, who in that hour or so had accounted for 5 (possibly 6) of the bag, which was as much as I had shot during all the previous days. "BB" and I both had the satisfaction of bringing off a right-and-left. In my own case a small lot of 3 geese came straight for me and I got one of them. Then the remaining two birds circled the field, and instead of making off, came round to have another look at the decoys, again they came right over me and this time I got them both.

And so the total for the trip rose to 44; with the possibility of still more to come as "BB" and Tom were staying on till Wednesday.

By 10.30 a.m. Alan and I, after a hasty breakfast, were on our way southwards, hurrying before the threatened blizzards expected from the far north. After a bitterly cold drive we reached Newcastle that night, and another long day's driving brought us home to Catfield.

CHAPTER 11
A HAPPY NEW YEAR
(1st JANUARY, 1953)

December 31st, 1952.

In view of the rain last night I guessed the Ludham Marshes would be flooded and that there might be a chance of a wigeon there, so I phoned Peter, and called for him just before 4. Sure enough there were a lot of shallow flood pools on the grass marshes and signs of recent visits by both duck and geese. It was a clear calm evening, with a nice pale sunset in the S.W. Mist started to rise from the marshes and hung in low thin layers all round us. Later, as the last of the day-light faded the full moon rose behind us — an orange ball breaking through the layer of mist — so that it never became really dark and the evening flight was prolonged. In fact, it is probably going on all night, parties of duck and geese moving about the marshlands seeking fresh feeding grounds. Apart from a snipe, the first bird of interest was a single duck which flew across my front. I took it for a mallard and dropped it with a single shot, but when Laddie brought it in it turned out to be a large cock wigeon. Other parties of wigeon were on the move and we both had occasional shots, and then we heard geese on the wing — clearly Whitefronts by their calls. By this time we had faced round as the only hope of seeing anything was to watch towards the moon and the light area of mist surrounding it.

The geese sounded quite close, but for a long time kept moving round just beyond the range of our sight, but suddenly I made out a skein moving towards Peter and I heard his shot ring out. Almost immediately another skein came over me from behind, and as I could see them clearly, I reckoned they must be in range, so I also fired. But neither of us had any luck and presently the geese moved away — their calls fading in the distance. My single wigeon was the only prize of the evening; but it was great fun, and especially so to be in contact with geese again.

January 1st, 1953.

The New Year has opened very quietly on the farm; no fuss or holiday, no celebrations or special events. The date is not really significant in our normal cycle of farm operations, though this time it has almost coincided with the completion of our last and main crop — sugar beet. The men finished topping the last acre yesterday, but that is still not the real end of it. There must be 20 tons of this topped beet lying in the field and another 80 in the main heaps in the farmyard. So it will be another fortnight before it is all delivered to the factory — which plans to close on January 14th, and I shan't get my last cheque till some time in February.

For myself, I had promised to keep the day free for a friend who wanted to have a rough shoot to get a few more of his pheasants. Last night he phoned that the shoot was "on", so at 10 a.m. I was over at Caister with my gun, Laddie and a sandwich lunch. His land is very like mine — woods, marshes and a little pond in the centre, and farm land round the outside, and the whole process of hunting his pheasants was very much after our own pattern at Catfield — except that he treated his guests more leniently and didn't give us so much hard jungle work in the rougher ground. The bag also was similar — similar to our own recent shoot on Boxing Day — 19 pheasants, 2 woodcock and 2 rabbits. Personally, I only had four shots, the results of which were, 2 pheasants, 1 jay and 1 missfire!

A HAPPY NEW YEAR!

It was after 5 as I came homewards through Potter Heigham, and I couldn't help thinking of the exciting possibilities of the Ludham Marshes. Last night the full moon rose at five — tonight it would be about 6, and though it was now dark and I had missed the dusk duck flight, there was a chance that both duck and geese would start moving again when the moon rose. So I took the car to the top of the lane leading down to the marshes, got out, and listened. It was still very dark and there was such a thick layer of cloud it seemed doubtful whether there would be enough light for shooting. But I heard the call of both wigeons and geese down on the marshes, and decided that I might as well go down and investigate.

Walking across the first marsh — where I had been last night — duck kept taking off almost at my feet, and I was quite unable to see them. I wandered round to all the various patches of flood water, but it was quite hopeless: I could hear duck getting up or flying round but never saw a single one. Then I heard geese on the wing; first a few, and later what sounded quite a big lot. But they seemed to be ¼ mile away and after a while sounded as though they were all down on the ground.

The best plan seemed to be to follow up the geese and find out where they were. I found my way to another large section of the marsh from whence the sound of the geese seemed to come. It was a large square chunk of marshland, bounded by deep drainage dykes on all four sides, and probably 50 acres in extent. It seemed to be a very worn and bare pasture, but it was hard to make out in the dark and several acres in the centre were under flood water a few inches deep. It was from this faint sheen of water that the noise of the geese seemed to come.

I edged closer to the edge of the water and then after a while the inevitable happened: the geese could see me long before I could see them, and with a roar of wings a big lot took off. They must have been on or near this flood water, and as they lifted I could just make out a dull cloud of them disappearing into the night. Then a few seconds later another similar lot took off — and I could see them too. I estimate that between 100 and 200 geese must have been resting on that marsh. It was still very dark but the invisible full moon behind the clouds just gave a faint gleam of light in the whole sky, and the even layer of cloud formed a nice uniform background.

I chose a strip of higher ground running out into the flood water, where I would not show up so conspicuously as standing in open water, and there I crouched down on one knee — Laddie beside me — and waited. Sure enough after a few minutes I heard geese approaching — obviously some of them wanted to come back to this flood area. In the next half hour or so several lots flew round; many I never saw; others I could just make out as they passed by to right or left. But I only had my game gun with ordinary cartridges (No. 6 shot) and it was no use risking long shots. After a while all activity ceased and I thought the geese must have moved away for good. And then I heard another party approaching; I could hear them getting nearer, and then a little flight of about 8 geese loomed up on my right. They seemed to be nearer than previous lots — I could make out the form of each separate goose — so as they passed by I stood up and let fly. I could clearly see the bird I fired at crumple up, and Laddie had it almost as soon as it hit the water with a splash. As I expected it was a Whitefront — but a very small young one, with no white front and no markings on its breast.

I waited for no more: I gathered my prize, found my way back to the car, and drove home in great jubilation. What a grand start for 1953!

CHAPTER 12

FISHING INTERLUDE

February 16th, 1953. — Kelso, Scotland.

This is the second fishing holiday I have taken in my life — apart from odd days and weekends which have come my way during the course of my travels abroad. There was, for instance, that Christmas weekend at Lago Traful in the Argentine (about 1935) when I caught the first salmon in my life, and several trout in those rivers that run down to the Atlantic from the Andes. Then there was a day or two in New Zealand in 1932, the chief of which was a day on Lake Taupo where one trolled for Rainbow trout — one caught them with comparative ease up to 6 lbs. or so; though the more lasting recollection is of grilling and eating them over a wood fire on the shore of the lake when the day's fishing was done. In 1949 I had several days after trout on the Polela — the river that runs through Michael's farm in Natal. And now — since 1945 — I own a small broad which is full of pike, as well as the usual selection of smaller coarse fish: and I have fished it two or three days in seven years! All of which goes to show that I am no fisherman, am never likely to become one, and am immune to the infection which strikes so many men, and seems to leave them stricken for life.

All this I realised on my way north yesterday. Late in the afternoon I collected an appropriate selection of clothes, stuffed them into a couple of suitcases, drove myself to Norwich and there took the train to London and thence the night sleeper to Berwick, whereas if I had been setting out on a wildfowling trip there would have been a very different type of preparation, and above all a very different feeling of excitement and anticipation.

It was the same last year when at the eleventh hour I took Michael's place for a week on the Thurso river in May and thus found myself taking my first real fishing holiday. In that week I fished solidly every day of the week, and ended up with three salmon, so I must have exposed myself fully to the fishing "bug". Yet though I enjoyed it all, and did comparatively well in what turned out to be a poor fishing week I came home unbitten and unscathed.

I'm afraid it will be the same this time. This morning Bill and I left the night train at Berwick at 5.30 in the morning, drove ourselves to Kelso in a car which had been left for us at the station, and were thus able to get in a full day's fishing on our first day.

This salmon fishing is a highly organised and closely regulated affair. On the Thurso it was all fly fishing and from the bank, and each day we were allotted a different beat of the river. Here it is all fishing from boats and at the present stage of the season it is all spinning. Moreover we have our particular beat of the Tweed — the Makerstoun beat — and there we stay for the whole week. This beat consists of about a mile of the Tweed and has six boats on it — stationed at each of the main fishable stretches of river. The beat also has two ghillies or boatmen attached to it. So this morning I went off with one ghillie and had the use of the three boats on the lower half of the beat, while Bill went off upstream with the other ghillie to the other three boats. Incidentally, I must explain that Bill has nobly lent me the necessary rods, tackle and other mysterious gadgets from his own surplus kit.

The procedure is that one gets out on to the river in one of the boats, the ghillie rows you to the likely spots in the river, and you then proceed to "spin" for salmon. After an hour or so when you have exhausted the possibilities of that particular stretch of river, you go ashore and walk along to the next boat. You then proceed to deal with the next stretch of the river in a similar way. A third spell in the third boat finishes the morning, and you then repair to a hut on the bank and eat your sandwich lunch. After lunch the whole process is repeated anew — a spell in each boat on each stretch of your beat.

I think I had now better confine myself to brief factual records of each day's fishing and leave further comment and general impressions till the end of the week.

This first day we caught three fish, two of 8 and 6½ lbs. respectively by myself, and one of 8½ lbs. by Bill. In addition I caught 4 kelts, 2 sea-trout kelts and 1 brown trout (all of which we returned to the river), and Bill caught about a dozen kelts. Anyhow we are quite pleased with this beginning, and feel that we have had an interesting day with quite a lot of fishing, though we have only three salmon to show for it.

February 17th.

There was quite a lot of rain in the night, so that the river was 2" higher today and rather more coloured. But the day itself has been mild and fine, with some lovely soft sunshine this afternoon. Bill and I changed our respective halves of the beat — and our ghillies — today. We both had far less sport: Bill landed a nice 12½ lb. salmon and caught or hooked several kelts, while I could do no better than two kelts, and a sea trout kelt which had to be returned.

But the beats lower down the river have been doing better and there must have been 15 or more salmon strewn around the hotel hall this evening — being packed up for dispatch by the evening post. So we are hoping that by tomorrow the fish population will have moved upstream to our beat.

February 18th.

Our hopes have hardly been fulfilled. The river was about 1" lower today and we set out with a good deal of quiet optimism. When we met for lunch Bill had caught an 8lb. salmon, but I had had a completely blank morning. Five times fish had plucked at my lure — a golden or silver sprat — but not in sufficient earnest to be hooked. Three times the same thing happened in the afternoon, while Bill similarly repeated his morning performance and landed another (7lb.) fish.

The fishing being so dull — for me — I found increasing interest in watching the bird life on the river. The number of mallard about is quite amazing — the river is full of them, and they are to be seen all day long flying up and down the river or resting under the windward bank or on rocks in midstream. I saw today goldeneye, goosanders and a single oystercatcher.

February 19th.

Conditions looked even more promising today; a lovely fine morning and the river another 2" lower, but again we only did moderately. There were certainly more fish about, and I personally had a lot of fishing — catching no less than six kelts, but after the fifth my luck changed and I caught a 7lb salmon. Then my luck left me again for just before lunch I got into a big fish and had him on for several minutes, and then when I really thought he was safely hooked, the line went slack and he was off. My ghillie was confident it was a fresh fish and put it at 14-15lbs. So the proverbial "big one" got away, as usual!

Bill on the lower stretch of the river had no luck at all.

We had to stop at lunch as we were both due in Glasgow this evening. So after a quick change of clothes we drove ourselves to Glasgow, joined the Scottish Company's staff party from 6.30 till 11 p.m., and have now just got back to Kelso at 2 in the morning.

February 20th.

Two somewhat tired and jaded fishermen staggered out of their hotel this morning, and it was half past ten before they were in their respective boats on the river. It was a dull chilly morning with sudden gusts of wind. The river itself was a few inches lower but in good fishing condition according to our ghillies.

Things soon began to go well; within an hour I had hooked a fish, which turned out to be a good fresh-run one and was soon landed. Then came a run of three kelts and then it was time for lunch. But there was still no sign of Bill, who was away on the upper beat, so I kept on fishing opposite the hut while waiting for him. Lucky I did so for at about 1.30 I got into another fish and duly landed it. By then I was too hungry to wait any longer for Bill so came ashore to eat my sandwiches.

It was after 2 before Bill came along, with his ghillie laden with salmon — four of them, 14 lb., 10 lb., 8½ lb., 6 lb., (mine were 9 and 8 lbs.). I left Bill to his lunch and hurried back to the river all eager to catch up with his mounting score. I fished all the three same stretches again but things were quieter now and it was late in the afternoon before I got a third fish — also 8 lbs. — in the middle of the reach. I stayed on till long after 5 in the hope of getting a fourth to equal Bill's score, but there was not so much as a touch and I had to call it a day — a good day. Bill turned up soon afterwards — with a fifth fish, so we drove back to the hotel with the boot of the car full of 8 fish, feeling very pleased with ourselves and quite prepared to swap yarns with any of the other people in the hotel.

February 21st.

News spreads quickly in a fishing hotel! This morning at breakfast we were greeted by fellow anglers — even those we had not spoken to before — with remarks such as "Is it true you got 8 in Makerstoun yesterday?" "I hear you had a wonderful day yesterday" etc., etc. Apparently it was a good day for our beat at this early stage of the season, and we naturally hoped the favourable conditions would continue for a second day. The water was a little higher and the wind a little stronger but to my inexperienced eyes everything looked very similar to yesterday; and I could see no reason why the fish should not behave as yesterday. But apparently fish — or at any rate salmon — are susceptible to minor changes in water temperature, wind, weather and a host of other factors in a way which is quite incomprehensible to me, but which comprises the mystery, the art and the fascination of fishing.

We were on the water in good time as it was my last day, but it soon became clear that we were not going to repeat yesterday's performance. During the morning I landed three kelts, and then just before lunch just managed to land a clean fish from "The Laird's Cast". Bill had caught two fish during the morning. After lunch I went back to "The Laird's Cast" and very soon had another fish out of it — the largest fish of the trip, 15 lbs. and for a moment I had hopes of approaching yesterday's score. But that was our last fish for the week; I went over all the best pools and stretches again, and had my hopes raised three times in that exciting moment when a fish takes your bait and you know you have him well hooked. But each time it turned out to be a kelt and he was duly returned to the river.

When Bill and I met at the car later in the evening I found he had had no more luck, and our score for the day therefore stood at 2 each.

And so ends a most delightful and interesting week — fishing all day and every day except for Thursday afternoon; a lovely river and good weather (we had no rain and never too much wind or water), and sport which proved better then we were entitled to expect. Our total bag was 19 salmon (11 to Bill and 8 to myself) varying from 6 to 15 lbs., and I suppose we must have landed between 50 and 60 kelts.

Tonight I am catching the night train to London from Berwick and should be home for lunch tomorrow.

So farewell to the Tweed, to the restless river and its treelined banks, to Makerstoun House standing solid and square — and rather austere — overlooking the river, and goodbye to all those pools and runs with their haunting names:

Willie's Bank
Hirple Nellie
The Orchard
The Dark Shore
North and South Clippers
The Laird's Cast
The Boat Pool
The Red Stane

February 22nd.

Home again — to feel a distinct feeling of spring in the air at Catfield. After lunch I took a walk round the farm to see what had been done during my week's absence, and for the first time for several months didn't need to put on any overcoat or other outer covering.

But before reverting to farm affairs let me try and crystallise my thoughts about this fishing game. It interests and intrigues me, and yet it fails to claim me as an enthusiast, and I cannot quite understand why! All this week I have inevitably been comparing fishing with shooting, and especially salmon-fishing with wildfowling. There is so much that is common to both sports and yet there must be still more in the subtle differences or I surely would have succumbed by now. Both take one to most attractive wild country; in fact the very rivers which are full of salmon are also — in their lower stretches and in their estuaries — the haunt of wild geese. Both salmon and geese are truly wild and worthy quarries; no element of artificial breeding and rearing (like pheasants), no organised battues as one gets with most game birds. Both bring one in touch with the mysteries of great migrations — geese to the Arctic and salmon to some distant ocean. Even the very measure of one's success is similar; my 8 salmon in 6 days is just the sort of bag I might hope to get with wild geese and I gather one can often go several days without catching a salmon just as one can with geese.

What then does fishing lack? Firstly I think I miss the spacious freedom one enjoys when out after geese. On the Tweed I was confined to the length of the river we had hired — a narrow ribbon of water perhaps a mile long. When wildfowling one feels almost as free and unrestricted as the geese themselves: all the coasts and estuaries below high-water mark are free, and one can often pursue the geese inland for the mere asking of permission from the local farmer. Imagine a casual fisherman asking permission to fish on a likely stretch of water that happens to take his fancy! This freedom in wildfowling applies to time as well as to place. One can chase geese at dawn and dusk throughout the day and even sometimes in the middle of the night (under the moon). Salmon fishing seems to be much more regulated in every way; one starts at 9, or perhaps a bit later, knocks off for lunch at one and then continues till about 5. The fisherman also seems to be far more closely controlled — both by law and by local custom — in his manner of fishing. At one time or place it may be all fly fishing; at another one may, or may not, spin or troll, or — as on the Tweed — the use of a gaff is forbidden.

In the second place I find fishing hardly energetic and vigorous enough. The exercise of casting and spinning all day is certainly strenuous enough on certain muscles, but it seems to involve only the hand and arm muscles, and the exercise itself is repetitive enough to the extent of being monotonous — apart from those exciting interludes when there is a fish on the end of the line. I miss the variety of exercise; the long tramps along the shore, the long stalks starting as a crouch and ending as a belly crawl, the frantic dashes after fallen birds or the still wilder scrambles to regain cover.

And that brings me to my third complaint — the comparative lack of variety. Half the fun of wildfowling is the choice of tactics and the planning that leads up to each particular hunt. One has to study the geese, their movements and their feeding grounds and decide whether to flight them, decoy them, stalk them or drive them. On the river one seems to be limited to the choice of various well-established pools or runs, all of which one fishes in one order or another, and the other main choice is in the detailed selection of the lure one attaches to the end of the line.

But in spite of all this and within these limitations, one must admit that there is a tremendous lot in fishing — a great deal more than in wildfowling. The factors which affect the behaviour of the fish themselves and the whole technique of choosing and presenting the right lure, comprise a far more elaborate and skilled art than anything to be found in shooting. At first it seemed almost unbelievable that slight differences of temperature, or weather, or colour, or height of water, could affect the reactions of salmon; nor could I see that a slight change in colour, shape or size of the lure could influence one's prospects of catching a fish. Yet all these subtle influences are well-established — not on the results of an odd day's fishing when the numbers involved could prove nothing — but on the accumulated experience and observations of generations of fishermen and ghillies over scores — if not hundreds — of years.

There is also far more to fishing in the range and variety of equipment used, which also adds to the interest of the sport. With wildfowling the position is fairly simple: there is only a limited choice in the type of gun to use, and only a little more room for argument in the type of cartridges, which has but two variables — the size of shot and the type of powder, and these two can only be varied in quantity within very narrow limits.

But in fishing the choice of equipment seems to be legion and the scope for discussion and argument correspondingly unlimited. There seems to be all sorts of rods and reels, lines and casts, traces and hooks with various minor gadgets such as swivels and leads. And when one comes to the choice of actual lures, whether fly, spoon, minnow or sprat, I can only compare an expert angler's collection with a schoolboy's collection of postage stamps or birds' eggs — innumerable varieties of size and colour on a general pattern. I can quite see that all this variety of fascinating equipment must form one of the main attractions of fishing; all this I can understand and appreciate, as also the skill required to handle a rod and line expertly, and the great interest to be found in studying the habits and behaviour of the fish themselves. It is a great art and sport, and I am really rather surprised that I have not become an enthusiast myself. But I haven't, and I feel that I am missing something.

One remarkable coincidence is worth recording about this fishing trip. When I found that our beat of the Tweed was the Makerstoun beat the name rang a bell and I remembered that our family came from a place called Stodrig near Makerstoun many generations ago. Sure enough there was a farm called Stodrig near the Makerstoun beat, and there was little doubt that I had come to fish in the exact district where my forebears had owned land and farmed centuries ago. In fact I like to think that some of my ancestors had probably fished the very same stretches of the Tweed as I had been doing; it seems more than possible that their lands may have included the very banks of the river where we have just been. For the family pedigree begins — so far as it can clearly be traced — with a Thomas Makdowell of Stodrig in the parish of Makerstoun who must have been born in the middle of the 15th century. For five more generations the family seems to have remained at Stodrig, and then for four more generations remained in the nearby district of Coldstream before moving south into England.

CHAPTER 13

A WILDGOOSE THAT CAME TO STAY
(1954)

This story really starts a year ago when we were given three eggs from a wild goose's nest. These we incubated under a domestic goose, and in due course three little goslings hatched out and were safely reared.

Now, a year later, we have three well grown handsome geese that live in a large grass pen, each with its flight feathers cut on one wing, to prevent it flying away. One is most certainly a gander; there is no mistaking the upright neck and aggressive masculine personality; another is equally certainly a goose; rather smaller in build and more modest and demure in disposition. The third we are not so sure about, it might be a more masculine type of female, or possibly a retiring male, dominated perhaps by the stronger character of its brother.

Anyhow it seemed a pity we had not got a fourth to make up two pairs. And then, nearly a month ago, an exciting thing happened : five wild geese turned up and settled in the field of winter wheat next to the goose pen. We left them undisturbed, so that before long they were introducing themselves through the wire netting, but after an hour or so the strangers flew off. Then, a few days later three geese turned up again, and again spent an hour or two hobnobbing with our own three through the wire fence.

We like to think that the original five were a family party of two parents and three youngsters, and that the parents were anxious to find some nice young companions for their children (with a view to possible match-making) before they themselves settled down to their yearly duty of family-raising.

On the second occasion the parents had no doubt now chosen their nesting site and were already absorbed in their domestic duties, so that the three youngsters were left to renew their acquaintance alone with their new found friends.

Each day we now hurried out before breakfast to see if our visitors had returned, but it was over a week before we heard or saw any further sign of them. And then one morning at breakfast there was a joyous clamour from the goose pen, and over the garden came sailing a single goose — in full view of the dining room window. As usual he settled in the field and then walked up to the wire netting. But this visit was the shortest of them all, and before long he was away again. It almost seemed as if the other two must have found mates for the season, and there was now just this one survivor, unattached and unsettled.

Next morning he was back again, and we began to think of ways of furthering the courtship, and of encouraging the stranger to stay. The pen was probably too small for the goose to overcome his natural fear of enclosed spaces and man-made fences, and he probably couldn't bring himself to land in it. So we gently drove our own three geese on to the front lawn, while the visitor was out in the field. The plan worked; in a few minutes the visitor took to the air and came gliding over the garden fence to land on the lawn. And there for a quarter of an hour, we had

As the flock increased the greylags frequently visited us at flight time
(evening flight over the house)

We usually have one or two pairs nesting each year in the marshes
(Greylag on nest by Catfield Broad)

the joy of watching the four geese walking about, a few yards from our window.

Eventually we managed to open the gate back into the pen without alarming the stranger, and hoped that our own geese would lead him back into the pen with them, but the manoeuvre failed, and the stranger obviously got flustered and flew off.

For a few days there was no further sign, and then one day last week two geese turned up again. This rather upset our theories about the family party but the really exciting thing was that one of the geese had landed in the pen. The other, as usual, was out in the field.

Then and there the idea of catching the goose was born, and with it came thoughts of Peter Scott's goose netting exploits. The pen was wedge shaped, and if we could get the goose to move towards the narrow point of the pen we might indeed be able to corner it where it would find itself with insufficient runway for a "take-off". But a net would certainly help, and it would take at least three of us.

The net resources of the establishment were quickly reviewed; the strawberry netting would be too frail; the "long-net" for catching rabbits was too long — and not deep enough; the tennis net was also rather shallow, and in any case a wren had built its nest in its toils where it hung on a nail in the summer-house.

What other nets had we? Why, the pig net — that would be the very thing; three or four yards square, loose mesh and amply strong enough. And so we set out to catch a wild goose in a pig net!

The goose that came to stay; with his three companions

One of them would come right up to our front door

The plan of campaign was simple: one of us would show himself beyond the blunt end of the pen, in the hope that the goose would start walking away — into the narrow point of the pen. The other two would wait under cover until the goose was well in the wedge, then they would advance into the pen and rush on the goose with the net held out between them.

Strangely enough it all went exactly according to plan, though with the unforeseen complication that our own three geese also walked into the corner. The final climax was rather like a rugger scrum with two men and four geese milling in a corner together. Our own three geese were quickly heeled out, leaving the stranger well and truly tackled.

A pair of scissors applied to the feathers of one wing ensured that he would remain safely in the pen, and now, a few days later, he seems to be settling down quite contentedly with his three companions.

CHAPTER 14
THE LAIRD'S FLIGHT
(1955 — 1956 Bruce's Year)

This year I took my youngest son Keith and his friend Bruce to Scotland on my usual goose-hunt, and this meant that the time available — between Cambridge end-of-term and Christmas — only left us a bare week in the north.

On our first day's travel we reached the Solway and found a warm welcome and a sumptuous meal awaiting us. We dined off smoked salmon, roast wild goose and blue Cheshire cheese, but turned in early as we planned to enjoy a short "curtain-raiser" on the marsh in the morning, before pushing on further north. At 5.30, Dick called us and showed us the way, some five miles, to a promising stretch of the Solway shore. But it was a calm, fine morning — with a lovely Solway dawn — and though we were on the right line of flight the skeins all passed too high overhead and I don't think any of us even tried a shot. But it was good to see the geese again and to realise that the hunt was on.

So we repacked the van, said au revoir to those three goddesses of English innkeeping — Betty, Martha and Jean, and to the not-so-godly Dick, and pressed on.

That evening, in another inn, we unpacked guns, decoys, and all the paraphernalia that goes with winter wildfowling and established our base for the next few days' operations.

I will not attempt to describe each day in detail. It was very soon apparent that there were very few geese on our favourite stretch of coast. Two of our first three mornings were reasonably wild and should have produced excellent morning flights, but though we broke our duck each day there were very few skeins and correspondingly few chances.

Nor did our usual tours of reconnaissance later in the day produce much promise. None of our favourite farms or fields were being used by the geese, and the few hundreds of geese that were in the district were mostly concentrated on a couple of "sanctuary" farms where we could not get permission to go after them.

Expeditions further afield were even more disappointing. The valley over the hills which often holds thousands of geese only showed a couple of hundred and even these were not using the usual farms.

So by the fourth day — with only five geese in the bag — things were looking grim. Our searches were pushed further along the coast — in both directions, and at last we found quite a lot of geese in a new district we had never worked before.

Most of the farms involved belonged to one landlord, and we were fortunate I think in getting permission to have "one day" at the geese. With geese it is usually sound to take your chances at once, so we had hardly thanked the laird before we were back on his fields planning next day's attack. We found the geese scattered over three farms, with one or two hundred in each of several fields — some grass, some stubble. With our glasses we studied these fields from a

Bruce and Keith down on the shore

distance, so as not to move the geese; and noted the various hedges and belts of timber where we could find cover. The plan was that each of us would go to a different field with two or three decoys, and lie up for the geese before dawn in the best hide we could each improvise from what was found on the spot. We hoped that by splitting our forces geese might be moved on from one of our fields to the others.

Keith and Bruce chose fields fairly near the coast which were both full of geese, and I took a stubble field rather further inland on higher ground, which also seemed to hold a lot of geese.

That evening we worked out our timetable to allow for the last man being in position by 7.30 a.m., after the van had dropped the other two at their respective farms. It worked out at the alarm clock being set for 5.30 a.m.

There is always an extra feeling of tension and expectancy on a morning when one sets out to wait for the geese in the fields. It is probably because of the greater probability of shooting a goose, and also perhaps because the morning's expedition is the climax to previous planning and reconnasissance — sometimes extending over several days.

On this occasion it was calm and clear when we got up, with the ground still frozen hard from recent frosts — not very propitious circumstances. I was the first to be dropped off the van and so had plenty of time to prepare for the flight. My stubble field was bounded by a post and wire fence on the side where I expected the geese to arrive, but there were a few scruffy thorn bushes scattered along it and I chose one of these for my hide, thickening the cover with extra sticks and tufts of dead grass. The decoys were placed forty yards out in the field, facing into such slight wind as there was.

The first light was now showing in the South East, and soon after 7 a.m. the first geese could be heard on the move. But it was nearly half past before I could see the first of them — a single bird; and as he came to have a look at the decoys he offered an easy shot — my first goose of the trip.

Soon after, as the light improved and the geese began streaming in from the firth, a wonderful flight developed. Skein after skein came in to my field from the west, mostly in small lots of a dozen to a score at a time. They came from Keith's direction and I could only hope that he was getting as much sport as I was before passing the geese on to me. When it was fully light I could make out his decoys in his grass field half a mile away, and from the numbers it was clear he had set up some shot birds to add to his stuffed ones. Presently I could see that a lot of the geese were settling in another grass field between us, so during a lull in the flight I walked across and put them all up. He told me afterwards that this manoeuvre added another goose to his score.

There were also a lot of geese collecting in another grass field between me and the coast and it was clear that many of them were within range of a plantation of young conifers bordering one side of the field. It looked just about the easiest stalk one could imagine — and so it proved. A long detour took me to the far side of the plantation and it only required a slow and quiet approach through the young trees to bring me opposite to the geese. Of course they either saw or heard me as I approached the edge of the trees but they gave me an easy right and left as they rose.

Back in my hide again a few late skeins still kept arriving and added a few more to the bag, but by 10.30 it was all over and at 11 it came on to rain and hail. In the bottom of my hide was a pile of geese under handfuls of dead grass, and for the first time in my life I had shot so many geese at a sitting that I had lost count! I knew I was in double figures, and was equally sure it couldn't be 20. In the event it proved to be 17 — four pinks and the rest greylags.

In due course we all met together and compared notes. Keith had had a good deal of shooting and got 5: Bruce had run into bad luck when farmworkers turned up to spread muck on an adjoining field. He only got 1. So the total bag was 23 — a record in my experience for three guns at morning flight.

After this cheerful change in our fortunes things went better for us. Next morning on the coast we collected another goose, and in the afternoon set out to explore a farm far along the coast where geese had been reported. Sure enough we found two to three hundred pinks in a group of fields and one of them offered a good chance of a stalk. So I dropped Keith and Bruce to try the stalk and went with a couple of decoys to a distant field the geese had been using in case they moved to it after the stalk. But nothing came my way, though the stalk came off successfully and I later collected Keith and Bruce with five geese — four shot at the end of the stalk and a fifth that flew over them later.

The next day was our final day and the boys were keen to return to this same farm and wait for the pinks with decoys at morning flight. Meanwhile I had found that geese on one of the "sanctuary" farms nearer our headquarters had started overflowing on to an adjoining grass field, and more fortunate still that this new field belonged to another friend of ours, who readily gave us permission to use it.

So at 6 a.m. they dropped me with a couple of decoys and a packet of sandwiches while they motored on to their distant farm. There was good cover between my two fields — a deep boundary ditch with several trees and shrubs growing along it. There was plenty of time to make a good hide before I heard the first geese at about 7.15. Then they began to arrive — many dropping in to the sanctuary field but some skeins circling over the boundary ditch and swinging over the decoys. It was not a big flight — perhaps not much more than 100 birds, but out of the few that gave me chances I managed to bag 6. They were all greylags.

We all met at our inn for lunch, when it appeared the boys had had a disappointing morning: plenty of geese, but all very wary and coming in at a great height before dropping into the centre of the field. The calm weather was largely to blame, probably aggravated by the disturbing effect of the previous evening's stalk. Anyhow they had only got one goose. And so the total bag for the six days came to 41 geese.

It only remains to add that we ended up that last day with an excellent little duck flight —

we had noticed mallard feeding on a flooded stubble and reckoned they would normally flight in at dusk. So we lined the boundary fence as the light began to fail, and within an hour or so had collected eight fat mallard.

Next morning with the van grossly overloaded with our spoils, we were heading for the south, home and Christmas.

CHAPTER 15
THE YEAR THAT WAS MISSED
(1956 — 1957)

Poor old Bird — So they set you
up in a corner did they? (The specimen is
stuffed trousers and top hat.

"BB"

Woodford Lodge,
Woodford,
Nr. Kettering.

October 18th, 1956.

Dear Old Mac,

It's grievous news you won't be joining us on the far goose grounds next January. Perhaps the enclosed drawing will bring a smile to the poor old bird.

But it is good to know it's only a primary missing, and that it will grow again and we must book you for 1958.

I had my "goose dream" last night — skeins so high they looked like midges, but I seem to remember that (in my dream) we searched the fields vainly for the gaggles, and all our familiar haunts were drawn blank.

C. sends her love and hopes you will soon be up to your old form — it's good to know you can be up and about again.

Love to Katie,

Ever,

D.

CHAPTER 16
TREBLE CHANCE POOL
(1957)

It was quite a small pool; not one of those large and complicated affairs. The prizes it offered were always quite modest; it never produced the huge dividends one reads about elsewhere. That Saturday, Keith and I thought it was time to try our luck at it again. After all, we need only invest about 3s. and we reckoned that we could do the job in about two hours. If we started at about three o'clock we should be finished by five; in time to rejoin the family for a cup of tea.

So at 3 p.m. we set out; prepared to expend half a gallon of precious basic ration in a good cause. For our pool was some distance away — in a grass marsh of one of the nearby Broadland valleys. Every winter at about this time if there has been sufficient rainfall, little pools or "flashes" of flood water appear on this marsh, and indeed on several of the neighbouring marshes. These flashes usually attract a few duck at evening flight; and so we each took a gun, a pocketful of cartridges, a dog and a wooden decoy-duck.

For the first hour or so, while it was still broad daylight, we walked round the neighbouring marshes to see whether there were any more likely pools, and if so whether any of these pools offered evidence of recent visitors. But nothing seemed more promising than our original pool in our original marsh, which had quite a few feathers floating about on it — mostly mallard by the look of them. Keith, however, found a group of flashes on the next marsh which looked almost as good and he decided to stay by them. So we parted, and each went to his own flash.

In the centre of mine was a raised patch of ground where my decoy could rest on the submerged grass in about an inch of water, head-on to the wind and secure from drifting to the edge. A gun-shot away I took my position to the north-east so that as I looked over the decoy and the water I was facing the brightest quarter of the evening sky.

It was a dull, misty evening, with an even grey sky that made a good background. The distant river wall and the landmarks on the uplands soon melted into invisibility, and one was left in the flat bare landscape with only an occasional tree to remind one of the bordering dykes and to provide bearings for the tramp back to the car.

Partridges were now calling on all sides as the coveys collected together for the night. A small stream of crows came drifting home to their evening roosts; some were carrion crows by their harsh double calls, while others looked suspiciously like "hoodies" in the failing light. I would gladly have tried a shot at them,, in the hope of reducing the number of these thieves and ravagers, but as usual they recognised the lone figure on the marsh for what it was and passed on one side or the other — not unnecessarily wide, but at a safe couple of gun-shots.

Next the snipe started flighting, and the air was full of "scrape-scrape" on all sides. I saw only one of them, and then too late to fire. Green plover also were on the move; several came tumbling past with that jerky, floppy flight; but still no sign of any duck.

It grew darker, and there were now some minutes of complete silence on the marsh as all the other bird life moved on or settled down for the night.

And then there was the sudden distant call of duck up in the sky — quite unmistakably wigeon. Somewhere in front of me the air was full of soft "whee-oo's" — "whee —, whee —, whee-ooo". Fortunately I saw them just in time — a tight wedge of about a dozen coming straight out of the south-west and heading over my right shoulder.

They seemed very high and showed no sign of circling or dropping in to my marsh. Looking back one can remember thinking in a split second, "They're too high for an ordinary game gun with No. 6 shot, but the magnum, with 3-inch cartridges, No. 3 shot and full choke should just reach them — it's worth a shot". And so I threw up the gun, gave a long lead of about four yards on the leader of the wedge, and fired.

The result was quite unexpected and very rewarding. No less than three blobs dropped out of the wedge and fell to the ground behind me. I was too surprised to think of my second barrel. Nor was there any difficulty in finding the three wigeon; they were all stone dead — two drakes and a duck; and even before the dog found them I could see their white breasts gleaming on the short dark grass.

Though I stayed a little longer no more duck came my way, and it seemed a pity to risk an anticlimax by being tempted with chancy shots when it was too dark. Besides, one was beginning to enjoy in anticipation the conversation that would take place when we met again at the car.

"Any luck, Dad?" — "Yes, I managed to get three wigeon" — "Three wigeon! But I only heard you have one shot!" — "Yes, I only had the one shot" — and so on.

At any rate that is why I shall always think of that little "flash" on a Norfolk marsh as my "Treble Chance Pool".

CHAPTER 17
AUTUMN IDYLL
(1957)

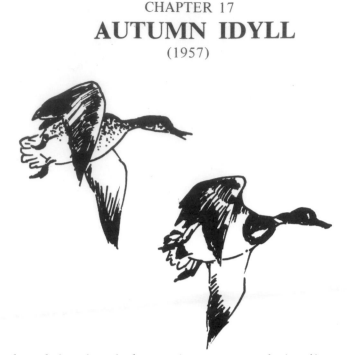

I had been advised that there had never been so many duck; all we needed was a wind and a cloudy day. The moon and the duck would do the rest. And so it was that I found myself driving down from Hertfordshire for the first flight of the new season. Near Thetford the skies cleared miraculously and the well-known ice-blue glaze of the Norfolk coast showed as a thin streak on the horizon. By the time I had reached my goal the thin streak had developed into a rapidly clearing sky, and any hope I still had for wind and cloud was not being borne out.

Perhaps you have noticed how spring is always discernible in one fine February day — an early harbinger of the warmth to come. I find autumn has an equivalent trait, and it was on this early September day that the melancholy fact was brought home to me that the end of the year was at hand. On that night I first had cold fingers and toes, the long planed streaked mist rose formidably over fen and pond, and the dry rustle of beech leaves in the plantation told me that the sap was dying back in the wood.

The four of us took our stations at 6.45 p.m. and settled down to wait for the birds. It was indeed an idyllic sky, but unhelpful to the flighter — a flaming sun behind banks of cloud, but clear blue everywhere else, and in the south-east a rising moon. Not a trace of wind. Bob was at twelve o'clock (nobody quite knows why that particular butt is labelled twelve, but there it is), Ted was at nine, Keith at three and I was on the north-east rim of the pond at six o'clock. Motionless between us on the water sat the two wooden decoys.

At first it was a picture of still life. One's attention wandered to the blackberries on the hide; rotten ones on the inside, spectacular fruit fit for the giant at the top of the beanstalk just out of reach. Beyond these, Ted's brown cap motionless behind the alders, and beyond him a dead ash with two pigeons calling softly to each other. Movement became increasingly apparent in the whining mosquitos, the gulls arrowing their highroad to the sea, an early bat flickering across the water.

Then with this alerted perception we heard man and machines. The hour belled out across the river, a train at a distant halt clanked and chuffed in quickening progression into some ever-fading but audible void, the lorry in the lane, the tractor moaning with its last load, a shout, another and the slamming of a door, the double chink of a safety catch pushed forward and back reassuringly. All the old sounds which pass so indifferently on the casual ear were now exaggerated.

Then, after a long hour, Bob's warning whistle told us to wake up, for there barely over the hornbeams and dropping straight towards the pool were twenty or so mallard. Always the un-expected, and how vast they seemed with the light behind them. Over Ted in his south-east hide the mist rose strongly and, with the moon behind it, it served as a blanket to all sight. Dark shapes would fly into it and seemingly not emerge. Splashes and bird calls seeped mysteriously through it; Ted was lost in it, the shadow of the alders swallowing up his silhourette.

Not till 9 p.m. did we rustle out of the hides and start to pick up. Three semi-domesticated geese which had honked nonchalantly on the mud at our feet while duck and shot spread over them rose hectically at our appearance, clamoured noisly for the next ten minutes and then, having made sufficient expostulation, retired to their home in the next field.

While this was going on we splashed along the bank looking for the marked birds, each gun grotesquely remote as he lunged in and out of the patches of mist and peered with splendid inability into black shadows. With only one torch, but with a good dog, we found 14 birds, probably a 100 per cent. pick-up, and headed for the farm. I had cold fingers and toes and relished the relaxing laziness of warming-up again.

Under a single bleak electric light we took final stock — and how bleak electric light is after moonlight — then padded in stockinged feet towards the cheer and warmth of beer and coffee. Now there was nothing for it but the post-mortem and reminiscence before three of us dispersed to our respective homes: Ted to Dorset and shortly outward bound to Assam, Bob to the North Norfolk coast and in five days to Germany, and myself to Hertfordshire.

CHAPTER 18
THE MOONLIGHT SHOOT
(1957 — 1958 Colin's Year)

This time it was the turn of my eldest son Colin to come with me. I had been looking forward to this holiday with more than usual excitement and anticipation. I missed last year's trip owing to illness, which meant that it would be over two years since I last shot a goose — a long time to wait.

We left home on January 6th; a day of terrible weather with low scudding clouds, driving rain and high wind. It cleared up a bit through Lincolnshire, and we even had a few gleams of thin wintry sunshine, but over the Pennines it was like a "cinema" rainstorm again. The whole countryside was soaking, sodden and often flooded. However there were consolations. The wind and rain would save us from any risk of fog, and the strong south-westerly wind should protect us from frost and treacherous roads.

We followed the same tracks and routine as we did in December 1955, reaching the Solway that night, and going down to the shore for the morning flight next morning. Unfortunately the wild weather subsided during the night and we faced no better prospects than two years ago. Sure enough a few geese came in off the estuary soon after 8 a.m., and I had one skein right over me — but too high even to tempt a shot. So it was back to breakfast and the road again. We reached our usual haunts in good time, and turned straight into the various side roads which went past all our favourite goose fields. Apart from a few faithful greylags on the old aerodrome we couldn't find a goose — until the last mile from base; where we came upon 200 - 300 greylags on a series of grass fields close under the hills. Most of them were on "sanctuary" fields, but some were overflowing on to more vulnerable areas, and it looked as if there were distinct possibilities ahead.

Later that evening, after we had unpacked and fed, we went back to those fields after the moon had risen — and listened from the car. Sure enough geese began flighting in under the moon, and though we never saw any (the sky was now clear and cloudless) we could hear a succession of approaching skeins every five minutes or so. With the moon only two days past the full there might be a chance of shooting by moonlight if we should have a night with suitable conditions in the next few days.

We turned in that night with a good deal of optimism — and set the alarm for 6.30 a.m. Next morning we went straight down to the coast and took up position by the short breakwater. As is usual at the time of full moon the flight was a poor one, and very late. The morning was calmer and bright and the few geese that flew in came high. Under the moon geese can feed almost all of the 24 hours, and the usual period of fasting during the night — with the resultant urge to hurry inland at dawn — is quite disorganised.

I was lucky to get a small skein right over me, and though they were at extreme range it was a chance to take. The leader fell to my first shot and crashed into the dense reeds some 30 yards behind me. Our other three shots all missed. This incident — of a goose shot on our first morning with the first shot of the trip — reminded me that history was repeating itself. Exactly the same thing happened on my first visit to this coast with "BB" in the winter of 1943-1944, and the lucky shot happened within a few yards of the same spot on both occasions. (See "The Field" — April 1st, 1944). The only difference was that this time it was a greylag, the other time it was a pinkfoot.

We had no more chances that morning and soon went back for breakfast.

The rest of the day was spent in a more thorough recce of the whole district (which resulted in only a few small parties of geese being located) and then in tracing the farmers whose fields the 2-300 greylags were using. We got the necessary permission from two farmers, controlling most of the fields, and decided to make plans for a shoot under the moon that night. After lunch we sallied forth with a billhook, quietly put off all the geese — which now seemed to lbe more like 400 — and made ourselves two hides in the drainage ditches surrounding one of the main fields. We also cached our decoys "on the site" so that we should not have so much to carry from the car in the dark. That just left time to slip down to the coast for the evening flight. A lot of geese went out to the estuary but very late and very high — and mostly pinks; all of which suggests that the pinks are feeding a long distance away, probably over the hills.

We made ourselves two hides — Colin in one of them

After supper clouds rolled up and it began to rain. By moonrise — 8 p.m. — there was a dense layer of cloud and no sign of the moon. So it looked hopeless for our moonlight shoot. But just before 10 p.m. the skies cleared and we decided to set out after all. By the time we reached the fields and had set up the decoys the clouds had rolled up again and though we waited till midnight there was hardly a goose on the move and if they had come it is doubtful if we could have seen them. So we packed up and decided to come back again at dawn.

Next morning broke dull and gusty but fine and we were in position by 7.30 a.m. It was nearly nine before the geese started to arrive and then a long protracted flight began which kept us there till 11. But we had not sited our hides too well and for some time we did not get many chances. Then I changed over to the other side of Colin and we had a spell with several skeins over us. The last little lot of 4 geese gave me a very satisfying right and left. The final score was 4 to me, 2 to Colin and a seventh bird picked up later far behind us.

The afternoon was spent in more recces including a trip over the hills, but the best discovery was a new big lot of geese on one of our "regular" fields nearer home. This held out prospects of another dawn ambush in a day or two. While getting the necessary "clearance" from the farmer we learnt that large numbers were feeding under the moon on a small stubble where he had dumped some old potatoes to be ploughed in. Obviously we should take the first opportunity of dealing with this situation — the moon was already past the full, and each night it would become smaller and rise later. A few nights only would provide suitable conditions. After dark the skies cleared and our hopes rose. At about 10 the moon rose also — in a crystal clear sky. Certainly the geese would flight — and the fields below them would be clear and recognisable, but so it seemed would any gunners lurking in those fields. We got out in good time — before the moon had lost its first orange glow, and already there were geese in the field and others calling above. There was

D. S. A. McD. in the other hide

absolutely no cover — bare posts and wire surrounding a large 50 acre field, an 8 acre patch of which contained the unploughed stubble and the rotten frosted potatoes. So there was nothing for it but to stand on the edge of this patch, with the decoys behind us. We had not long to wait; geese were on the move all the time, and most of them seemed to be making for our patch. At first they were difficult to see as the clear sky gave a slate-blue background, but later on slight cloud developed and a watery haze surrounded the moon — so that we had almost perfect conditions. We were out there for over 3 hours and all the time geese kept coming in and offering us chances — when we could see them. I must have fired about 30 cartridges. The final count was 12 geese — both pinks and greys with at least two down in the distance that we never found (we looked for them next morning). It was a memorable night and quite the best evening I have ever had under the moon. Two incidents stand out; a shot of mine which brought down two greylags, and a shared "right-and-left" with which Colin and I concluded the proceedings. Two pinks came gliding in low; I just saw them in time and got the first and while I was falling over backwards trying to follow round for the second Colin finished it off for me. Two very tired but delighted fowlers crawled into bed about 2.30 a.m.

Morning flight a few hours later was clearly out of the question and we slept on till breakfast called us at 9. All that day we continued the search, scouring the countryside for likely prospects. The best bet seemed to be a party of geese using one of their favourite fields which had a convenient ditch running round two sides of it. We had often ambushed there before and I don't think that field ever failed to yield a goose. So late in the afternoon we put the geese off and examined the ditches for suitable hides. There was absolutely no cover on the side we would have to use — except the open ditch itself, so we would have to improvise some additional cover. A farmtrack leading into the field — rather like a Norfolk loke — provided the solution with its bushy hedges, and we relied on a few minutes' work with a billhook in the morning.

There remained nothing left to do except to go down to the seawall for the evening flight. But the geese came out high in the calm evening and gave us no chances. The only consolation was a single mallard which came streaking in from the estuary and fell to my second barrel.

After dark we waited anxiously for the moon again, as we reckoned the geese would again return to the "potato patch". But at 11 the moon rose unseen behind a thick bank of cloud, and though we waited till 11.30 the skies failed to clear and we decided to call it off.

THE MOONLIGHT SHOOT

Next morning we drove down to the farmtrack in good time, collected each an armful of branches from the hedge to make our hides, and had them in place and thickened with dead grass in good time before the geese began to flight. But the weather had changed again; the morning broke clear and bright with very little wind, so the geese flew high. Most of them seemed deter-

The geese flew high

mined to press on to further feeding grounds and very few even hesitated at the sight of our decoys. Eventually a pair of geese swooped down — I never knew where they had come from. The first I knew they were almost on the ground with their paddles down and Colin was firing both barrels — but to no effect. Then a little later a skein of a score or so came circling down, and as they swung round in front of my hide it was my turn to fire, and again there was no apparent effect. But on watching the departing skein I saw one goose lag behind, and eventually glide slowly to earth. Sure enough, by following the line on to the next farm I found the goose dead on the ground — a large greylag. By now the flight had pretty well ceased so we collected the decoys and went back for lunch.

In the afternoon we could find nothing very encouraging to tackle. In the end we found a bunch of over 100 greylags on a field next to the main road. So I dropped Colin off the blind side of the van, opposite the geese, and waited for him to disappear behind the roadside hedge. I left him there to wait for the geese to lift at dusk while I went off to find something else for myself. But I could find nothing and so went down to the coast on the chance of a shot at the evening flight. When I got back I found Colin had had several long shots at his geese but they had crossed the road too wide of him on either side.

Late that night we had a last sortie under the moon. The sky was clear again, the moon a bare semi-circle, and it didn't rise till after midnight — which took us into the Sabbath. We only heard two lots of geese on the move and after an hour we came home without firing a shot. Next day, being Sunday, was one of rest and reconnaissance only. But soon after lunch "BB" and Tom turned up — earlier than we had expected — and we began laying plans for the next day. In the end "BB" and Tom decided to follow the traditional practice of going down to the coast for the first morning flight, while Colin and I chose to have another go at the geese on the fields where we ambushed them on our second morning. This time the weather was far less favourable — fine and still with high thin cloud and a bright sunrise. Quite a nice lot of skeins came our way but they seemed quite uninterested in our field and in the decoys set out behind our hides. After a couple of hours — and only two or three ineffective shots — we gave it up. Meanwhile small lots of geese had dropped into neighbouring grass fields. One lot offered a possible "drive" so Colin was sent off on a long detour to get as near them as possible, while I went round in a wide arc the other way. At a pre-arranged time I moved towards the geese and put them up. They went straight over Colin who promptly dropped one — a large greylag. Half an hour later we were able to repeat an almost identical manoeuvre and again Colin got his goose. The other two got nothing on the coast.

That evening we repeated Saturday night's exercise, and this time all four of us lined the main road at dusk. The geese stayed on late and it was a curious sensation to see a line of four men crouched behind a main road hedge while a stream of cars and lorries roared by with blazing headlights. 200 yards the other side of the road some 50 wild geese sat on a field of winter wheat waiting for their chosen moment to get back to the safety of the estuary. Eventually, with a chatter of geese-calls, they lifted and flew off to our right flank and gave none of us a chance. That night Colin had to return home, so after supper I drove him to the nearest mainline station to catch the night sleeper to London. In our five shooting days together we had collected 23 geese and a mallard.

In the morning we tried the shore again. It was a poor flight and only a few skeins came anywhere near us. Two of them passed over "BB" who was the only one of us to fire his gun, but with no result. After breakfast we motored inland to see if geese were still feeding on two fields we had located the previous day, and to confirm that they came to them in the morning. We had found large flocks of both greylags and pinks smothering two fields that had grown potatoes last summer, and one of which was now showing the green shoots of winter wheat. In this latter there was a 2-course meal awaiting the geese; green blades of wheat and the soft pulp of the small potatoes left in the field. I had never before seen greys and pinks feeding closely together in the same field; in this case they were almost intermingled. More remarkable still; with the greys was a party of six barnacle geese — a good ten miles from the nearest open estuary. We found the geese again feeding and got the necessary permission from the owners of the two fields.

For the rest of the day there was little we could do. But we heard of a farm still further afield where greylags were reputed to flight along a river at dusk. So we went there and waited by the river for a couple of hours. We heard quite a few geese and presently a lot of goose-talk broke out in a potato field the other side of the river. I could just see the geese through my glasses, and took up position opposite them, hoping they might flight down to the river at last light. But they went on chattering for over an hour and then got up and flew off into the dark at right angles to me.

So ended a blank day — but with plans organised for a dawn ambush on the two potato fields on the morrow.

It seemed fine when we got up at 6.15 and we were soon speeding over the hills to the distant upland farms. But over the summit we found fairly thick mist and we wondered whether the geese would be able to find their favourite fields. After leaving the cars at the first farm we started on the long track to the potato fields, laden with decoys, guns, flasks and sandwiches, glasses and two very useful strips of camouflage netting produced by Tom.

We had already decided on our positions by ballot and a sketch plan of the fields. "BB" was in a little corner of scrub where the two potato fields joined two adjoining fields. Tom was 70 yards away along one hedge, and I a similar distance along another. "BB" had ample natural cover. Tom and I each rigged up a small hide for ourselves whose basis was a camouflage net held up by four sticks at the corners. I could just sit or kneel under mine, and during the morning I couldn't help comparing myself with a wart-hog! I would be crouched just outside the hide, waiting for geese, and on the first approaching honk I would scuttle backwards under the netting and stay under cover until the critical moment came for me to scramble out again and take a shot.

For the first hour or so there was a steady stream of small skeins, mostly coming in low through the mist, and usually not visible until they were within about 100 yards. It was most exciting, and rather eerie, hearing the air full of goose calls and never knowing quite when or where they would suddenly loom into view. We all had a number of chances, and soon had several down. Then there was a bit of a lull and I for one managed to eat my sandwiches and swallow the hot tea. After a while the flight continued, and at an increased tempo; especially as the mist began to disperse. The geese were all greys, except for a few skeins of pinks which came over late and high and never made a serious attempt to come in. We stayed on till midday and then collected our gear and spoils and made our way back to the vans. We found the score was 19, 8 each to "BB" and myself, 2 to Tom and 1 picked up at the end which might have been anybody's. Truly a memorable flight; the best I have had with "BB" but not up to the 23 that Keith, Bruce and I got two years ago.

After the shoot it was amazing to see the way the geese had ravaged the field of winter wheat. In a few days the geese had trampled the whole field flat and grazed the wheat bare to the ground except for a strip on one side where they had obviously kept about a gunshot away from the main road on that side. The whole effect — and it must have extended to about 10 acres — was that of a muddy farmyard completely covered with the footprints of flocks of tame geese. No wonder so many of the local farmers readily give us permission to shoot — and scare away — the geese !

After lunch we did a short tour of the coastal area to check on the whereabouts of other geese. We found a fair mob of pinks — about 200 — by Puddy Tat Hill, which should be ripe for ambushing any day now. We also found nearly as many on the "potato patch", which set me thinking how we could deal with these geese now that the moon had gone.

This patch was set in the middle of a large area of perfectly flat farmland — perhaps 50 acres — with absolutely no cover. Only a post and wire fence separated one piece of grass from the rest of the area. Concealment seemed out of the question, short of digging an elaborate gun pit. The only hope lay in disguise.

Next morning while the other two went down to the coast again I took myself to the potato patch with an empty beer case (to sit on) and one of the camouflage nets (to wrap myself up in). In addition there was the usual clobber of gun, cartridge belt, glasses, flask and sandwiches, four stakes for the net, and of course the four stuffed decoys. With the decoys set up I sat on my box facing the coast and the brightening dawn and hoped I would look no more offensive than a heap of rubbish in the field — albeit a very conspicuous heap.

It was a bright dawn with flaming red clouds over the distant hills turning to orange and then yellow as the sun approached the horizon. Skeins of geese soon appeared against the clear patches of sky and began heading in my direction. Some passed on, but many came to my patch and headed straight for the decoys. At the last moment they all sheered off and just wouldn't come within shot, though I did try two or three long shots. By nine it was fairly obvious that my plan wasn't working and I decided to pack up and get back to base in time for breakfast. And only then, in the full morning light, did I discover that I had set two of the decoys within a few yards of a dead goose on the ground — no doubt one from our night under the moon, but now lying in a large area of scattered plucked feathers — the work of carrion crows. So I don't know whether it was my huddled form or the conspicuous signs of a dead companion which scared the geese away.

We could find nothing at all promising in the rest of the day. At evening the other two tried the potato patch — this time in hopes of a flighting duck, while I found a small bunch of pinks near Puddy Tat Hill and managed to work my way up a burn till I was within 200 yards of them. Late in the dusk they lifted and went out to the coast, but they chose the opposite direction to that which I had anticipated. So ended another blank day.

For the morrow we decided to return to the scene of the wonderful flight over the hills. Reconnaissance had shown that the geese were already using the same two potato fields the day after our onslaught. We could find no other promising alternative, and after a day's rest the fields might provide another profitable flight. If we could get another goose each we should be satisfied; if we got two each we should be surprised and delighted.

So we made another early start and were well in position by 7.45 a.m. This time the weather was clear and chilly with a fairly strong N.W. wind. The geese were late in arriving and we were able to see them a long way off — very different to the previous conditions of mist. For a while we only had small occasional skeins and few gave us fair chances. In any case the shooting was bad and I for one began to get irritated and frustrated that I could not hit a bird, or at least bring one down. At last a skein came slap over me, rather lower, and I got a right and left. At once one's whole outlook changed. It was a lovely fine day; pleasant company, glorious sport! For another two hours the skeins kept arriving and there was never a dull moment. Whenever one of us left his hide to collect a fallen bird there would surely be a shout from the others :- "More coming! — Hurry up; get back to cover!" At one stage, during a lull, "BB" and I were caught out in the open when a large skein suddenly appeared literally "out of the blue", gliding straight down towards our field. Movement was out of the question, so we dropped on our knees by a group of stones and with our heads well down hoped we would look like two large boulders.

The geese circled above us, suspicious and hesitant, but eventually they came low enough to justify a shot and between us we got one. A little later another low skein gave me the chance of ending the morning as I had begun it — with a right and left. At 11 we packed up and took all our gear and the slain back to the vans. The total bag this time was 17 (myself 8, Tom 5 and "BB" 4), of which three of the geese were only winged and brought back alive for transfer to Norfolk. It was indeed a most remarkable morning, far exceeding our expectations. All the geese were greys, except for one pink, and it was amazing how keen they were to continue with their feed on these two fields.

I can't say that we made any special effort to organise a further outing after lunch. We made the usual tour of the coastal fields but found nothing to entice us out of the car. With inland prospects so poor it was clearly a case for another visit to the shore in the morning.

So on my last morning we went down to the coast again and waited for the morning flight from the mud flats. The pinks came in first in large skeins and at a safe height, but it was Saturday morning and all the local fowlers were out in force. Each skein was greeted with a fusillade from the over-optimistic gunners, but I never saw a single bird brought down. Later the greys started coming in, usually in smaller parties and occasionally at a more reasonable height. We all had a few long shots, but the lowest skeins managed to slip through where there were no guns. At nine the flight eased off and Tom and I decided to get back to firm land and rejoin "BB" at the van. And then, as we were collecting our things a lone bird came swinging along over the reeds. At first I thought it was a gull, but Tom had also seen it, and even as I cocked my hammers I heard his shot ring out and saw the goose crumple up and drop into the reeds.

That made exactly 60 geese in our ten days shooting of which I found I had accounted for 30. On the morrow I was due to start homewards so the rest of the day was spent in cleaning and packing guns and in knocking up a crate in which to carry home the five pricked greylags we had collected.

That evening the wireless forecast gales, frost and driving snow, and this warned me that I should have to pay for my holiday with a bitterly cold and unpleasant drive home — three days of it. But it was well worth it.

CHAPTER 19

BEGINNER'S LUCK
(1958 — 1959 Simon's Year)

There is no need to describe the usual trek north. I got away on December 28th, feeling very "Christmassy" and rather jaded, and picked up my nephew Simon in Newcastle. The next day's drive through the Cheviots and the Border country soon revived the sluggish liver and swept the mind clear of its worries. We began talking "geese" and before the day was out had found several hundred greylags scattered over three or four farms within reach of our base. One lot was on a field of corn that had obviously never been harvested and which lay in a tangled mass of straw. Birds of all sorts were feeding on it — gulls, rooks, jackdaws, pigeons, starlings — and geese. It looked an ideal opportunity for an ambush at morning flight and we went straight to the farmhouse to seek permission to shoot on his land. Alas — someone else had had the same idea and had been promised a go at the geese the very next day! Although we were offered a day later in the week we had no great hopes of a successful repeat performance.

In any case I had explained to Simon that the first rule of these trips is that one goes down to the coast on the first morning — to seek a goose the hard way, and to see what the area holds.

So next morning we were down by the tide line soon after 7.30 and waited for the flight to begin. The estuary was disappointingly quiet — very little goose-talk out on the water, and the weather was only moderate — some wind and threatening showers, but not enough to keep the geese really low. In the end a few skeins started to move up the river but only one turned inland and crossed our stretch of coast. And it went slap over Simon! As usual I saw the goose start to fall just before I heard the shot — so Simon had shot a goose with his first shot of his first fowling trip! It's just as easy as that!! However, jubilation was soon tempered with frustration: at the end of the flight I moved up to Simon and found him still searching the reed bed for his goose. We both searched methodically and thoroughly, but we never found it though it had fallen a mere 25 yards or so into the reeds.

The rest of the day we spent in a thorough recce of all the usual goose farms, including those over the hills, but we found very little more. There was nothing over the hills, and no sign of the usual big armies of pinks; apart from a small bunch on a grass field all the geese we heard or saw were greys. The old aerodrome held its faithful contingent of greys — about 200 of them, so at dusk we got between them and the coast, in the hope of a shot when they lifted. But they were probably half a mile inland from us and we misjudged their line of flight, by about 100 yards. Still hopeful we made another sortie after supper and went and stood in a grass field where another bunch of greys had been feeding all day. We hoped they might return when the moon rose at about 10 p.m. But a bank of thick cloud hung in the south-east and blotted out the moon and no geese seemed to be on the move. So we gave it up at midnight.

Next morning we had arranged to decoy the geese on a field close to our H.Q.; where Colin and I had two good mornings last year. This time we profited from our previous experience and had our hides better placed. A wonderful flight developed between 8 and 9 a.m., and carried on intermittently till nearly midday. But the weather was against us — clear skies, very little wind and perfect visibility, so that the geese came in very high and took their time in inspecting everything below them. Many hundreds — possibly a thousand — started to drop towards our field, but most of them either turned away at the last moment or passed on high overhead. We didn't have many chances and only fired about a dozen cartridges between us. In the end we had got 4 greylags, of which Simon shot (and collected) one.

In the evening we repeated our attempt to intercept the geese flighting off the aerodrome, but again we were 100 yards astray in our calculations and the geese passed safely out to the estuary on our left. That evening a new hazard was added to the normal range of problems that beset goose hunting; we had been invited to a Hogmanay party by one of our local farmer friends — a retired naval officer. This kept us up till about 1 a.m., and on our return to base we found our quarters deserted and locked, and the family away at a party of their own. Fortunately we found an unlatched kitchen window. Getting up a few hours later was more difficult than usual — in fact I overslept by half an hour and never heard the alarm clock. My head was also still in a protesting mood and made things more difficult than usual in checking the normal items of clothing and gear. In fact I found myself later on without the one most essential piece of equipment after weapons and clothing — binoculars. To go fowling without glasses makes me feel only half dressed — I am lost without them. For scanning the countryside they are, of course, indispensable, but even when waiting for morning or evening flight they add enormously to my own enjoyment of the proceedings. There are always distant skeins to follow; rafts of geese or duck on the water, and even other humans to be studied at times. — the tactics of rival gunners on the coast, or the movements of farm workers as outdoor work on the farms begins for another day. On this New Year's Day of 1959 we had fortunately decided to go further along the coast for morning flight, where the walk out across the fields is shortest — and we were just in time. We took up position by the Long Breakwater and a lot of geese began to flight in soon after 8. A small skein flying along the tide line nearly took me by surprise and I was a few seconds too late in taking the last bird of the nearest leg of the V. It dropped into the water, and as the tide was ebbing fast with a strong wind helping it the goose was carried out to sea faster than I could have gone out after it. I had hardly reloaded when a single goose came along and this I dropped safely on the mud. My first two shots of 1959 had brought down two greylags, though only the one was retrieved; it seemed indeed a very Happy New Year! A little later I watched a skein of about 20 going in over where Simon should be, and this time there was no question of the instantaneous death that reached up into the sky and struck one of the geese. It fell like a stone — into the reeds; but Simon told me afterwards that he had no difficulty in finding it; he walked straight on to it. I don't think either of us had any more chances, but it was a much better flight than Tuesday's with lots of greys in the estuary and skeins moving in all along the coast. We hurried home, to be in time for breakfast and again found our quarters apparently deserted! But in fact they were all a-bed, some not having returned till 8 a.m.!! So we started to get our own breakfast, till the son and daughter of the house struggled down to help us, looking very much the worse for wear. We ourselves did little more for the rest of the day — a short recce to keep an eye on the various lots of geese; a few calls on farmers to smooth the way for future occasions; and a long rest after lunch. At dusk we kept our third rendezvous with the aerodrome geese. A storm was blowing up and we couldn't locate the gaggle with any certainty. In fact I began to be extremely doubtful if the geese were there at all. But at 4.30 to the minute they all rose with a roar — 300 to 400 of them, and this time they were very nearly over us. They came hurtling down wind — at terrific speed and already at a great height, and though they were obviously beyond range I couldn't resist speeding the nearest bird with a charge of BB.

Next day — our fourth — was a long and interesting one, though it yielded no spoils. The best proposition at dawn was to decoy on a grass field behind Taylor's farm, where we had seen up to 40 greylags every day since our arrival. But it was a difficult field — large, square and without the slightest cover. A post and wire fence ran round all four sides, so we fell back on a variation of the old technique "BB" and I developed in 1945 — "stubble-man and cover-man". Simon was made to lie down flat along the bottom of the wire fence, while I covered him with a camouflage net tastefully decorated with a few wisps of dead grass. (This exercise normally takes place in the middle of a stubble-field!). My job as "cover-man", was not only to cover up the stubble-man again each time he had leapt out of concealment to take a shot, but also to act as look-out from some distant point of vantage, and to signal the movements and intentions of approaching geese by a series of whistle blasts. So much for theory. In fact, we had hardly got ourselves organised when three very early geese came sailing in. I was just able to give the appropriate signal before they passed slap over Simon, who sprouted like a mushroom out of the ground and delivered a charge of shot into the nearest bird. But it was either too high or too tough, or perhaps just lucky, for it recovered and passed on its way with the others. After that theory went to pieces; two lots of geese dropped into distant parts of the field and I had to embark on a long tramp round the countryside to put them up, with the idea of driving them over Simon. But they flew wide and Simon had no more shots; and no more skeins came in, though several passed overhead at a great height. It was another still bright morning with no wind and the odds all in favour of the geese.

After that we set out on a tour of other feeding grounds and found a large party of pinks on a grass field alongside a side road. The only hope was a drive, so after finding the farmer and getting permission I dropped Simon off the blind side of the van, into a deep ditch, and then took the car out of the way and started on the usual detour round the geese. But before I was ready to move the geese a man and boy started walking across the field and the whole plan was wrecked. The geese flew off at right angles.

At our next spy from our favourite look-out point up the hill road we noticed an albino goose in a gaggle of some 50. Although it was over a mile away I was sure it was a greylag, as it was in a field regularly used by greylags, and where we had identified the geese in the field as greylags every day since our arrival. (We were now waiting for this lot to build up to a large enough number to justify a dawn ambush with decoys). With no other lots of geese vulnerable to attack we decided to go over the hills and explore both old and new haunts. We soon found several big lots of greys in the next valley but only one gaggle seemed to offer a stalk, and when we traced the farmer we found he was away from home. Eventually, after lunch, we contacted him by 'phone and as he was co-operative we immediately set out back over the hills again to try and stalk the geese before they moved at dusk. But when we arrived on the scene the field was bare — the geese had flown. However the sky was soon full of other skeins, moving out from other fields, and in the next few minutes something like 2,000 greylags flighted down the valley. Quite a number passed right over us, and we even tried a few long shots, but the geese were probably safely out of range. For some time big and small lots were flighting about in all directions, and we were still hopeful we might get a fair chance but we never fired another shot. But this new farm clearly offered interesting possibilities and we promised to call again.

The next day was Saturday, and Simon had arranged to call on a family of school and college friends who lived on an estate up in the hills. We were told to arrive in good time so that we could have a walk round (which suggested the odd pheasant) and so it was clear we should only have time for a quick dawn flight before setting out. We therefore went down to the coast where there is the shortest walk from car to tide-edge and agreed that we must leave the coast at 9 a.m. sharp, whether the flight was over or not. Again it was a still clear dawn and conditions were not promising. But we could hear a lot of geese in the estuary and as we reached the open shore we could see large numbers quite close in on the mud and directly opposite us. Almost before I had trampled out a small clearing in the reeds I heard geese on the wing and an early skein appeared over the reed tops. I dropped one bird in the mud just in front of me and hit a second very hard, but I saw it swing back to the sea and land far out on the mud. Two carrion crows soon took up station a few yards from it, hoping for an early death to turn the goose into an easy meal for them. But the goose seemed to be only winged, and managed to waddle out to meet the rising tide. The last I saw of it, through my glasses, was swimming strongly out to sea. We had no more chances and were back for breakfast by 9.30 and the open road by 10.15 after a change into more civilised clothes.

The walk-round with Simon's friends turned out to be a walk along the river for duck. It also transpired that geese were using some of the fields along this river and that the boys had got several the previous night by waiting for them at dusk. Tactful references to our own interest in geese, and to the convenient presence of four decoys in our van led to the suggestion that we might repeat the dusk rendezvous with the geese. So after walking the river banks for duck Simon and I and one of the boys met at the field the geese had been visiting at dusk. It was a large flat grass field with several flashes of flood water still unfrozen, and a few trees along one side. We made ourselves inconspicuous under the trees, put the decoys out in the field, and awaited developments. Presently there was a great clamour of geese, and we could see several hundred rising into the air down the river. We later learnt that our host had come across them on a field of winter wheat and had put them up on his way to the river a mile further down. These geese split up, and from then on the valley was filled with the calls of geese. As the light failed some of them came to our field, but only a few were within range — no doubt due to the hammering they had received the previous night. At any rate I had four shots and got two, while earlier on I had got a very high single mallard. No one else had any luck and when all the geese calls had died away we packed up and made our farewells — but not before we had been promised another day with the geese. So ended the week's shooting, with a total score of nine geese (all greylags) and the one mallard.

Next morning (Sunday) I put Simon on the train homewards and motored on to inspect the field where the greylags had risen last night. It was a huge square field of winter wheat following potatoes, so that there was the double attraction of frosted potatoes and young green wheat shoots.

The geese were there in force — I estimated about 600 of them, and there was promising cover on two sides; a thin thorn hedge on the west and an old sunken roadway with whins and brambles on the east. I went on to discuss plans with the laird and we agreed that it would be advisable to tackle the geese as soon as possible, i.e. the very next morning. So after warning the tenant farmer and the keeper of our plans we arranged to meet "on the site" at 7.30 a.m. next morning.

By the time I returned to base "BB" and Tom had arrived and I was able to assure them that their first morning's shooting was already organised.

Morning came crisp and cold and clear. A hard frost made the road sparkle with countless ice crystals in the glare of our headlights, and we reached the wheat field in good time with the dawn just beginning to show in the south-east. I explained the lay-out to "BB" and Tom and let them go ahead to place the decoys, while I waited for the owner's contingent. Promptly on time Andrew turned up with a friend, and we all then made our way across the frozen field and spread out along the western thorn hedge. The cover was ideal — not only was there a hedge, but a deep ditch ran along it with clumps of whins and furze so it was easy to find almost perfect natural hides. With five humans to conceal the odds were weighted in favour of the geese, who also had the advantage of a clear, cloudless and almost windless morning. They came all right — in a steady stream for about an hour, but at a great height. The decoys drew them well and nearly every skein headed straight for the stuffed birds on the ground, but when high overhead they made cautious circles of inspection and only a few got as far as making that last deliberate glide-in.

Andrew and friend, Tom, keeper and "BB"; After the morning flight

So there was not a great deal of shooting, but we all had our share and the final bag was 12 — Tom 4, "BB" and I 3 each, and 2 between the boys: all greys.

We just got back in time for lunch and were content to spend the afternoon in checking up on the whereabouts of geese nearer home and laying on a similar ambush for next morning. We found a small party of greys on a field next to the sea wall and waited for them to lift at dusk, but they went out to the estuary diagonally and were the usual 100 yards wide of Tom.

Next day was full of surprises. We had planned to decoy the geese that Simon and I had seen feeding on a field of ungathered corn on the evening of our arrival a week ago. But in the meantime the geese had dwindled in numbers: no doubt the field was beginning to be stripped of all remaining grain, and we also knew that other gunners had twice assaulted the geese during the past week. Finally the hard frost of recent days no doubt left all the straw frozen to the sodden ground and any grain firmly embedded in ice. However the geese had begun to spread on to adjoining grass fields and one of these had held gaggles every day we had passed by. But on this final morning not a single skein made a serious attempt to come to the field, and only one single bird and a party of three swept in to land by the decoys. In spite of sitting shots at 40-50 yards range by "BB" and myself all four geese escaped. We gave up in disgust at about 10 and could not remember when a morning with decoys had last drawn a complete blank. We then set off to find other geese.

We had seen a cloud of several hundred rise from fields a mile or more away, and after some searching found a couple of hundred pinks on a large open grass field. A farm track led to this field and at the end of the track was a bunch of the usual Scotch circular corn stacks. It looked as if the nearest geese might be within range of these stacks and that a stalk was "on". So I drove the van on to the next field and dropped "BB" off on the blind side with the stacks between him and as many as possible of the wide spread of geese. We had a grandstand view of the whole operation from the car which, of course, we did not dare move or leave. A long belly-crawl took "BB" to the safety of the stacks, and after that we could see his large round hindquarters edging up from stack to stack until he disappeared from view. In a few more minutes the air was full of a cloud of geese though we hardly heard the two shots muffled between the stacks. We raced up in the van and found "BB" chasing crippled geese right and left. He had got 4 — the nearest at over 60 yards range. This unexpected and successful stalk was the second surprise of the day. After lunch we went further afield in our searches, and tried several farms over the hills. At the last we noticed a few greys on a field of winter wheat next to the road. We called at the farm to tackle the grieve, and at the same moment the owner also turned up. A closer inspection of the field revealed many more geese in folds of dead ground and it was clear that it was providing a strong feed. The owner gave us all facilities and we promised to come again at first light with our decoys. This was our third surprise — a most promising ambush discovered late in the day and ripe for immediate action next morning. On our final drive round those parts we saw hundreds — probably thousands — more greys moving to their sleeping quarters at evening flight. At one point on the road we were straddled with long weaving skeins flying right over the car — in easy range; and a little later we found a large bunch of greys all sitting down on a grass field and apparently settled down for the night. That gave us ideas for a new form of evening flight — inland.

Another surprise awaited us next morning when we began to load the van in the dark: both back tyres were flat! We suspected "BB" of having let the air out so that we should have to go in Tom's car which has a heater!! It was still bitterly cold, though not quite so piercing as the day before when there had been 12-14 degrees of frost with a slight wind. We reached our wheat field in good time and found a perfect lay-out. In one corner of the field a square acre of young conifers jutted out, and the geese had been feeding right up to the plantation fence. So we had perfect cover under the young firs and the only difficulty was in sticking the legs of the decoys into the frozen ground. The field was on the top of rising ground overlooking a long valley with snow capped mountains in the distance. We had a grandstand view of the morning flight and watched skein after skein set off up the valley. In the clear atmosphere we could probably see them several miles away, and much further, of course, with glasses. There was plenty of time to take cover whenever a bundle of geese started to head towards us, but in fact very few came our way, though several lots settled in the grass fields below us. At length a single bird came circling around and gave Tom a long shot. Later 2 skeins came to the decoys, and between us we

The field was on rising ground overlooking a long valley

got 4 more. We stayed on hopefully till 11, but by then there was no sign of further movement; the sky for miles around was empty of geese and there was complete silence, with all the many hundreds of geese safely feeding on the ground in their various chosen fields. We could see several lots up and down the valley, but none seemed disposed to make any further moves. So we returned back to base for lunch, leaving our decoys in position, together with the 5 dead geese "set up" with the aid of pointed sticks. We were back again by 2.30 but there was still no movement and no sound of geese and we soon gave it up. There was then only time to try the fields near the estuary and we started off to see if the usual geese were on the aerodrome. But when we were nearly there I happened to spot a small party on a field further down the coast. It seemed easier to judge their likely line of flight than that of any geese on the vast expanse of the airfield and we changed our destination accordingly. To add to our hopes it started to snow, which should help to keep the geese low. But as usual they came out some distance beyond us, though at comfortable treetop height.

Next morning it was the turn for morning flight on the coast again. The recent hard frosts had made a big difference to the tidal area. Instead of struggling laboriously through the mud of the reed beds one was able to walk easily and confidently on the hard frozen surface. The fringe of short reeds was now white with a crackling of ice and last night's flurry of snow. While I was still on the sea wall I heard geese coming towards me and I was just able to slip one cartridge in before two vague forms passed only a few feet above me. But I couldn't see along my own gun barrels, and in any case it is always difficult to swing an 8-bore on such a close target. At any rate the geese went on — squawking in protest. A minute later while I was in the midst of the reed bed another early skein passed close overhead, but it was still too dark to take proper aim. Again I missed. Arrived at the edge of the open mud I could hear plenty of geese ahead of me, and could make them out with my glasses, sitting in groups on the mud, a mere 100 yards or so out. Presently, with better light the flight started and several skeins came in over our stretch of the coast. I dropped a grey with a long second barrel and marked the line of the fall carefully: presently in a lull of the flight I searched for it, but couldn't find it. Later a pair of geese gave me a fair chance, and I dropped one in the reeds behind me. I was too intent on marking this one to risk a second shot at the other goose. However I found the shot goose — a pink — at once, though it was only winged and had wriggled under the dense tangle of matted reeds. Two wing feathers only stuck out and gave away its position. After the flight Tom came over with his two spaniels and helped to search for the greylag. Eventually we found it — straight on my line, but further than I had calculated. This gave great pleasure to Tom, and I had to suffer several repeat descriptions of the incident — what a wonderful old dog "D" was; how he had an instinct for finding lost birds if left to himself; and how he came in grinning all over his face — he was so pleased with himself. (I can never understand how a small spaniel with a large bird in his mouth can contrive to grin at the same time). The others had had no luck, though a few shots.

The rest of the day we spent in reconnaissance far and wide. At one point we thought we had found a stalk, but the geese moved before we could make our plans. We also found 250 pinks on a grass field which looked driveable. "BB" and Tom crawled into position and I put the geese up, but they gave difficult high shots and passed on unscathed. We even visited the distant wheat field we had ambushed the morning before, but that no longer held any geese.

Next morning it was overcast and trying to snow when we looked out and it seemed that we might at least have really good conditions for morning flight. "BB" and Tom had decided to go down to the coast again, but I had declared in favour of another morning with the decoys next to the sanctuary farm. The weather got wilder and stormier as I got into position, and it needed a screwdriver and hammer to punch holes in the frozen ground for the wire spikes on the decoys' legs. The geese were punctual, in spite of the poorer light, and a large skein soon battled into the wind towards the sanctuary field. Unfortunately they came so wide of me, and so low, that they never saw the decoys but went straight to the far side of the adjoining field. Further skeins followed in a steady stream and, of course, all went straight to the big lot already on the ground. It looked as if I was in for a blank morning, but eventually one or two lots came in via my side of the field, and others started moving across from one field to another before settling down to feed. At any rate I had a few fair chances, and at last I had a nice skein right over me which yielded a goose. The weather now began to clear and quieten and the geese all seemed firmly settled for their morning feed — some 300 of them in a fairly solid mass right at the far end of the field in front of me. There was nothing I could do about it — except to settle down myself in my hide and hope that something might induce the geese to move. In particular I knew that "BB" and Tom would now be back for breakfast and that they would soon set out again by car to check where all the geese had got to. I was confident that their first call would be to see how I was getting on. Sure enough at about 10 I saw their van coming along the distant road — and stop opposite the geese. They got out, having obviously sized up the situation, and started making aggressive gestures at the geese. At first a few birds rose, but merely flew another hundred yards or so away from the road and settled again. Then a single bird got up and came right across the field. It crossed my dyke just within range, and going like a bomb with the wind up its tail. I was rather surprised when it fell to my shot. A few moments later the whole mass of geese rose. The field in front of me seemed to spout geese from one end to the other; in a few seconds they had formed up into long weaving skeins, and the whole lot came heading straight for me. It was a perfect "goose-drive", with me in the centre and a line of geese stretching 100 yards to left and right. Although they looked easy shots they had gained a good height in their quarter mile flight towards me, and I knew it was no good shooting till they were almost overhead and at their nearest. I got my first bird but missed with my second barrel at the departing line. There was no point in staying on after that, so I packed up and rejoined the others awaiting me at the farmyard. As I expected they had had an excellent flight on the coast and had come home with three geese themselves.

After such a satisfactory morning we made no more serious assaults on the geese, but spent the afternoon in an extensive recce by car and checked on our dispositions for next morning's flight.

This we had arranged to take place on the local laird's land, where we had watched geese building up on a stubble field. On this last inspection we found a fair number of birds on the stubble, but also a much larger number on a nearby grass field. This complicated matters as there was no cover at all round the grass field, but a ditch with a few hedgerow trees on the seaward side of the stubble field. We therefore decided to lie up in this ditch with the decoys on the stubble. The laird's eldest son was to join us which in turn meant that the keeper would also probably be sent along, but when we called at the rendezvous soon after 7 next morning we learnt that the young laird was "bedded" with some indisposition and that the keeper was not expected to accompany us. Although we are always very willing to join forces with local landowners — in return for their great kindness in letting us shoot on their land — we are always relieved when we are left to ourselves. Extra bodies to conceal add to our difficulties, and the average gamekeeper is often far from expert when it comes to dealing with wild geese.

Yesterday's stormy weather had given way to clear skies again and the geese soon began to stream in at their usual safe height. One or two lots came to our field but mostly they flew in beyond the end of the field and then turned at right angles and flew along behind us a good two gunshots from the line of the ditch and trees. However one or two were less cautious and came straight over the trees, and "BB" and I each managed to bring one down. By this time I could see that most of the skeins were going straight to the grass field and settling there; it seemed most important to check this tendency and to try and move these geese back to the stubble. So I left "BB" and Tom in the ditch and set out for the grass field. About a hundred geese were already there and, of course, soon flew off as I got near; some of them swinging round towards the stubble. But further skeins were still streaming in from the mud banks and heading for the grass field. There was absolutely no cover: the only thing to do was to "freeze" against one of the posts of the wire fence and hope for the best. Some of the flights did in fact swing round rather too close to the fence before they spotted the danger, and in this way I managed to get several long shots and to bring down two more geese. Later I returned to the others, just in time to see "BB" get another goose from a pair that came straight to the stubble.

So our last morning produced another five — all greylags. Amongst the morning's skeins we saw again the white goose — a good five miles from where we had first seen it. A closer inspection through glasses showed that it had black primaries, so we came to the conclusion that it could not be an albino but was more probably a snow goose, no doubt an escapee from someone's collection.

"BB" and Tom were to stay on for another week, but after lunch I had to leave them and set out for home.

This winter — the first time in these many years — the weather defeated me. At Edinburgh I found that all the roads to Newcastle were blocked, and with appointments awaiting me in England there was no alternative but to take the train. I was lucky to get on to that night's car-sleeper service, and next day drove home from my fowling holiday — from London! Our total score this year, up to the time I left, was 41 geese shot and collected and nearly all of these were greylags. The big armies of pinks were only just beginning to collect when I left. I had had 11 shooting days — 5 with Simon and 6 with the others, and my own contribution had been 19 geese — all greys except for the one pink shot on the coast.

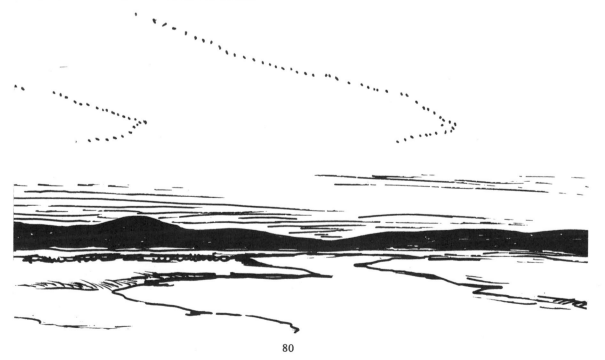

CHAPTER 20
PATRICK'S FIRST GOOSE
(1960 – 1961 Henry's Year)

We made up a party of four this year; myself and Keith with his friend Ted and my nephew Henry. Four is rather a crowd for some goose hunting expeditions, but with two cars one can avoid this by operating as two separate pairs, and this is particularly useful for the important task of reconnaissance.

I set out on Saturday, December 10th, to meet the other three at Bawtry on the Great North road. Passing near the Wash at Fosdyke I looked out hopefully for the first sight of geese, and sure enough a small skein appeared in the distance, to be joined by a larger bunch of 100 or more which rose from a potato stubble. This indeed emphasised that my trip had started, contact was established: the hunt was up!

For the next week I knew I should be seeing the weaving skeins every day, and for many hours each day I should be hearing the music of their clamour.

We stopped that night on the Northumberland coast and were up early next morning to try a curtain raiser on the Fenham Flats. But it was rather a disappointment, we saw a few ducks and heard the odd wigeon, but there was no sign of geese and none of us even fired a shot. So we hurried back to breakfast and pressed on northwards, each car doing its own tour of reconnaissance as it got into our usual goose country.

Henry was with me and I took him along one of the inland valleys which usually held geese. Before long we found the geese – about 2,000 of them on a large stubble field across the other side of the valley. Amongst them we could see a single white goose. Nearer home we heard other lots and reached the estuary in time to see a few out on the mud flats. Later it started to snow.

Next morning we went down to the coast as usual. There was only a slight dusting of snow, but it had been freezing fairly hard, and most of the tracks through the reeds would bear us on the frozen surface. There sounded a fine lot of geese in the estuary, but the nearest ones moved out further on to the mud as they heard us crunching our way through the tall reeds. Eventually the morning flight was disappointing, only 3 or 4 small lots came anywhere near me and only Ted had a shot. The big skeins all sounded as if they moved up towards the head of the estuary. There was however a pricked goose skulking about in the short reeds in front of Henry – I saw it walk in from the mud with the first light. I told Henry later on and sent him after it, but the goose took him by surprise and flew back to sea again. It was no use staying on – the geese had all moved in – so we went back for breakfast and then organised a series of recce trips to find where the geese were feeding. Ted and Henry were sent off to follow up the geese I had spotted on the way up the previous afternoon while Keith and I checked on the laird's estate. We could hear geese on the blind side of some rising ground, and a walk to the top of the ridge disclosed about 1,000 pinks feeding on the flat grass fields below. We then called on the laird and were invited to join forces with him and his young son for a morning with the geese on Wednesday. That still left the next day (Tuesday) unprovided for, so we drove on to another area over the hills where there are a series of good goose farms. At first there was no sight or sound of anything, and then luckily something disturbed the geese and we saw a large cloud of them rise from a distant field, circle, and then settle again. We soon tracked them down to a field adjoining the farm of a man we knew well, and it seemed that to decoy them over the boundary should be a practical proposition. When we got back to base and met Ted and Henry they also had good news: they had found a thousand or more geese still on the field where we had seen them yesterday; they had traced and found the farmer, got permission to shoot and brought back sketches of the lay-out of the fields with hedges, tracks, cornstacks, etc. In fact we decided to follow up this alternative next morning in preference to the other as there seemed to be a bigger lot of geese and better topography.

Meanwhile we still had time for the evening flight on the coast. We had found a small lot of geese between the railway and the sea wall, and placed ourselves where we estimated they should cross the coast. We guessed well: the skein came right over Ted and Keith, and I saw one goose falling after the shots. But it apparently recovered and reached the mud. Soon after a single bird came heading straight for me — silently and low. I completely missed with the first shot but got it with the second: it fell like a sack just in front of Henry who was coming up behind me and was just getting ready to deal with it. So our first day was just saved from being a blank.

After tea we packed the van all ready for an early start in the morning.

It was cold, dull and misty as we took the road at 6 next morning; in fact just freezing. We were all in position in good time with the decoys set out both in front and behind us but the mist seemed to upset the usual flight and only a few odd geese turned up at first light. As the light grew I was not too pleased with our positions, so we all moved further along our hedge and re-set the decoys. Still no geese came our way, but it sounded as though quite a number were somewhere in front of us. Presently we heard them all get up, but apparently settle again. I told the others to stay put while I tried to work round the geese and move them. They saw me through the mist

We lined our original hedge again as the mist was thinning. Henry and Keith

before I saw them, and lifted with a roar. But again they settled only a few hundred yards further on — in the next field as it transpired. Working along the hedge I could at last make them out, sitting in the middle of the field. Some of them also saw me, and again they took fright and lifted. This time they scattered in several directions, and some skeins came straight for me — not realising where the danger lay. I only had to "freeze" into the hedge and the nearest skein came straight over me and gave me an easy right and left.

After that the geese kept on the move, and we also kept moving round the field trying to put the geese over each other. In this way we all had several shots, and before long I heard two dull thuds in the distance following shots. Keith and Ted each had a goose down. Later we moved back to the decoys and lined our original hedge again as the mist was thinning and the decoys seemed to be drawing the geese better. Keith and I each had a very high goose out of a pair that came over the decoys, and then Keith got another extremely high single bird. In this way we hung on till nearly 3 p.m., when we packed up, slipped down to the coast for a blank evening flight and finally got back to base at 5 p.m. — 11 hours since we had set out. The total score was nine — all pinks. It had been an interesting and enjoyable day; geese on the move nearly all the time and a changing mist to add uncertainty and a touch of mystery to everything.

The next day — Wednesday — was booked for our "combined operation" with the Laird. We called at the "big house" at 6.30 a.m. as arranged, but found only Patrick the younger son awaiting us. The Laird had a chill and had cried off (this seemed to be a hereditary failing — the elder son had similarly withdrawn two years ago). So we collected the keeper and drove on to the nearest farmyard overlooking the wonderful stretch of grass fields which the geese were using. One of the main objectives of the morning's operations was for Patrick to shoot his first goose, and the keeper had laid his plans accordingly. Keith and Henry were sent off to the right; Ted was taken off a couple of fields to the left, while Patrick and I were left in the centre. A small "hide" had been built for us in the corner of a young plantation of conifers, while all round us were the grass fields on which the geese had been feeding My position in the hide with Patrick — in a quasi-professional role — was no doubt intended, and certainly accepted, as a great honour; but it had its drawbacks. In the cold and misty morning the flight was slow to develop but eventually there was a steady stream of geese flying along the series of grass fields and passing over one or more of our three groups. We could hear them coming and eventually they would loom into sight but usually at a safe height. I was itching to fire at the nearest skeins which I reckoned were just in range for my 3-inch cartridges with BB shot, but at the same time I didn't want the boy to fire at hopeless chances with his 16 bore and 4 shot. So I restrained my itching finger and waited for some lower skeins to give Patrick his chance. Eventually he got a goose down and I felt that my main duty was done, and that it was now a case of "free for all". To our left Ted seemed to be having indifferent sport, but on our right a regular fusillade suggested that Keith and Henry were in the thick of things. At about 9 the keeper came along and indicated that he was then expected to take Patrick home. Patrick was clearly in two minds, but in the end the call of filial duty, a warm house and a hot breakfast won the day. No sooner had he departed than I got a single goose and then a right and left with 3 consecutive shots. We all stayed on — with our sandwiches — till nearly eleven and by then things had quietened down and we all foregathered at the van. Apart from Patrick's goose and the keeper's 4 or 5 the rest of us had collected 15, Keith with 7, myself 5, Henry 2 and Ted 1. They were all pinks, though one of the keeper's was a bean goose — the first I had seen at close hand.

After lunch we all returned to the all-important task of reconnaissance. The three boys went over the hill to check the geese Keith and I had found yesterday. I set out for the scene of yesterday's battle — in case we needed to try it again. But the valley was full of mist and it was quite impossible to spot anything; in any case it was doubtful whether any geese would have dared to penetrate the solid blanket that hung over yesterday's fields. Eventually I found the geese — 3,000 of them as near as I could estimate — all collected in a field high up the valley side and well above the mist. But they were on preserved land where I knew we had no hope of access. Fortunately the boys came back with better news: they found the geese all right, not only on the same field as yesterday but also on another field about a mile away. We decided to split our forces in the morning and wait for the geese in both fields simultaneously.

We set the alarm extra early for next morning as we did not dare risk the road over the hills with its black-ice surface, but took the longer road round. It was under a clear sky with sparkling stars that we dropped Keith and Ted at the first farm, with four of the decoys. Henry and I went on to our further farm. Picking my way through the farmyard in the dark I stumbled on a frozen clod, and with both my hands full of gear (gun, decoys, etc.) I took the full force of the fall on my knees and elbows. My thick thigh waders no doubt saved me from serious damage, but it was all very painful, and subsequent kneeling on the frozen ground was sheer agony.

The flight was disappointing. Some geese were already on the field when we arrived — possibly fog-bound all night, and as it got light we could see them collecting on a large grass field across the shallow valley. New arrivals continued to join them till there must have been several hundred there. Presently Henry volunteered to set off across country to move them. Meanwhile other geese — greys — were beginning to appear in the distant sky from the opposite direction. But they all dropped into their own grass field much nearer to us. During the morning 2 or 3 small lots came to our field and showed some slight interest in our decoys, but nothing gave us a fair shot, and I only fired a few cartridges in desperation.

Keith and Ted seemed to be having some shooting and we soon gave up our own positions as hopeless and drove over to join the others. They had had quite a reasonable flight, with several skeins over them at a fair range, but they were both shooting badly and only one greylag was collected — by Ted. Keith got a couple of mallard, though, when following up a wounded goose along a burn — but the goose got away. There was considerable despondency about all this — only 1 goose instead of the half dozen they should have got.

I took the afternoon off, to rest my painful and swollen knees, and left the boys to their own devices. They went back to the morning's fields, in the hope that some geese might be on the move again at dusk. They did get a few shots, but with no result.

Next morning we decided we would try the coast again. A thaw was now forecast and we hoped that for our last morning on Saturday we might find a potato field that had thawed out and was attracting the geese.

The weather was true to forecast on Friday morning, and we looked out to a black and damp countryside instead of the white and frosty scene of the last few mornings. We spread out along the usual stretch of coast and listened to the usual dawn chatter of geese out on the mud. But from my position in a small inland of tall reeds on the right of the line the flight seemed a small one. Only one lot came near me, except for a small skein that slipped out to the mud from behind me and took me by surprise. I never fired a shot and didn't hear any sound from the others on my left. But when we gathered together at about 9 I was pleasantly surprised to see both Keith and Henry coming in with a goose each. They had had a fair flight and several shots. We got back in time for a proper breakfast for once, which was a pleasant chance from the two rounds of sandwiches which had been our routine for the past 3 mornings.

After a shave and change I had some business to attend to at a nearby town and left the others to carry out the usual recces in search of something for our last morning. We met again at 3.30 in time for the evening flight but the boys had bad news. They could find no geese on any of the usual and more reliable farms, and the best they could offer was a bunch of greys on inaccessible land across the upper reaches of the river. They thought they might be decoyable to our side of the river as they flew in to the fields at dawn. It was possible, but not very promising, and it seemed a case of either this or another final visit to the coast with the inevitable competition of all the local Saturday gunners. But before going down for the evening flight Keith and I did a quick recce of the "home beat", and there — as sometimes happens at the eleventh hour — we stumbled on a good lot of geese (200-300) feeding on a potato stubble not a mile from our H.Q. The thaw had softened the potato gleanings and the geese were feeding on them eagerly; no doubt their first good meal since the last few days of hard frost.

But the farmer presented a problem. Several years ago I had tackled him for permission and had been turned down. A year or two later "BB" had tried his luck and had been allowed on the land. So there was at least some hope. After tea Keith and I drove round to his house and I knocked on the door to beard him. To my surprise and embarrassment he greeted me as an old friend; said how glad he was to see me again, and at once assured me of a welcome on his fields! It was obvious he mistook me for someone else — perhaps "BB" or one of his party. However he never asked my name and I played the hand as it was dealt to me.

On the way home Keith and I walked round the potato field in the dark with a torch, stepped out the lengths of the sides, inspected the boundary fences and ditches for cover and decided on the general plan of attack. This was clearly the best proposition for our last morning; we went back and briefed the other two, packed the van ready for the morning, and went to bed in good time with the alarm set at the more reasonable time of 6.15 a.m.

All was well as we set out next morning: the thaw still held and there was a promising breeze. We were in position in good time, three of us in a deep ditch along one side of the field, while Keith acted as long-stop at the far end with his 8-bore.

The well-known flight line close under the hills

At 8 the goose began to fly in, mostly following the well known flight line along the fields close under the foot of the hills, but some coming in diagonally direct from the coast. Being greys they came in small and medium skeins well spread out; in fact the flight continued till about 10, and several hundred geese came towards our field. But our cover was not too good, and the wind dropped as the skies cleared, while four bodies are a lot to conceal from 1,000 or more piercing eyes. Very few geese were deceived long enough to come right in to the decoys, so it was usually a case of a long shot at extreme range before the hesitant skein began to climb away again. But we all had our chances and between us we got 7 down. One of them was only stunned or slightly wounded, as when I found it sitting by itself in the middle of a distant field it got up again and flew out to the coast.

So ended our week with a total bag of 33 geese and 2 mallard.

Soon after midday we had changed, packed the van and car, and had set forth on the long drive home.

Our two novices Henry and Ted had proved apt and keen. They were not completely new to the game as they had been out on the Wash before, but they had still to shoot their first goose — which of course they both did on this trip. I think they both enjoyed the whole strenuous campaign and cheerfully adapted themselves to the rather austere daily routine — with possibly slight reservations. One of them displayed a well known hereditary weakness for filling his hot bath to the brim — with disastrous results for subsequent bathers, and all the three younger members seemed to feel the cold. One was discovered sleeping in bedsocks, and the blast of superheated air which came out of their bedrooms each morning when called was a measure of the smallness of their rooms and the efficiency of the electric fires which they left blazing all night. However there were excuses; one was on leave from India, another had been born and reared in South Africa, and Keith himself had a graveyard cough which suggested a hospital bed as a more appropriate place for him than a freezing ditch on a December morning. Food also seemed to be somewhat of a preoccupation. On the second morning there was a plaintive enquiry at 12.30 as to the prospects for lunch. As we were then 20 miles from base it was suggested that we should pack up and make for the nearest town and there buy ourselves the best lunch that the best hotel could provide. As geese were still on the move the suggestion went unheeded and the party was kept out in the field till about 3 p.m., and only after evening flight on the coast were they returned to base. That, one hoped, would enable the apprentices to get into proper perspective the relative importance of their stomachs and goose shooting!

But seriously, the bags we achieve in the limited time at our disposal, and under the conditions of free-lance shooting that we follow, are only possible through our policy of intense concentration and hard work. We go out after the geese at every suitable opportunity and those opportunities we have to seek and make for ourselves. The rest of the daylight hours are spent in reconnaissance and in the planning of future assaults. Apart from a regular evening meal at the end of the day the rest of our eating is haphazard and irregular, and often based on a couple of rounds of sandwiches and a thermos of coffee taken with us when we first set out before dawn. Always we have to be planning a day or two ahead for it is little use setting out each morning unless:

1. We have ascertained by observation that a worthwhile number of geese are using a certain field.
2. We have traced the farmer or owner and obtained permission to shoot.
and 3. We have studied the hedges, ditches or other cover surrounding the field and worked out a plan of action. This sometimes requires close inspection on the spot, after the geese have left in the evening.

Of course when these conditions are lacking we can always go down to the coast, as indeed we always do on the first morning, and often on one or two more, as there is a satisfaction about shooting a goose when it first comes in off the mud or water that does not quite apply to inland shooting.

"A goose on the shore is worth four on the fields".

CHAPTER 21
FRESH FIELDS
(1961 – 1962 Sandy's Year)

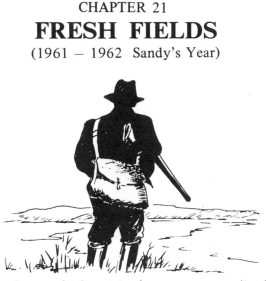

Once again as the time for our fowling trip drew near we realised how much we are at the mercy of weather conditions at the turn of the year.   Christmas had brought hard frosts, to be followed by snow at the New Year. Road conditions became chaotic and dominated the news in both the papers and on the wireless : "50 main roads blocked", "villages cut off", "train services disrupted", "airports out of action", "scores of cars abandoned".   Keith, trying to get back to Berkhamsted on the Sunday (31st December), after our Boxing Day Shoot, only got as far as Cambridge : Colin returning next day took 8 hours instead of the usual 3½. On top of all this I had got a dose of flu, and it therefore seemed foolish to set out for the North on the Tuesday as planned.

So we delayed our departure for 24 hours, by which time we hoped the roads would be cleared and my flu past its worst. In fact, apart from some packed snow on the Norfolk roads and a bad patch on the coast road near Dunbar, we had a good run north and on the second day met the forecast thaw coming into Scotland from the north-west.

I had two nephews, Henry and Sandy, with me this year – Henry, an old hand from last year, but Sandy a novice to this type of fowling, though he had made trips to the Wash. He had still to shoot his first goose.

We had arranged to spend the first few days in a new area ; one that I had long known of, and visited in autumn, but had never tried in winter.   On the way we passed through our usual hunting area and made a quick recce of the feeding grounds. Sandy and I could find nothing, but Henry located a big bunch of geese – several hundred – on a tangled stubble close under the hills. (It was the same field that had offered a similar encouraging sight to Simon and myself almost exactly three years ago!) We hoped that they would still be there for us after the weekend.

At our new H.Q. we were told that a few geese were feeding on two fields quite close to the house, so we started our first day with a "de luxe" variety of fowling.   The alarm was set for 7 a.m. ; a quick cup of tea in the kitchen ; and by 7.20 we were walking across to the nearby fields. We set up our decoys on a potato stubble behind us and two other guns took up position behind the next fence in front of us – with a large grass field between the two lines of guns. Things were slow to start but after a long wait a thin line of 5 geese appeared coming up from the bay straight towards us. They came straight and low – heading for the decoys, and passing (as it seemed) close over Henry. I waited for the shots – would he never fire? – and still the geese pressed on, till they were over the fence and safely out of range!   At the subsequent court of enquiry we could get very little sense out of Henry – merely some talk about being so doubled up at the base of the fence that he couldn't uncoil himself in time to get his gun into action!

The geese swung round beyond the decoys, went back beyond the other guns and settled in a distant field. Later they were made to move, and came forward again over the far fence, where one of the other party got a clean right and left.

87

Later a pair came along on my left and passed over me very high. I was doubtful whether they were in range, but itching fingers at the first possible chance made me fire. One goose fell, and was retrieved by Sandy a quarter of a mile away. Next a single goose came along and passed over the two boys but escaped. And then, finally, a larger skein of a dozen or more came straight for the decoys and gave the boys another chance. One bird fell to the last of the four shots and was credited to Henry.

After breakfast we set out for a walk along the marshes by the bay. There were plenty of wigeon, some eider and a few mallard; also a pricked pinkfoot which just evaded us. Our only score was one mallard as it swung back over the guns.

In the afternoon we did a recce further afield by car but found nothing, and then in the evening the boys went back to the foreshore for the evening flight, but with no result.

The outlook for the next day was indeed grim, as there seemed very few geese about. The boys decided to go back to the fields again, while I decided to sample the shore to see what the bay really held. It was a clear morning with a keen frost but no wind — so prospects could hardly be worse. I could, however, hear a few greys out on the mud and soon after 8 the first skein of 17 lifted and faced the shore. With their usual uncanny skill they chose the one section of the sea wall where there was no one below them, though I had counted 9 other gunners out on that Saturday morning to right and left of me. Every furze and whin seemed to hold a concealed fowler and later on they loosed off at every duck that came streaming back to the bay. Most of them were quite 100 yards up, and passed on quite oblivious of the shots below them, speeding on their purposeful way till they were well out over the estuary, when they planed down in easy contemptuous glides to the sanctuary of the open water.

Back at breakfast I found Henry and Sandy also with clean guns, only one small party of geese having come anywhere near them.

The prospects for the rest of the day now seemed grimmer than ever. There was very little sign of geese in the area; we had no previous knowledge of the neighbourhood or likely feeding grounds and weather conditions were unhelpful. In such circumstances when one hasn't a clue what to do in particular, there is one golden general rule — go out and find the geese.

So with a thermos of coffee and a packet of sandwiches we set out after breakfast, the boys doing a circuit clockwise to the south, and myself doing a similar circuit anticlockwise to the west. We would meet at a certain village some 15 miles inland and compare notes.

It was all new ground to me but a lot of it looked good goose country; broad valleys with large square fields. Some of the fields of winter wheat had oil drums all over them — a sure sign that the farmers had been having trouble with geese. It was while motoring along the side of the second valley that I suddenly noticed the unmistakable grey mottled effect of geese on a distant stubble. To stop the car and check through glasses brought instant confirmation; and then two fields further on I saw another 100 or 200. I pressed on to the rendezvous with the boys — to be told they had found nothing — and gave them the good news. In high spirits we retraced our route back to the geese and then set about finding the farmers. Both were at home for their Saturday dinners, and both proved co-operative. We met again on the high road, overlooking the scene of battle and planned our campaign. The geese were too far out from any walls or ditches to make a stalk possible, so a drive was the only solution. We took the nearest field first and sent Henry and Sandy off on a long approach — on hands and knees behind stone dykes — to the point nearest to the geese. I watched from a safe distance and when they were on their last stage I set off on a long detour to get behind the geese on the far side. Unfortunately (as it then seemed) the main mob took alarm before I was properly behind them and they all flew off to the side, but fortunately settled again with the other mob two fields away. Two smaller parties stood firm and eventually flew off over the boys, but they were rather wide and high and they passed unscathed. The four shots were too far away to disturb the geese in the other field, so a second drive was soon under way. This time Sandy and I crept up into position, and found an easy approach in dead ground right up to the stone wall bordering the field. Henry went round by car to the next farm and then set out on foot to move the geese. This time the plan worked perfectly — the geese were in a long field running under a hill: I felt sure they wouldn't try to fly "uphill" but would turn away from the hill across the open valley (where Sandy and I were). I was watching the nearest geese through a chink in the coping of the wall: they were all feeding peacefully, some of them sitting down and resting. Then their heads began to stick up and I knew Henry must be coming into their view. In another moment the usual babel of goose talk broke out and they were all on the wing. The whole 300 or so came straight for Sandy and me. I heard Sandy fire, then they were over me, and I took the first bird right overhead. As I saw him pack up I swung on to a second and saw him follow suit. Then out of the departing skeins another bird lagged behind and finally collapsed in a distant field. It was Sandy's second bird and was in due course retrieved — so that we both had a right and left; in Sandy's case, the first geese he had shot. On the way back to the road with our spoils we saw five geese ahead, back in another stubble, and tried yet another drive (Sandy's turn as beater) but this failed completely. Back at the cars we suddenly realised we still hadn't had lunch, so set upon our sandwiches and coffee at 3.30 p.m. ! And even as we ate, and talked and went over the details of the last two hours of excitement, a skein of 12 geese came swinging in over the hills and began dropping in to their feeding grounds again. Time and again they circled, and at last pitched in a fresh field — a barley stubble.

It had come round to my turn again as beater, so Henry and Sandy were sent off on suitable lines of approach while I went round to the opposite point of the compass and did the usual pincer movement on the geese. I got to within about 200 yards of them in the failing light; then I saw all their heads go up. A few nervous squawks and then the whole skein took off — and headed straight for where I knew Henry must be; I saw a goose turn away from the skein — a few seconds later the two shots reached me — and with my glasses I followed the goose to where it pitched in the distance. Henry had also marked it, and on following our two lines of direction we met at the point of intersection — where the goose duly awaited us !

So ended a most interesting day — with five geese in the boot of the car (all greys) and a new stretch of goose country opened up. As we plodded back to the cars flight after flight of mallard came streaming over the hills to pitch into the barley stubbles all round us. We were tempted to join battle again, but decided that fortune — and the farmers — had been kind enough to us already — and we would call it a day.

On the morrow we moved on to our old quarters of previous years. We set out immediately after breakfast and spent the morning exploring a long stretch of country full of goose valleys. The fields of yesterday's goose drives were again full of geese and we found several more big lots feeding on barley or potato stubble all the way along our route. We must have seen quite 1,000 geese during the morning — all happily feeding and undisturbed on the Sabbath morn.

At our old H.Q. we found "BB" and Tom had already arrived. Henry was to join them in the hotel, while Sandy came with me to stay with friends who had kindly offered to put us up. After lunch the boys set out on a recce of the distant valley that had produced such good sport for us last year, while I did a tour of the Home Beat. We both had promising reports to exchange later; the boys found several hundred geese on the farm next to last year's scene of battle, and I was able to check that at least 100 pinks were feeding on the Laird's farms nearer home. But these could both wait another 24 hours. In the morning we would go down to the coast as usual.

It was still and mild, with no snow or frost when we set out next morning, but a fair breeze got up and heavy clouds rolled along from the west as the dawn broke. "BB" and Tom were a mile further along to the west of us.

Geese were just beginning to "talk" as we staggered out through the reedpath to the edge of the mud, and as we came to the last of the reeds we could hear a lot of geese close in. In fact we could see them through glasses barely 100 yards in front of us. So it was impossible to advance any further, or to spread out along the coast. We all three crouched down within a few yards of each other and hoped that some of the geese would presently lift and come in over us. And that's exactly what happened — suddenly there were six or seven shapes looming into sight over the reed tops and we all let fly ! I saw my first bird crumple and greedily swung to fire at a second — instead of carefully marking where the first fell in the faint light. As a result when the flight was over I never found this goose in the vast expanse of the reed bed. The other two now spread out along the coast and a very fair flight developed — parties of greys and a few pinks — keeping up a nearly continuous flight for about an hour from 8 to 9 a.m. But most of them went in further up the coast, and though we had a few shots we were unable to bring anything down. Later we found that "BB" and Tom had shot 4 geese, though they only retrieved 3. "BB", I was sorry to find, had been guilty of gross delinquency. Firstly, he went after a wounded goose with an empty gun and the goose recovered sufficiently to fly out to the mud; secondly, he failed to follow up this goose at once, but preferred to come back to base and attend to the needs of his stomach. After breakfast, when he returned, he found unmistakable evidence in the mud that some other more valiant fowler, with a more enterprising dog, had gone out and collected his goose.

The next step was to lay a plan for the morrow. The boys volunteered to go back to yesterday's valley, trace the farmer of the fields the geese were using and lay on a morning ambush. This they did and were back by 2 p.m. — with two hours of hunting time still in hand. I could suggest only one thing — a return to the scene of Saturday's goose drives, in the hope that the same operations could be repeated. So we set off — a journey of over 30 miles — and were greatly relieved to find the same fields again full of geese. Henry and Sandy crept up in dead ground to the stone dyke of the field where the main body of geese were feeding, and I drove on to the next farm and then set off across the fields to put the geese over the boys. All went well — the geese lifted — went straight over the two hidden gunners, but alas only 1 goose fell — to Henry.

All this had not disturbed another smaller lot of geese in a second field of stubble, so while Henry went off to collect the car Sandy and I tried a simple pincer movement on the remaining geese. Sandy worked round on one side, I on the opposite side, and we hoped that one of us would put the geese over the other. As it happened, I showed myself first, the geese took off, and though Sandy had not got very far on his side he was near enough to shoot and managed to get his goose.

After that we stayed in the fields to wait for the duck flight that had so tempted us on Saturday (having meanwhile got the farmer's blessing). Not so many came in this time but we all had some shooting and added a couple of mallard to the day's bag.

Next morning required an early start — 6.30 a.m. — as we had some 20 miles to drive to the farm that the boys had found and "cleared" for the morning flight. I knew the area well and could visualize the ground and the general layout from Henry's sketch and a study of our maps. But one always feels somewhat at a loss arriving on a strange field in the dark and having to decide how to place the guns and the decoys. But at least I knew where the geese would come from — the distant estuary and also an inland loch, the two flight lines converging on this field of winter wheat (following potatoes) that they had been feeding on for the past few days.

We put Sandy in the corner of the field — the apex facing the oncoming geese; with Henry on his left and myself on the right. We were hardly ready before the first distant "quink-quink" told us that pinks were on the move. For an hour we experienced a splendid flight, with most of the skeins passing over us, though a few were wide on our flanks, or rather too high. I had more than my fair share of the luck, and most of the shooting. Every year, on these fowling trips, one or two incidents stand out in sharp recollection and will no doubt remain in my memory so long as memory continues to function. This year, like the right and left on Saturday I shall always remember the right and left this morning when a pair of pinks appeared coming straight for me, then swung slightly to my right and crossed the fence at comfortable long range.

At about 9 it was all over and we returned to the farmyard and our cars, where we fell upon sandwiches, soup and coffee — the latter laced with rum. It had been a fairly wild morning with storm clouds rolling up, and as we left the fields a driving storm of sleet and rain lashed and chilled us, which made the rum bottle particularly welcome.

After that we toured the next stretch of the valley to find where the geese had settled — found them, and got permission to go on this new farm if we wished. On our return to base there was just time after lunch to do a quick recce in another direction to lay plans for a similar ambush on another lot of geese next morning, and this we eventually decided to do rather than harass again the geese we had hammered this morning.

To finish the day we went down to the coast for the evening flight, but nothing came our way.

Our bag in the morning was 8 pinkfoots — 3 carrying rings — and as the boys only claimed 1 each, I was duly credited with 6.

Next morning required another early start, for though it was only 10 miles to the feeding grounds we knew that the geese would be pinks which are always early at morning flight.

The light was just beginning to show in the S.E. as we trudged across the fields and set up the decoys, and already there was an occasional squawk from an early goose in the darkness above us. The boundary fence of posts and wire had a few thorn bushes strung along it, and these provided convenient cover for us. We had only just taken up position when the first small skein passed low and silent over Henry — who confessed afterwards that his gun was still in its cover. A minute later and another skein loomed out of the dim light in front of me. I was ready for it and

The boundary fence had a few thorn bushes strung along it
D. S. A. McD. and Sandy

dropped a goose with the first shot of the morning. Thereafter there was hardly a dull moment for the next couple of hours. A steady stream of skeins appeared out of the east and came steadily up the valley towards us. While still two fields away one could often see them react to the decoys and change course so as to head straight for our sector of the stubble field. The early lots were usually in fair range, but as the light strengthened the skeins kept higher and seemed to realise

Henry and Sandy

that by that time of day there should be a large concentration of geese on the ground — and not merely a handful of decoys.

We all had plenty of shooting, but it was remarkably erratic; we all missed some of the easiest chances and yet at other times spectacular high shots came off.

By about 10 we had all got through a belt of cartridges and retreated to the cars for our usual sandwich breakfast. The score was then 13 geese — all pinks except for 2 greys. The boys then returned to their hides while I went in search of the geese, which had seemed to settle a mile behind us; there was always the chance that I might put them up and that they would return to their first feeding ground. I knew the lay of the land well, but my glasses showed no sign of the geese from all the well-known vantage points on the roads. But I also knew there was a stretch of dead ground hidden from all the main roads and tucked away in the bottom of the valley. There was one place on a minor road whence it could be searched with glasses. Sure enough — there were the geese — hundreds of them — on another stubble. I hurried to the farm in question, found the farmer and got his permission to shoot (on the morrow) and made a more thorough study of the geese and their field from a vantage point behind the farm. There were probably 1,000 geese in that field — all pinks as far as I could tell, including one almost cream-coloured. All this I reported to the boys, and as we discussed plans and prospects for the next morning further skeins appeared out of the sky and glided down to join the others on the ground. These newcomers seemed to be as numerous as the ones already on the ground, so that we had visions of 2,000 geese heading for the new field in the morning. And then, to round off the morning, a single greylag came heading for the decoys, anxious to join up with some of its kind. It offered an easy chance as it crossed the fence, but I regret to record that it required three shots to bring it down.

Back at base we found that "BB" and Tom had had no luck on the coast. In fact the day yielded nothing more though further recces were carried out after lunch and the boys stayed on for the evening flight on the sea wall.

We had to get up even earlier next morning (5.45 a.m.) as it was a longer drive to the new farm, there was a longer walk to the goose field and we had been none too early the previous morning. "BB" and Tom decided to join us, making a formidable party of 5 guns, but thereby increasing the odds in favour of the geese as five bodies are five times harder to conceal from geese than a lone fowler. As it was there were geese on the move as we reached our field well before dawn, though we were convinced that these geese must have spent the night roosting on the field instead of returning to the estuary the previous evening. We couldn't see them in the dark sky, though the air was full of their cries and many must have passed close overhead. It was a large field of barley stubble, but the boundaries were bare post and wire fences offering very little cover. We lined the eastern fence with the decoys in two groups behind us, and geese soon started coming in. Before long one small lot came close over me and were just visible in the faint light. I dropped a goose with the one shot that time and sight allowed. And then developed a tremendous flight with skein after skein of pinks converging on our field. But the storms and gales forecast by the wireless had not materialised, and the geese came in high. We did not get much shooting as the geese would not drop into range till they were well over any boundary, and the decoys did not seem to have much effect on the big battalions. At one stage, after a lot of cautious circling, skein after skein glided down into the centre of the field till there must have been about 2,000 pinks in a solid mass on the ground. I had then moved round to the far side of the field, and when I put them up they climbed and got away without suffering any casualties. Later, some smaller parties and single birds were attracted to the decoys and enabled Henry to get a couple and Tom a neat right and left. Then a single goose came circling round and gave Sandy his chance. Finally, as we were about to pack up a pricked bird was seen out in the field and duly collected — though who had shot it was impossible to say. The final score was therefore 7 and though this was a small toll to take from perhaps 3,000 geese, there was every compensation in the continuous sight and sound of wild geese constantly moving across the sky; first converging on our field, then circling until someone chanced a shot, and then departing into the distance, perhaps to return again later in the morning. But by 10 o'clock all movement ceased; the geese had found other feeding grounds, and we too were getting hungrey!

In the afternoon we did some desultory recces; "BB" and Tom tried a drive of some geese on the Commander's winter wheat, and later when three of the geese returned Sandy and I tried the same manoeuvre — but both efforts failed. Sandy stayed on to wait for the evening duck flight on an adjoining stubble and got three mallard.

Next morning we had to start on our way homewards ; but there was time for a couple of hours before breakfast, though clearly it had to be something close at hand. The fields below our quarters provided the obvious answer. A few geese had been dropping into these fields over the past few days and I did not think the two abortive stalks yesterday afternoon would have upset the geese. It was a miserable morning — rain that turned to sleet but not enough wind to keep the geese low. We had excellent cover — an 8-ft. open drainage ditch between two fields, so we put the decoys in two groups — one in each field — and stood in the bottom of the ditch between them. But very few geese came ; the usual early pair of greys glided in silently before we were ready, and later a small skein circled the decoys but just kept at extreme range. We all held our fire, hoping they would come nearer next time round, but at last they settled safely out of shot. Then another pair of greys came along, and though Henry had two shots the geese were again at extreme range and passed on untouched — taking the gaggle on the ground with them. Meanwhile skein after skein of pinks had been passing high overhead, making for the hills and the feeding grounds beyond, but showing no interest in our area. So it was that our last morning was a blank.

Our total bag for the 7 days' shooting was 36 geese — mostly pinks — and my own share was 16.

Two hours later, as we packed the car and made ready to depart we saw the sky suddenly fill with large numbers of greys, which began spiralling down to the fields we had just left, until there must have been at least 500 massed together almost exactly where we had set our decoys !

But this was no normal morning flight — it was clearly a case of a large concentration of geese having been disturbed on the fields to which they had flighted at first light and now moving en masse to a new feeding ground.

So we left them, undisturbed by the car which took us on our long journey southwards, passing close by their field.

Au revoir   grey goose !

CHAPTER 22
THREE GENERATIONS
(1963 — 1964 Katie's Year)

This year both Colin and Keith wanted to go north after the geese, so we made it a family party. Colin brought his eldest boy Chun, aged 13, eager to introduce him to the mysteries of goose hunting. Katie also decided to come — to the consternation of some of her family. I can only imagine that repeated spells of goose-widowhood over the past thirty odd years had at last strained her feminine curiosity to breaking point.

The only time we could all manage was a week just after Christmas, so we set off on Saturday, December 28th and reached the Borders that evening. Next morning the boys went down to Budle Bay for the morning flight but saw and heard little — certainly no geese. We were well up into goose country by midday and did the usual tours of likely areas to try and get an idea where we should find geese. The boys in their car were to press on further north while Katie and I would make a detour along one of the western valleys. Sure enough as we drove up the valley we soon saw several skeins flying up the river high above us. Some dropped into fields just below us, but the main lots flew on and soon left us far behind. A few miles on we stopped and searched the broad valley below us with glasses. On the large open fields it was soon easy to find the geese — several hundreds of them massed in the centre of a stubble field a mile away across the valley. But it was new ground and we should have to find out later whether it was accessible to us. A little further on we found a small lot of pinks on a potato stubble quite close to the main road, Although they took no notice of the stream of passing traffic as soon as we stopped the van to watch them they took alarm and lifted.

At dusk we met the boys by the main estuary to see what happened at evening flight. But there was no sign of returning geese, and little sound of them out in the firth. As reported by "BB" who had been up before Christmas, prospects did not look very promising on the home grounds.

Nevertheless in the morning we went down for the traditional dawn flight on the coast. In the dark it was all unusually quiet — no sound of goose talk out on the mud, though as the light improved I could make out a small party of geese close in near the reeds on my left. Later a few geese began to move, but it was some time before a skein came near us. Then a bunch of greys passed in front of Keith on my right. He had a couple of shots and one bird swung back towards me; clearly hit but not fatally. It offered a fine chance, passing behind me over the reeds with the wind up its tail. I gave it a long lead, and it crashed with a dull crump into the reed-bed. I marked the line carefully and trod out a path through the dense tangled mass of reeds. But though it is not difficult to mark a line it is much harder to estimate the distance at which a bird falls when one is hemmed in by reeds 7-8 ft. high. I tried again, estimating the half-distance and doubling it, but in the end I had to wait till Keith came along with Fen. The dog soon found the goose — a large greylag — bang on the line, but ten yards beyond the point I marked.

After breakfast we set out on the usual search for geese. At midday we noticed large skeins of pinks moving up the estuary, and eventually traced them to the furthest grass fields on the Laird's estate. There must have been at least 500 of them. This was too good an opening to miss, so we called on the Laird and arranged to go after these geese next morning.

Another recce after lunch showed that a few hundred pinks were also feeding on their usual farms over the hills. This seemed promising enough for Wednesday and we therefore got the farmer's permission accordingly. The day ended with the boys going down to the coast for evening flight but they had no luck.

We got up early next morning in high hopes: the Laird's fields had never failed to provide good sport. We collected Patrick and the keeper at the Big House at 6.30 — Patrick now a tall youth of nearly 17 — and took up our positions in the grass fields much as we did three years ago. Keith and I went to the right and stood behind a tall thorn hedge, Colin and Chun found cover in a strip of timber dividing two of the grass fields, while the keeper took Patrick off to some other point on the expected line of flight. But the whole operation was a complete failure. Not a goose came in to the fields at dawn, and it was late in the morning before a big lot of pinks rose from somewhere up-river and flew off far down the estuary. We could only guess that they had been feeding all night under the moon, and would not come in again till they had digested their full crops and developed a new hunger. But though we waited till nearly noon there was no sign of a flight and only a couple of single birds gave us an excuse to let off our guns.

Further checks later in the week indicated that the geese had in fact completely abandoned these feeding grounds for the time being — a practice apparently that they often adopt early in the New Year. A few days before our arrival a couple of thousand had been using these fields, and I have never seen such a vast area of grass simply plastered with goose-droppings. The 500 we found on Sunday must have been the last of the horde having a final feed before moving on.

With Wednesday now provided for we set about laying plans for Thursday. After lunch the boys went off to follow up the geese that Katie and I had found up the western valley: I went off by myself over the hill to check on the geese that they had found on Sunday. I found they had been feeding on a potato stubble, but they seemed to have cleared up all the remaining potatoes and there were only a few fresh droppings about. The next field was a grass field and there were plenty of droppings, so it seemed the geese had not yet finished with this area. I also found a score of recently fired cartridge cases by the ditch between the two fields, and a dead goose far out on the grass, so it was clear that we were not to be the first on the scene. This was not too promising, and the boys came back with news that we could not go after the other geese as the farmer had definitely let the shooting.

That evening was Hogmanay and we saw the New Year in with friends in the district, and forgot about geese for a few hours.

The party cost me a morning flight as I felt quite unable to face the dawn next morning. The boys were undeterred and went off down to the coast again. There was a better flight with plenty of geese out in the firth and on the move. They had a few chances but had no luck.

Over breakfast we decided that we would go after the pinks over the hill that night — under the moon, provided of course conditions were suitable. That left no plans for Thursday, so we set out again on another tour of reconnaissance. On our way we happened to meet the owner of the farm over the hill. We told him of our plans for that night, and he in turn mentioned that a lot of greys had been feeding on his father's farm a mile or two further on. He even gave us his father's permission to go after them! We followed up this clue at once; soon found the geese on some large fields of permanent grass and carefully checked the general layout of the ground through our glasses. It all looked quite promising with straggling thorn hedges for cover and a fairly obvious line of flight. We booked this in our minds for Thursday morning.

Back at base we had an early evening meal and set out once more over the hills for the potato stubble. The moon was now three days past full, so it would still rise early, but late enough to give a dark period between sunset and moonrise. This led us to hope that there might be a well-defined "moon-flight" when the geese got hungry again after their day's feeding and found enough light to venture inland again. But for the first hour or so there was thick cloud, and though the moon must have been "up" it was still invisible. Fortunately there was a fairly strong wind which kept the sky pattern continually changing. Presently the cloud cover thinned; an occasional star appeared, and we left the warmth of the car to set up the decoys and take up our positions. We put 4 decoys on the potato stubble in front of us, 4 on the grass field behind, and took cover in the deep ditch between the two fields. It was still another hour or so before things began to happen. Then a pair of geese swung in, and got away unscathed. After that several small skeins came in and we all had some shooting. It was all very exciting — as it always is under the moon. Ears and eyes are stretched to the limits of their perception, and usually it is a distant "quink, quink" which first heralds the approach of geese. Presently, after a few more calls, ever louder, a skein looms into view, gliding down towards the decoys. For a few seconds the birds are in sight and in range and one takes one's chance. In this way we shot 4 pinks, including the first goose shot by Chun with his 16 bore. Not a big bag, and not a lot of shooting, but very exciting and very satisfying. After another hour the sky thickened again, a solid bank of cloud obscured the moon, and we all packed up at about 11 p.m.

After a short night's sleep we were up again at 6 to deal with the greys. Past the scene of battle of a few hours earlier we pushed on to the new farm where the greys were feeding. We chose the downwind corner of the field where we had seen the geese and took up positions in the two hedges flanking the corner. The decoys made an enticing group on the grass in the angle behind us. While we were getting organised two more figures loomed up in the half-light and proved to be two other fowlers who had also obtained permission to shoot on this farm. They were very much put out at finding us in possession and took the situation with poor grace. They took themselves off to another part of the field, changed later to a position on our left flank and before long departed altogether. In due course the morning flight developed with many skeins moving along the valley below us, but most of them passing along to our right. But several swung up the hill to our field, and out of one of the first skeins I got a nice right and left. Then another lot came low over the hedge where I was tucked in under a thorn bush, but it took both shots to stop the goose I picked. The others also had their share of shooting but somehow failed to get any geese. After a couple of hours the flight seemed to have finished and we collected our gear and went back to the car and our sandwich breakfast.

On our way back to base we called at the scene of the moonlight shoot to see if any shot geese had been left on the ground unnoticed, and just as we came away a large mob of pinks — several hundred strong — came swinging into view and settled in the grass field. Then another still larger army of geese appeared out of the west and after much circling and hesitation settled in a large corn stubble on the other side of the potato stubble. There must have been 1,500 pinks in the two fields, and it was clear that they had not been too disturbed to remain in the area. After all, our midnight shooting had only harassed a very few skeins, and it looked as if we could tackle them again on the same ground.

But, as a second-string, Colin and Keith drove on to a new area, where they had seen geese settling by an old mill up on higher ground. They came back with lukewarm reports — signs of a few geese, but difficult fields and bad access roads. Prospects were not too good. We were running out of time and opportunities, and had only 8 geese in the bag so far. A repeat moonlight flight seemed the best bet, but the weather was far from promising. We checked with the nearest Meteorological Office and were assured there was little chance of any break in the clouds before dawn. So we had to wait till dawn and the usual morning flight.

So on our last full day we set out yet again over the hills, but depleted in numbers as Chun had caught some form of chill and was left in bed in the charge of his grandmother. Even so, three was rather a crowd for the one length of ditch by the potato stubble, and it seemed better to divide our forces. So I took myself off with a couple of the decoys and lay up under a hedge a mile away from the others. (This was the hedge where Henry and Sandy had such good sport with me two years ago and got 14 geese). There is a distinct flight line on this farm, my belief being that the geese follow the line of a small burn which flows right through the centre of their favourite feeding grounds, and which they can no doubt easily see either in the first light of dawn or by moonlight. This hedge, which is really a post and wire fence with a few scruffy thorns in it, runs down to the burn at right angles, and one is usually sure to see some skeins passing over it if geese are using the area at all. The decoys, set out on the grass behind me, would I hope draw a few skeins down low enough for a shot.

I never saw the first geese; a few pinks passing high overhead while there was still hardly any light. But a minute or two later a couple of shots drifted down to me from the direction of Colin and Keith. The same thing happened several times until I had counted a score of shots from the two boys. By now I could watch the skeins coming and from time to time one would head for my decoys, losing height all the way, and eventually give me a chance. I think four skeins came within range, and with my eight shots I got three geese — all pinks. Meanwhile a steady fusillade was taking place in the distance and it was obvious the boys had struck it lucky. The sky was now hardly ever empty of geese; skeins came weaving up and down the broad valley in search of feeding grounds. Often I would watch them turn towards the distant potato stubble and start to circle in; then three or four shots would show that the decoys had brought them right down and that two figures pressed against the side of the ditch had sprung into action. By ten o'clock things quietened down and I packed up my own gear and went back to the car in the farmyard. Colin and Keith were also beginning to pack up, but even as I reached them more geese appeared in the distance and we all dived for cover again. Only one skein came low enough for a shot – a small party of 4 – and I had the pleasure of seeing Colin and Keith each bring down a goose. Keith's bird landed with an enormous splash in the ditch within a yard of Colin, thoroughly soaking him. One wonders how he would have withstood a direct hit from a 7-lb. pinkfoot dropping like a stone from perhaps 150 feet!

This made the boys' score 9 for the morning; 12 for the three of us – one of the best morning flights we have had. As we left for base and lunch more geese continued to arrive, and we realised that the ground might well provide one more outing – a final session under the moon on our last night. But a check with the Met. Office dashed our hopes – 10/10 cloud and no hope of moonlight before dawn.

There was nothing left but a quick outing at dawn, as we all had to be on our way south before midday.

Keith and I went down to the estuary, to the stretch between the breakwaters, while Colin – nothing daunted – dashed over the hill to the distant potato field. It was a miserable morning; dull with slight mist turning to rain, and low unbroken grey skies. We heard a few shots down on the coast as we walked across the fields, followed by the roar of a large pack of greys as they rose and flew out to the open water. Someone probably trying a stalk at first light. After that silence descended and we hardly saw a goose. There seemed no prospect of a flight developing and we soon gave up our vigil. Back on the sea-wall we could see large rafts of geese out on the distant water, but there was no sign of movement, and no indication that they had any intention of leaving the sanctuary of the estuary.

Colin also drew blank and was back at base as soon as we were. By eleven we had breakfasted, packed and were on our way home.

Our bag of 20 for the week was quite reasonable under all the circumstances. The period around full-moon time is always very chancy. It plays havoc with the regular dawn and dusk flights as the geese can often feed at any hour of night or day. If they have fed all night under the moon they may well stay out at sea for most of the following day. On the other hand one cannot always be sure of moonlight. We were lucky to strike a patch of some two hours when the moon and the cloud cover were suitable for both the goose and for us; but two other nights were quite impossible owing to continuous unbroken cloud.

The holiday period of Christmas and Hogmanay is also a bad time in that the geese then get more than their usual dose of harrying by local gunners. They are more wary, more unsettled and seek their feeding grounds further afield. We only shot one goose on the shore – all the rest came from distant farms at least 10 miles away.

But the week came to an end only too soon. After 10 days or a fortnight I have had enough to begin to feel the strain, and conversely the first few days are required to adjust body and mind to the unusual and irregular hours of meals and sleep and the curious times for physical activity. The latter part of the first week is when all adjustments have been made, eyes and ears have recovered their old acuteness and skill, and in general I find myself as physically fit as I can hope to be. A week seems hardly enough; one longs for a few more days while the wave is at its crest.

But there it is. Another fowling trip becomes a memory; to be added to the ever-growing list of such trips and memories.

CHAPTER 23
A GOOSE'S MEMORY
(1964)

Every spring we rear a few Mallard ducklings and Canada goslings in a pen on the lawn, with a barrel to shut them up in at night, heated by an infra-red poultry lamp.

In 1961 we raised a clutch of four Greylag goslings with the Canadas, but unfortunately lost all but one of them in the following winter when a fox appeared in the district. The surviving Greylag grew up very tame and spent much of its time round the house and orchard, mixing with the domestic poultry. Last spring it disappeared for some weeks and we feared it had come to grief, but it turned up on May 22nd on the little goose marsh — with three goslings in tow. A Greylag nest in an adjoining reed bed was then found to be abandoned, with one addled egg and the remains of several shells, and I had no doubt that it was this tame Greylag which had been nesting there. (I had not cared to go near enough to the nest to recognise the goose for fear of making her desert the nest).

So the three goslings were picked up and brought to the nursery pen in the garden — leaving the goose in a state of considerable agitation and distress. To our surprise, within an hour or two

Family of Canada Geese on the Goose Marsh

98

Canada Goose at her nest

the goose had flown into the garden, found her family and was thoroughly contented with her mixed brood of ducklings and goslings in the wire pen. Her own three were reared successfully and in due course joined the local population of Canadas and Greylags — with rings on their legs for identification.

This spring the old goose disappeared again in April, and a search of the reed beds found a goose sitting on a nest within a few yards of last year's site. On May 5th my old friend turned up on the goose marsh, this time with five goslings, and again a check on the nest showed that it was abandoned, with pieces of hatched eggshells. But this time the goose had her gander with her.

We picked up the goslings as before, and this time neither the goose nor the gander seemed greatly perturbed. It was rather a cold day, and there were already a score of ducklings and a dozen or so goslings in the usual pen in the garden. So they were all driven into the tub, the five new goslings put in with them to get a "warm-up", and the pop-hole closed.

I left them all together — out of sight in the tub — and went off to do another job. Coming back in ten minutes' time one can imagine my surprise at finding the goose waiting inside the pen! She must have flown into the garden and dropped into the few square yards enclosed with wire netting.

It seems a clear case of accurate memory. The garden is quite out of sight of the marsh though only a few hundred yards away; and the goslings were, of course, completely enclosed in a solid tub. But the goose must have remembered what happened last year, and guessed that the

Canada Goose with nest of eggs

In time the Canada Geese increased to about 40 and some of them would fly in to the lawn
(Note 5 Egyptian Geese in the background)

same thing was happening again; there she was, waiting for me to open the pop-hole and let her brood out!

Moreover, in an hour's time the gander had joined her in the pen to complete the family. But there is a sinister sequel to the story. Examination revealed a ring on the gander's leg which shows that he is a son of the goose — one of the three goslings she reared last year. Moreover, I doubt whether he is 100% pure Greylag. He is rather larger than normal and somewhat on the pale side. It suggests that the goose may have contracted a liaison with a Greylag-domestic hybrid the previous year. If this is so, then the previous pattern of evolution is being reversed: instead of a domestic strain of goose being developed from the wild goose, we are witnessing the "breeding-out" of the domestic strain from a Greylag family. In a generation or two, at this rate, we shall arrive at a substantially pure Greylag generation.

CHAPTER 24
THE HOUNDS OF HEAVEN
(1964 — 1965 Keith's Year)

This year Keith and I decided to break new ground. For years we have gone to the same area in Scotland — an area which has provided grand sport and which still holds thousands of geese. But it is beginning to get spoilt. More and more people are coming to it, including an increasing number of trigger-happy sportsmen from the nearby towns: the geese are moving further and further away to more distant and secluded feeding grounds: and we had pretty well exhausted the possibilities of the area.

It was time to seek "fresh woods and pastures new".

We knew the west coast of Scotland also had great possibilities, especially out on the Hebridean islands, and Keith had seen something of these possibilities on recent holiday visits. So we decided on a trip to one of these islands.

I left London on November 30th by the night train and arrived in Glasgow next morning after a rotten night in a jolting sleeper. Next day I spent on business — at the Glasgow Factory — feeling extremely tired and jaded. That evening Keith arrived by air and by 8 p.m. I was awaiting him at Renfrew with a hired car already packed and fuelled for the next stage. So we drove off into the night, heading north, and eventually reached a small village on the west coast.

Meanwhile prospects had improved. When I left London I had only the vaguest idea of what lay before us: the first night's bed was assured, but after that the diary was blank. I But Keith had at the last moment secured accommodation on the island and I had made some telephone enquiries from Glasgow which had resulted in the prospect of obtaining permission to shoot over some promising areas. I thought of the recent T.V. programme in London in honour of Churchill's 90th Birthday and the excerpt from "Oklahoma" which it included:

"I have a wonderful feeling
Everything's going my way".

On the last stage of our journey that evening we caught a clear glimpse of a wild cat by the side of the road. There was no mistaking the ringed tail in the light of the headlamps.

Next morning Keith took me out at dawn to show me the local estuary with its population of greylags. It was a most attractive area, with a small bay, tidal estuary and surrounding merse, backed by a valley of fertile farm land. We watched a hundred or so greylags flight in, and though we could legally have taken our guns on the foreshore, we knew the local laird was a strict protectionist and disliked having his geese shot. So we contented ourselves with watching, and later photographing the geese. It was a very pleasant curtain-raiser and we returned to breakfast well satisfied to have made contact with geese so soon on our journey. We also had the luck to see a Hen Harrier at quite close quarters.

THE HOUNDS OF HEAVEN

After that it took us a day to travel by road and boat to reach our island, and it was completely dark by the time we disembarked with the car. This made it impossible to spy out the land for the morrow, and the only hope was to collect some local information that night.

So we sought out the factor of one of the island estates and found him most helpful. He in turn passed us on to the gamekeeper, and the latter was equally helpful and co-operative. In fact he was the first gamekeeper I have come across who really knew and understood wild geese and appreciated the sport of shooting them. I think he had his doubts about us though, for when we explained that we only had a few days and were, therefore, anxious to start on the morrow, he tentatively suggested meeting us at 10 a.m. — or "maybe 9 o'clock if that is not too early". When we pointed out that that was much too late — that the morning flight would be over — he came clean; and from then on we dealt with each other on level terms. So we parted with high hopes for the morning, and made our way to our hotel where a hot meal and a good night's sleep soon made up for past deficiences.

Next morning we collected the keeper in good time — about 7.15 a.m. and he guided us to one of the sea lochs on the island where we had already guessed — from a study of the map — that there should be a good concentration of geese. It was a wild morning with a strong northerly wind, and as we took up our positions behind the sea wall a violent hailstorm broke out. It was impossible to face it and we had to huddle under the bank with our backs to it until it blew over. Fortunately it cleared before the morning flight began. We could hear plenty of geese out on the sandbanks, and presently I heard shots coming from Keith's direction. Then one or two small parties of greylags passed over on my right, but barely in range. Next the barnacle geese started to flight and I had a few long shots without success. Keith seemed to be having a much busier time and as it got light I could see large skeins streaming in from the sea in his direction. Eventually, a skein came right over me, crabbing sideways against the wind, and I got a very satisfying right and left.

When it was all over Keith came along with his five barnacles and one greylag. So our first encounter yielded 8 geese at morning flight; this indeed was some island!

After breakfast we took a packed lunch with us and spent the middle of the day exploring the whole island and finding the areas that held geese. These areas seemed to be all over the island, wherever there was a patch of good farmland with large grass fields. The Whitefronts — which were all of the Greenland variety — were often in small parties and the largest lot we came across was about 300 strong. Greylags were also present in small lots, but there was one big mob of 500 that we found late in the day. The most fascinating geese, however, were the barnacles of which there were several thousand. I think I have only twice seen barnacles in the truly wild state before; in December 1952, I reported a single barnacle with a small party of greys in Perthshire, and in January 1958, I saw 6 barnacles in the midst of a large concentration of pinks and greys on a potato stubble.

The barnacles seemed to be very gregarious, and reminded us of pinkfooted geese. We found two or three lots of over 1,000 and several in the 500-750 bracket. An individual goose is handsome enough, but when packed like a solid carpet on a green field in sunlight the grey of their backs has a distinct bluish tinge. Moreover, their white cheek-patch, which on a dead bird seems to be merely a rather grubby off-white, when seen en masse in bright daylight, takes on a delightful pale primrose sheen. And their call — again suggestive of pinkfeet, but less distinctive; this indeed was like the yelping of puppies. Surely of all the British geese the barnacles have the strongest claim to be called the Hounds of Heaven.

In the evening we joined the keeper again. He had offered to take us to a loch in the hills where the whitefronts often flighted at dusk. This was another new experience for us: I had not realised that this species liked to roost on small inland lochs. We took up position in the heather downwind of the loch and waited for the geese. Surely enough they came; perhaps a couple of hundred altogether; beating up the hill into the wind and swinging down to the loch like coveys of giant Martian grouse. I had all the luck this time and shot 6, though we only found 5 at the pickup. Keith had 2 down but only retrieved one.

At any rate, a total score of 14 for the whole day, including three varieties, made it a memorable occasion for us both.

By contrast the next day was a blank. We went to another loch for the morning flight; a large one on the lower ground which was supposed to hold greylags. A few whitefronts came down from the hills and settled in a sheltered arm of the loch, and there was a massive flight of barnacles (and, I think, some greylags) from the distant estuary to a large field on my left. But though I went across and moved them we neither of us had more than a few unlikely shots. Then after the usual midday "recce" and attempt to do some photographing, we again went up to the hills to try another small loch for whitefronts. But only a single bird came near, though several skeins passed over to the side of us bound for some other loch in the heather.

Next day was our last, and we had more or less agreed with the keeper to go back to the large loch on the low ground and try a new position to intercept the dawn flight from the sea. But Keith and I had found two farms several miles down the coast, where a narrow strip of grass fields lined the estuary; and these fields held geese — in one case about 600 barnacles. We felt sure the geese would return next morning, and it seemed easy to anticipate the line of flight. So we backed our own fancy and got down to the coast about 7.30 a.m. just as light was beginning to show in the east. I took the first farm and Keith went on to the second. I found wonderful cover — a deep, narrow ditch running out to the shore, with clumps of gorse on both banks. I only had to stand in the bottom of the ditch and my head was just above ground level with broken masses of gorse all round me.

I was near the downwind point of the field, nearest to the coast, so wherever the geese came from they were almost certain to make their final approach over my corner. Just before 8 a.m. the first skein came swinging in, straight and low — and I missed completely! After a bit of a pause the flight continued, and nearly all the skeins headed straight for me. With my next 8 shots I dropped 6 geese — all barnacles. After the fifth I was thinking of stopping, but then, of course, another skein came into sight before I had even unloaded my gun, and so, of course, I had to have another go. After that I did deliberately stop — 6 geese at morning flight is quite enough — so I collected my spoils and tramped up to the road to wait for Keith and the car. I had heard him shooting in the distance, and at 9.30 a.m. he turned up with 2 whitefronts and a barnacle in the car. Apparently several hundred whitefronts had come his way, but only a few barnacles, whereas all the geese I had seen were the latter.

After breakfast we had hoped to meet Ted off the incoming 'plane but we found the weather had grounded the air-service and there was no news from Ted — presumably stranded in Glasgow. We had hoped he would arrive in time to join us at evening flight, but this was now impossible and we had to go without him; to the scene of our first morning's flight. Here we waited for the reverse flight — the geese returning to the estuary from their feeding grounds. One or two skeins began to move along the coast but too far out over the sand for me to reach them. So I got out to the edge of the saltmarsh and crouched in a small gully. Presently an odd goose came along and I dropped it. Later another came along, and though I hit it hard it carried on and landed on the sand far down the estuary. I went after it, found it again, but it was still able to fly and took off out of range.

Meanwhile the main body of geese had come out from the land en masse, and I should think that anything between two and three thousand geese must have streamed over Keith. He had time to fire four shots at them, but they were too high and I would have been very surprised to have seen anything fall.

With the last of the light I moved back to some patches of flood water on a field over the sea wall, and waited for the duck to come. Teal, wigeon and mallard began to stream in — several parties of each. I managed to get one mallard and three wigeon before the light failed. Keith came in with one mallard.

That night there was a pleasant surprise for us at the hotel: Ted rang up to say he had found a charter 'plane coming to the island next morning and had arranged a seat on it. So at 10 a.m. on Sunday morning we collected him — and awarded him top marks for economy of luggage. He was already dressed for the fray, carrying a gun in one hand and in the other two Wellingtons stuffed with his pyjamas and toiletries.

Of course there was no shooting on the Sabbath, so we armed ourselves with the usual sandwiches and set out on a tour of the island for Ted's benefit. We showed him geese here, there and everywhere, took some more photographs and ended up with a grandstand view of the barnacles coming down to the saltings at evening flight. We must have seen at least 2,000 collect; interspersed with curlew, mallard, wigeon and a few greylags.

We had also been studying form for Monday morning. Keith and I would·be unable to shoot;

Keith having to catch an early boat for the mainland with the car and surplus luggage, and myself having to be suitably dressed ready for a meeting in a London office that evening. But it was Ted's one and only chance. We eventually settled for the strip of coast that produced such a good flight the previous morning. None of the fields held any geese on Sunday, so it seemed they had been driven away from the field where I had awaited them. But Keith was convinced that he had been on a flight-line to other feeding grounds, and as they had not been disturbed on these distant fields it was reasonable to hope that they would still fly in on the same line. So, in daylight we showed Ted the lay-out, told him where to lie up, and on Monday morning I took him there in a car borrowed from the hotel.

I could hear geese moving in his direction before I could see them, and presently two shots rolled up from the coast below me — to be followed, I thought, by two faint thuds, though I could hardly believe that one could hear the fall of a goose at that distance. Later I watched a skein flying past where I knew he must be, and suddenly one of the clear hard shapes of a goose turned into a ragged bundle and dropped to the marsh below. A few seconds later the sound of the shot reached me.

Meanwhile I was in dire trouble with the borrowed car. In moving it to the edge of the farm track, to make way for any early morning traffic, I had failed to see in the dark the concealed drainage ditch running alongside the road. My front wheel slipped in and I found the car literally and firmly ditched. There was nothing I could do single-handed — except make matters worse — so I had to wait till it was daylight and then seek help from the nearest farm. A tractor was soon forthcoming and by the time the flight was over we had the car safely on the hard road again.

A jubilant Ted appeared with three geese; two whitefronts and one barnacle. So I had heard his first two geese fall!

We then had comfortable time to catch our 'plane to the mainland. By that evening the return to sophisticated civilisation was complete. After a call at a City office, a bath and change (and, most important, a belated shave!), I sat down to an excellent dinner at Claridges, for December 7th was the date of this year's traditional Smithfield Dinner.

NOTE: Although barnacle geese are on the "protected" list of birds, we were assured that there is on the island a special dispensation from this regulation. In view of the large numbers of these geese and of the report that their numbers are on the increase, we were satisfied that they could well withstand a reasonable amount of shooting. We therefore went our way with a clear conscience.

CHAPTER 25

ISLAND OF GEESE

(1965 – 1966)

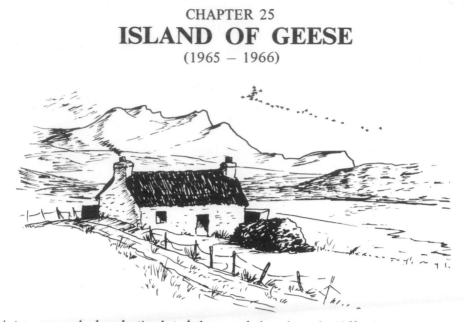

As winter approached and stimulated the usual thoughts of wildfowling I became aware of an irresistible urge to pay a repeat visit to the island that Keith and I had "discovered" last year. Keith was of the same mind, and so we began to plan for a whole week this time.

The end of November was the only time that suited us both, and this was to coincide with the sudden spell of cold weather and N.W. gales that swept the country. The day before we were due to set out a belt of snow clamped down on northern England and all roads to Scotland were blocked — except the A1. By this time we had decided to do the whole trip by car, after much cogitation and the balancing of the various factors involved in going by train or air, hiring a car in Scotland, or taking our own. In the end considerations of cost and reliability, together with the freedom to take ample clothing and equipment, turned the scales in favour of our own car.

On Friday, November 26th, we set forth from Tring after an early lunch and made for the Great North Road. Somewhere near Corby we had our first sight of geese — a couple of skeins high up and far away to our left. They were probably Canadas or Whitefronts but too far for identification by sight or sound.

Beyond Doncaster we ran into the belt of snow, and by Scotch Corner there was about nine inches of it, though the road itself had been cleared. We stopped for a quick meal and confirmed that only the A1 was reasonably sure to remain open. Any thoughts of Bowes Moor and Beattock, or Carter Bar, were soon dispelled. So we pressed on along the coast road, through Edinburgh, and eventually reached our hotel in Stirling just before 2 a.m. This had been the longest day's driving I had had for many a long day, though with two drivers it had not seemed too bad. The speedometer showed 440 miles. Twice before I have driven nearly as far singlehanded — and on similar errands. Once, many years ago, I had left the office in Berkhamsted in the evening and motored up to Wigtown on the Solway overnight, arriving in time to knock-up Bob McGuffie for the morning flight. That was just over 400 miles. On another occasion I was returning from a fowling trip in the east of Scotland and came through from Bridge of Allan in the day — just under 400 — to Catfield.

We were too tired to unpack the car at Stirling and crawled upstairs with only our overnight cases. My last thought before falling asleep was one of panic lest the car should be pilfered and our all-important guns stolen! Precious permits from two more landowners on the island were also at risk in my briefcase. But morning found the car and its contents still intact in the street.

We still had a long way to go so an early start was essential. There was no fuss about having breakfast at 7.30 a.m. — a full kitchen staff seemed to be on duty, though no other guests had appeared by the time we left at 8; what a joy to travel in Scotland in winter, when all the summer tourists with their caravans and coaches have departed, and the hotels and shops seem genuinely glad to welcome the occasional traveller.

ISLAND OF GEESE

Saturday was a glorious bright winter's day; the mountains of course, all mantled in snow, with bright blue sky behind them, and warm autumn tints on the woods and bracken. I took Keith through the Carse of Forth and along the side of Flanders Moss. Years ago the Moss used to hold several thousand pinks, and I once had a memorable night there waiting for them to flight under the moon. A friend had taken me there, and we were joined by the daughter of the local inn-keeper — the first time I had ever been out fowling with a girl! I think we got five geese that night. But today we could see no geese in the Moss, nor any throughout the length and breadth of the Carse. Only by the Lake of Monteith did we see a few greylags in a field and then a skein high up in the sky. We had no time to linger however; there was a long way to go; and the roads were covered with ice or snow for quite long stretches, so that high speeds were out of the question.

We had allowed five hours for the second day's driving, and in the event we reached our little port in plenty of time. On the way we again found a score or so of seal bobbing about in the sea at the same spot where we saw them last year. With just their heads showing they looked like so many small black footballs. In the afternoon the weather thickened up again and we had quite a choppy crossing to our island; in fact by the time we arrived there was a full gale blowing and the skipper had considerable difficulty in making fast to the pier. For a time he held on with only one hawser from the bows, while the stern swung out in the wind before they could get another line across. At last all was well, our car was swung ashore, and we felt considerable relief that we had at last reached the island — with the car and all our gear intact. We made straight for the factor who had been so helpful last year, and found that we could have three days on the farms of his estate. The headkeeper though was a new one, so we had to go and introduce ourselves to him and agree a plan for Monday. This was soon fixed up, and so at last we reached our hotel and found a warm welcome awaiting us from mine host — backed up with a glass of malt whisky and a huge hot meal. By then we were ready for bed, and I think I had the longest and soundest sleep I have had for many a long night, only just managing to appear for breakfast at 9. We apparently had the hotel to ourselves, so meals were ours to command, whenever and however we required them.

The joy of arriving on a Saturday was that it gave us the whole of Sunday to recover from our travels, carry out a thorough reconnaissance of the goose areas, and make contact with new

December sunshine and Atlantic breakers

Atlantic coast on the Island of Geese

"prospects". Saturday's storms had abated by the morning and we had another bright wintry day to begin with. We spent the whole of Sunday in the car, with sandwiches and a flask of coffee for our lunch, inspecting all the main areas where we had found geese last year. Many of them again held geese — especially the fields used by the whitefronts, but the distribution of the barnacles was quite different, and on the whole there did not seem to be quite so many. In one area we saw several grouse by the side of the road, and at one point we had grouse sitting on the top of stone walls on either side of the car! We stopped and photographed them while one of them scolded us. At midday we explored a distant part of the island where we had an introduction to a keeper. The man turned out to be a stalker first and foremost and was busy with his hind-shooting programme, but the estate also held grouse and a few wild pheasants, with some duck down on the coast and woodcock in the New Year. But it hardly seemed the place for geese — rough tumbling country, covered with scrub woodlands and only the occasional field or rough pasture. However they claimed to have the goose shooting over some farms in an area we knew to be promising, and so we fixed up to have a day with the keeper on Thursday. We were shown over the main house of the estate; a typical Scotch shooting lodge standing on a small headland, and looking out over an inlet of the sea on either side. All round was rough grass and marshy valleys running up between irregular masses of dense thickets or stunted woodlands. Both Keith and I were struck by the resemblance to the East African bush, and the keeper said that other visitors had made the same comparison. Moreover within a few hundred yards of the house, and in the short time of our visit, we saw all three varieties of deer — roe, fallow and red deer; several of each species, including three large stags, one of which was a twelve pointer.

There was still another task we had set ourselves, and that was to go and watch two hill lochs at the other end of the island that looked (from the map) as though they might attract whitefronts at evening flight. We left the car on the nearest road and each took one loch where we waited till it was dark. But nothing came to my patch of water and Keith reported only a dozen or so whitefronts flying in to his. A negative result but none the less useful for that.

Next morning the hunt started in earnest. We had arranged to do the same morning flight as last year — probably one of the most spectacular ones in the whole British Isles. A long arm of the sea runs in between rising ground on either side and ends in a flat valley at its head, consisting of acres of flat grass fields, devoid of all hedges or trees and with no more cover than an

ISLAND OF GEESE

A long arm of the sea runs in between rising ground on either side

occasional post and wire fence. It is ideal for geese, both for feeding and security: their only hazard is to cross the protective sea wall — a grass bank just high enough to conceal a gunner if he presses himself flat against it. For our part the hazard was to reach the sea wall. An overnight frost had turned the narrow roads to black ice, and the keeper who was to have joined us ended up with his Land Rover in a ditch. But we got there just as the first geese were on the move (soon after 7 a.m.) and spread along the bank to intercept the morning flight. It certainly was spectacular: for about an hour a steady stream of geese flew in to their feeding grounds, in family parties, in small skeins, in large skeins, in hundreds. There was a gale blowing, straight in from the estuary; and assuming it was a 60 m.p.h. wind, and the geese were coming in at their normal 40 m.p.h. air speed, then these geese were hurtling past us at 100 m.p.h. All this, and the piercing cold which froze our clothes and numbed our fingers, made for very poor shooting, so that by the end of the flight we had only collected six geese. One of these was a "pricked" barnacle which we retrieved alive and hoped to take home to Norfolk. However the great majority of the geese passed inland on our right, and only a minute fraction of the streaming skeins offered us a possible chance.

The middle of the day was spent in the usual tours of reconnaissance, but the northern stream of stormy weather continued, and several times during the day violent sleet and hail storms lashed the countryside, making observation impossible and imprisoning us in the car till they passed. In one of the calmer spells we found a large gaggle of whitefronts in a field next to the road and seized the opportunity of taking some cine-film of them. Then at 3.45 p.m. we joined up with the keeper again who took us up to the hill loch where the whitefronts roost at night. Another violent storm broke out, so that we were forced to shelter in an old deserted bothy. Fortunately the sleet cleared just as the light was failing, but the wind continued at gale force and whipped the waters of the loch into choppy waves which drenched the hillside with spray. We stood shivering by a stone wall waiting for the first geese to show up, but we began to doubt whether they could possibly reach the loch against the powerful wind. Moreover we could hardly imagine geese resting on the turbulent waters of the loch. So after a while we decided there could be no flight, and started to make our way downhill to the waiting Land Rover. And then, by a stroke of luck, I happened to catch sight of a struggling, weaving bunch of geese battling their way up a valley to our left, where some high ground on the northern side clearly broke the force of the storm. But the geese never reached the loch, and a second skein following the first showed that they were dropping in to the head of the marshy valley, just short of the loch, and in the lee of the hill. We struggled across ourselves, to get in the line of this new flight, and sure enough for the next ten minutes an exciting flight developed with a stream of skeins following the earlier ones. I managed to get four, including a right and left, while Keith on my right added another. And so an evening which we had nearly abandoned yielded another five geese — all whitefronts of course — making a total of eleven for our first day.

Next morning we planned to go to the two farms that Keith and I discovered last year. One of our "recces" had shown that geese were again using the same fields; barnacles on my farm and whitefronts on Keith's. But this time we exchanged farms, so Keith stopped off first and I went on to the further one. The wind was still strong, though the snow and frost had gone from the low ground overnight, and we only had one short stinging hail storm to contend with. The direction of the wind however — still northerly — was almost exactly the opposite to last year's south westerly, and it was more difficult to anticipate how the geese would fly in. Certainly it was a more difficult flight, and I think not such a steady and sustained one. Geese came to my field from both the north and east, and tended to drop into the far side. But a few came speeding downwind on the old flight line and I got a very high one early on and a couple more towards the end of the flight. Meanwhile Keith had collected a couple, and also a wigeon, though he also got two more geese that he failed to find. Altogether five geese against last year's nine.

Our warm hotel with hot breakfast awaiting us was more than usually welcome that morning as my thigh waders had filled with water early in the proceedings. The only cover I could find had been a small ditch running along one of the field fences. I could just stand on the bottom, but when the first geese came in sight I naturally crouched as low as I could and before I realised what had happened both boots had filled up.

After the usual midday recce and a picnic lunch in the heart of the barnacle country (Keith found a mass of some 3,000 which he photographed) we had to go back to base to collect my boots from the hotel kitchen and then set out again to try the evening flight at the sea wall. The weather was kind this time, and though the wind was still strong, we had our backs to it waiting for the geese to fight their way back to the sea. As so often happens at evening flight the outlying geese tended to mass together before flighting, and eventually the great majority came out in two large mobs — probably a thousand in each. But the wind kept them down to a reasonable height and Keith got a couple out of the mass that went straight over him. The other mob came out on my right and I doubt whether the extreme flank were in range to my shots. However earlier on I had got a greylag out of a small bunch that came out by themselves. We also found by the sea wall a lively pricked barnacle that was no doubt one of Keith's wounded birds from yesterday. So we came home with four more geese.

Wednesday brought a complete change in the weather — a sudden absence of wind. When I woke there was no rattling of the windows and no battering of rain or hail on them. As we crawled out of the hotel the air was mild and the sky clear and full of stars. Only the twinkling pattern of ice crystals in the car's headlights showed that there had been a slight ground frost. It proved to be the first day I kept dry and warm from dawn to dark. We went to the sea wall again, but in the clear still morning the flight was as disappointing as Monday's had been spectacular. The estuary was full of geese, but they were far out except for a few greylags, and when they did begin to flight they mostly came in at a great height and beyond the two ends of the sea wall. Very few came near us and we had very few shots. One nice skein came slap over me and I got one barnacle out of it, dropping it with a thump almost at my feet, but that was our only score for the morning.

After breakfast we set out to try and find a stalk or a drive on the fields. We first found a bunch of whitefronts on a field that looked "driveable". There seemed to be plenty of dead ground below the field, so Keith set off to work round close to the gaggle and then I would put them up. But the geese must have had a sentry posted as they took off long before Keith got near them and while I was still watching his progress from the car. Then we set out to search the fields flanking the estuary and found large concentrations of barnacles spread over several fields, probably between one and two thousand geese altogether, and a long drive was planned. Keith drove me several fields past the geese and then went back and got down into a creek behind the geese; we must have ended up a mile apart. At the prearranged time I started to walk across the fields towards Keith, and parties of geese began to get up and move forward as I reached the next field to them. A regular snowball effect developed, each mob of geese joining up with the one next ahead of it until at last the whole 1,500 or so were collected in one field. Then the next ''flush'' took them over Keith and I saw a goose drop out of the sky long before I heard the shot. But the goose fell on the shore and managed to reach the water, where it proceeded to swim across the estuary with Keith wading after it. Unfortunately the bird could swim faster than Keith could wade and the unequal contest had to be abandoned.

We moved on and soon found another drive — a bunch of whitefronts and barnacles on a stubble above a little cliff. Keith set off to push the geese over me, and very soon a small party of white-fronts came over at an easy height. As I was expecting a much bigger lot I held my fire waiting for the main body of geese to appear. When they did they were further away and higher, and so I missed an easy chance. Moral: Two geese over you are as good as 200 or 2,000: you have only two barrels to fire and can rarely expect to get more than two geese out of a drive. Next we tried waiting in a little grassy marsh by the canal that always seemed to hold geese. There were both whitefronts and barnacles on it this time, but as they were unstalkable we put them off, set up two decoys and waited in some gorse bushes for the geese to return. But it was getting rather late in the day for this sort of manoeuvre and nothing happened for nearly an hour. Then Keith heard geese on the ground in the distance, and set off by car to find them and put them up, in the hope that they might see the decoys and come near enough to give me a shot. Instead he found they were easily stalkable — over the crest of a hill. He only had to approach from the far side of the hill and as he came over the top the geese were in range and he dropped three as they jumped. He came back to pick me up and seemed a little shamefaced about his exploit — it had all been too easy!

Finally, to finish the day, we went again to the loch in the hills to wait for whitefronts to flight in. This time the loch was smooth and calm and we expected the geese to take their usual route over the heather. Very few came; first a party of three slipped in low, between me and Keith and out of range for both of us. Then a large skein came in high on my left, and finally a couple of geese came in over Keith and his was the only shot fired — to no avail. Altogether rather a disappointing day (by our latest standards!) with only a few shots fired and only four more geese to add to the score — now standing at twenty-four for the three days.

Next day we were due to move on to new ground, and the estate in question sent their head-keeper to take charge of us. They came to our hotel at 6.45 a.m. in their own Land Rover and led the way to a hillside where we had often seen geese. Another violent rain storm broke out as we drove along, but fortunately stopped by the time we set out on foot up the hill. It must have been pouring for hours: we left the cars in a flood on the roadside, and the track up the hill which led to an old ruined bothy was more like a mountain torrent than an old cartway. It was soon clear that our guides didn't know much about goose shooting; they had made no efforts to find out what geese were in the area, what fields they were using or what flight line they were following. Keith was left in the shelter of the old bothy, and I was taken round various rough fields in search of a stone wall that had provided suitable cover on some earlier occasion. Fortunately we had brought two of our decoys with us, and I reckoned they would do more to provide us with chances than all the haphazard efforts of the keepers. For a long time nothing happened, then a small skein suddenly appeared from almost behind us, and a few more lots were seen moving in the distance. By the time it was fully light I could see that the decoys were badly placed, and so I asked the keeper to lift them and place them on a wide expanse of smooth green grass where they would stand out better, and where they would be nearer Keith as well as myself. And then, while we were both out in the open near the decoys, a couple of barnacles suddenly appeared, heading straight for us. Sudden movement was out of the question: the keeper dropped to his knees, with his dog huddled close to him, and I squeezed up behind him as though we were a boulder. The three of us must have looked like some grotesque and shapeless piece of modern sculpture — ''Three figures waiting for the sky to fall on them''. However it deceived the geese who came straight on — over the decoys out on our left front. At the critical moment I straightened up on one knee and took the leading goose with a charge of No. 3, and the second as it climbed away with the BB shot which I normally keep in the second barrel. Both geese crumpled up in mid-air. Later on two single barnacles also came to the decoys and were accounted for by Keith. Finally,

111

as we were packing up, the keepers already on their way home, and Keith half way down the hill with the spoils, a skein of whitefronts came circling round and landed on the grass near where the decoys had been. They dropped on to dead ground, and left me with a short stalk from where I had been watching them by the bothy. A few yards on hands and knees, a few more flat on the ground, and I was able to reach a boulder round which I could take a peep at the geese. I reckoned they were just in range, but only with BB shot. So a quick change of cartridge in the right barrel and then up on my knees for the shot. The first shot dropped one bird as all their heads went up, but the second failed as the geese jumped. As a matter of interest I stepped out the distance to the shot bird — 68 yards.

By this time it was nearly 10 and we hurried back to base for breakfast. After that we did another tour by car, exploring several new areas and finding new fields on some of the minor roads which often held parties of geese. We also called on another farmer to lay plans for the morrow and left with him and his neighbour the four barnacles we had shot that morning: in both cases they were much appreciated — which is not always the case.

In the late afternoon we rejoined the keeper who had arranged to take us to a bay on the coast where there was supposed to be a good duck flight. Into the bay ran a little valley where a burn from the hills tumbled down into the sea. The duck were said to flight in from the sea at dusk, and fly up the valley to their inland feeding grounds. A few duck did appear, and we had perhaps half a dozen shots between us, but it was rather disappointing and we only got one mallard drake.

The next day was our last, and we faced it with some despondency. There was only one limited area where we still had permission to shoot, and that was where we had been the previous morning. To return to the same fields a second day running is always a chancy business, and in this case we knew there were very few geese feeding in that area. Moreover the day dawned mild, with little wind and clear skies, so any geese on the move would be sure to fly high. So we waited by the derelict bothy, our two decoys out on the patch of clear grass in front, and nothing came our way — except for a single squawking goose that passed high over Keith and gave him a remote chance. That was the only shot we fired, except for another long shot at a couple of mallard that dropped into a burn just as we were loading our gear into the car.

The middle of the day remained bright and sunny so we took the chance to use up some films on geese in other areas, including a huge concentration of some 2,000 barnacles out on a remote farm at the mouth of the estuary.

2000 Barnacle Geese

ISLAND OF GEESE

For the evening flight we felt just as pessimistic as in the morning. We had arranged to wait for the evening flight of whitefronts in a small loch in the hills. But it was in the same area, and during the day we had found very few geese within likely flighting distance. This loch was new to us, but when we got to it we found a delightful sheet of shallow water set in a large shallow saucer of hill pasture. A quick inspection in the failing light showed plenty of goose feathers blown on to the lee shore, and quite a fair sprinkling of goose droppings on the close-grazed grass; some of them quite recent. So our hopes rose, while we set our two decoys in the water and reasoned out which way the geese were most likely to approach the pool. By now the sun had set, the sky was still bright and cloudless and a moon just past the first quarter was well up in the east. The light northerly wind was hardly likely to have any effect on the flight. For a long time we waited, with no sight or sound of geese, except for one large skein flying along the coast out at sea. It was now nearly dark except for the moonlight and it really seemed as if our last day was going to be a blank, as indeed we had feared. And then a whistle from Keith told me that he had heard geese on the move. A little later I could hear them too as they came nearer. A few moments later a small skein loomed into view, heading straight for me as I crouched a few yards from the water. It was the easiest of all shots at geese — a bird in level flight straight overhead at reasonable range. One throws up the gun when the skein is nearly overhead; and as soon as the gun is lined up on the selected bird swing it back so that it blots out the target, press the trigger, and a dead goose should hit the ground with a resounding thump a yard or two behind you! The only problem at night is to see the target in time and to be able to aim a gun correctly when you can't see the fore-sight. A little later a larger skein came in over Keith and he also got his goose. Both geese to our surprise were barnacles, and a still larger bunch of them came swinging round the loch for a while, but cleared off after we had each had a shot at them. We stayed on a little longer as the moon gave just enough light for shooting, but there seemed no sign of further geese and we reluctantly decided that this was the end of the day, and the end of another wildfowling holiday.

There only remained the long haul home. We left in typical West Highland weather, low cloud and steady rain, but as soon as we reached the mainland we soon ran into slush and sleet, and as we climbed over the first pass this turned to snow and treacherous roads. The hills were deep in snow and deer were down by the roadside. Our second skid took us into the parapet of a bridge and delayed us for the best part of an hour while we struggled with a crumpled wing and other damage. Fortunately the main frame, steering and engine seemed to be intact and our only major disability was the loss of a headlamp. Eventually we reached Newcastle at midnight, the coastal route via A1 being again the only reliable way back south, and another day's driving took us both to our respective homes.

A brighter note on which to close this account is the fact that our two "pricked" barnacle geese survived the journey in their tea-chest, and are now safely penned on green grass again — on our lawn at Catfield.

CHAPTER 26
THE END OF AN ERA
(1966 — 1967 Ted's Year)

It was a foregone conclusion that we should try and return to our "Island of Geese" this season. Keith had a few days' holiday still in hand, and so had Ted, who was to be the third member of the party. Ted had been initiated to our particular type of fowling two years ago when he turned up on a Sunday, shot three geese on Monday morning, and was away again within 24 hours.

The only dates that suited us all were in early December, so we met at Euston Station on Monday night, December 5th, myself having slipped away from the Smithfield Dinner somewhat early, and feeling rather overdressed, still in my dinner jacket!

After last year's strain of the long drive by car, and the hazards of ice and snow on the roads, we had decided to do the main journey to and from Scotland by train, and to collect a small hired van in Glasgow. This left us with a tight schedule of rail-road-steamer connections and tension mounted when our train arrived half-an-hour late in Glasgow. But at least it was clear, wet and black, when I peeped out of the window at Kilmarnock and the roads should give us no trouble. The van was not ready, though, when we reached the hire depot, and another precious half-hour was lost. However, we reached our little port in comfortable time, only to find that the steamer also had been in trouble and would be at best an hour late.

Eventually we reached our island and drove to the factor's house to report our arrival. The factor, we found, had been called to London, and so we pressed on straight to the gamekeeper's cottage and fixed up details for the morning.

There was not much argument about this. With no chance of daylight reconnaissance, the obvious choice was morning flight behind the seawall — the same seawall that we had crouched behind on our first morning on each of our last two visits. That settled, we moved on to our H.Q. and found mine host "Uncle Alec" awaiting us in the bar, and a hot meal to follow.

Next morning the alarm went off half an hour later than I thought I had set it, and mild panic ensued as we tumbled into our clothes. But we were in the van ready for the fray within ten minutes of the alarm, and in the event it proved to be a rather late flight, with nothing moving before 8 a.m. It was mild and lightly overcast, with very little wind, so conditions were not too good, but plenty of whitefronts began to appear, swinging in from their hill lochs and dropping into their feeding grounds behind us. A few greylags also came in from the estuary, and then, from about 9 to 9.30 the main flight of barnacles took place. It was a curious mixed flight, with parties of geese suddenly coming back over us from inland, and others flighting along the seawall. We stayed on till 10 a.m. and then met at the van with our spoils — four barnacles for me; two whitefronts and a barnacle for Keith, and a couple of greylags for Ted; a total of nine with three varieties.

By this time we had arranged to spend the middle of the day at a potato stubble which the keeper claimed had been attracting large numbers of geese. So we hurried back for a late breakfast and then set forth again.

But before meeting the keeper we did a quick recce to see what we could find for the morrow.

The two farms across the bay offered the best prospects as they had served us so well, and provided such good flights, on both previous occasions. Sure enough, the grass fields on the first farm were covered with geese, both whitefronts and barnacles, and they were using the two fields on either side of the deep ditch that gave me such excellent cover on the first occasion two years ago. So there was no need to explore further, nor to plan tactics; it would be a case of the mixture as before.

Back at the keeper's we transferred to his Land Rover and drove up to the potato field. A couple of hundred geese were on it — whitefronts and greylags — and quickly departed as we came in sight. The idea was to put out a couple of decoys, lie up in the boundary fences, and wait for the geese to return. After a while a few small lots did appear, but mostly swung round high and wide and gave us very few chances. By now the weather had deteriorated, with steady, heavy rain, and I for one was beginning to feel wet, cold and miserable, with rain running down inside my long boots. So we took shelter in the wood at one end of the field and fell upon our sandwiches and coffee. It is, of course, always on such occasions that chances come along, so I went back to my hide in a clump of gorse bushes while the others finished their lunch. And sure enough, within a few minutes a skein of whitefronts came flying in, circled the decoys and then flew off again. But they passed just close enough to me and I got a goose out of the departing skein.

At 3 p.m. the keeper collected us in the Land Rover and we moved on to the next assignment — evening flight at the hill loch used by the whitefronts. The rain had eased off, but there was only a fair crosswind, so the geese came pretty high and hardly offered possible shots. Quite a lot came though, and at the height of the flight the sky in front of me was filled with perhaps a score of skeins, coming into view half a mile or so away in the failing light. It was a case of trying to spot a lower skein and letting the higher ones pass unmolested. At last I picked what seemed the most likely skein and as it passed high overhead I chanced one shot, giving the target a lead of several yards. To my great surprise the goose packed up and fell like a stone, or perhaps even more like a diving Gannet as it folded its wings and fell with a terrific splash into the loch behind me. It was quite the highest shot I have ever brought off at geese with a 12-bore, and for that reason is one of those special shots I shall always remember. Keith on my right also got an extremely high goose, though to our surprise it was a barnacle; we did not think barnacles roosted on this loch.

So ended our first day with a total score of 12 geese.

That night the wind freshened and increased to gale dimensions. Several times I was wakened by the violent rattling of the window frames in my bedroom and the fierce tattoo of rain on the glass. We set out in good time in the morning and made our way to the familiar ditch between the two fields. Ted took up station in the middle, Keith took the seaward flank and I was on the landward side. A couple of decoys placed in the field behind us (i.e. upwind) should help to ensure that the approaching geese would come over the ditch to the second field and not drop short in the field in front of us.

It was a good thing we were early this morning as the first goose talk came out of the darkness at barely 7.30 and I was lucky to spot the first skein gliding in from my right. I dropped a goose with my first shot (always a good beginning to a day) and it fell only a few yards from me. After that there was quite a long pause before the main flight got under way. Then for perhaps half an hour we enjoyed a morning flight under almost classic conditions: rough weather and skein after skein battling in against the wind — first whitefronts coming down from the hills on our right — and gliding in to the field behind us. Later the barnacles started to flight, but in their case coming along the coast on the left of our line. At one stage a party of barnacles landed far out in the field behind us, and I took advantage of a lull in the flight to climb out of the ditch and put them up — lest they decoy all further geese to them. While out in the open a violent hailstorm swept across the fields and I found it impossible to stand upright. Great vertical curtains of rain and hail swept across the countryside as I struggled back to the shelter of the ditch. Down in the ditch it was quiet and dry by comparison; one's head being almost hidden at ground level, while clumps of gorse gave further protection, both from the weather and also from the searching eyes of the approaching geese. Altogether it was an excellent flight and after collecting the distant victims we found we had added another 11 geese to the score — five to me, four (and a mallard) to Keith and a couple to Ted.

Back to base for breakfast, and then we set out on a more thorough reconnaissance of the main. goose areas. We took the usual sandwiches and hot coffee with us and, of course, kept our guns with us in case an opportunity for a stalk or drive cropped up during the middle of the day. This year the distribution of geese seemed very different from what we had found previously. Several areas that had held large numbers of geese before were now bare, and whole districts seemed deserted. What geese there were seemed broken up into smaller lots, and we could find very few greylags. Local opinion held that there were just as many geese as usual on the island, so no doubt there must have been large numbers in some areas we had not discovered.

Eventually we found a big mixed lot of whitefronts and barnacles on a large field by the "canal" A drive seemed possible so Keith and Ted dropped off behind the cover of a wood and I drove on till I could leave the car and make my way across country to come up behind the geese. But they would not fly forward into the strong wind — they just rose almost vertically and then swung back to left and right. I left Keith and Ted with a couple of decoys and they lay up under cover hoping that some at least of the geese would return. But this also proved unavailing, though Keith was lucky to get a greylag out of a bunch that rose from an adjoining patch of roots.

Meanwhile I took the van back to the nearest garage to fill up with petrol and then collected the keeper to join us for the evening flight. This we had arranged to take by the seawall on the far side of the estuary, where we hoped the geese would flight back to the sands under the shelter of the high ground to the west. Failing geese, we expected there would be a duck flight in the opposite direction as there had been when we tried this area two years ago.

When we got down to the seawall at about 3.30 geese were already on the move, and a most exciting evening developed. Violent storms kept sweeping across the estuary, and this seemed to upset the geese and disrupt their normal flight out to the sands. Some headed out to the sea and then swung back to the shelter of the land; others came flying along the fields inside the seawall. In fact, geese seemed to be moving in all directions. In the midst of all this a particularly violent squall drove the duck in from the estuary long before their usual flight time, and we found our-selves in the midst of a combined goose and duck flight. As I only had goose cartridges I pre-ferred to concentrate on the larger quarry and managed to bag a couple of barnacles. But in a lull between skeins I had a nice right and left at mallard and later a single one. Keith came in with no less than four barnacles, a mallard and a wigeon while Ted was top scorer with two white-fronts, one barnacle, a mallard, two wigeon and a pintail. Altogether it had been quite one of our most memorable days — an excellent morning flight and a quite exceptional evening one.

For our third and last morning we went back to the seawall again at the head of the estuary. The wind had kept up during the night and had increased to gale force when we turned out. In fact, the little van laboured in top gear when driving into the teeth of the wind, and when we walked across the marsh to take up our positions, it was as exhausting as struggling uphill. We reckoned the geese would flight in on the far side — under the shelter of the high ground, so we all moved well to the left this time; at least I did, and must have ended up nearly a mile from Keith on the right flank with Ted in the middle. As dawn broke the wind ceased, the rain held off, and we had a comfortable, dry, outing until a sudden squall overtook us as we were coming in. It was a late flight, hardly anything on the move until 8 a.m. Then an excellent flight developed with skein after skein lifting off the distant estuary, until, at the height of it; the sky in front of me was filled with weaving lines of geese beating in for their morning feed. As on Wednesday morning, quite a few came back from inland or flew along the seawall, so that one needed eyes all round one's head. For myself there was the added satisfaction of shooting better so that by 9 a.m. I had collected six barnacles — a number which I have often told myself (and others!) is quite enough to shoot at a sitting. But there were also three geese which had dropped out far in front and behind me, and which I had not relied on retrieving. But the keeper found one with his dog out on the saltings in front of us, I found another far behind me, dead, right on the line I had marked, and the third we also found where it had fallen dead half a mile away, and then, as we were trudging back to the van a skein of barnacles came straight for me — right out in the open — and I got one out of it, making a total of 10 for the morning. Keith had got a couple, and Ted one, though he was unable to find it.

The middle of the day yielded nothing — geese were back on the large field by the canal, but we could do nothing with them.

So we came to our last outing — a repeat of the previous evening's vigil by the seawall. Although we all gaily talked of concentrating on the duck flight, we found the geese behaving much as they had done before, and of course it was impossible to ignore them. We had hardly climbed out of the Land Rover when a skein of barnacles came heading straight for us. Ted was the first to get his gun loaded, and proceeded to give a perfect example of how to shoot a wild goose — to the applause of his critical but admiring audience! He ended up by shooting four during the evening, while Keith got one, and I finished a spell of poor shooting by getting two with one shot out of a skein that passed low to the landward side of the seawall. The ducks did not behave so well, but we got four wigeon and a mallard between us. There only remained a check of the total bag at the keeper's cottage, the distribution of the spoils and a reluctant farewell. Then back to base, a good meal and an evening's packing ready for an early departure in the morning. The total bag for the three days was:

> 39 Barnacle geese
> 10 Whitefronted geese
> 3 Greylag geese
> 8 Mallard
> 6 Wigeon
> 1 Pintail

We were on the road again just before dawn, and passing round the head of the bay could just see the massed ranks of geese out on the mud awaiting the moment for their morning flight to the fields. We had also said a sad farewell at our hotel, as "Uncle Alec' had taken to his bed the night before, and it was only when we said goodbye to his wife over an early cup of tea that we heard that a slight heart attack was suspected. In the last three years we had developed a great affection for Alec — he seemed a worthy successor to the many other hosts who, over the years, have provided us with a friendly and hospitable base from which to carry out our daily forays.

It was fine and fairly calm as we cast off from the pier for the journey back to the mainland, and as we left the open sea the day was bright and crisp, with blue skies and clear warm colours on the hills. Only the high tops showed a sprinkling of snow. Several items of interest broke the monotony of the sea and road journey: wild goats on some of the cliffs, little parties of eider ducks in the sea lochs, our friends, the seals, at their usual point, a couple of buzzards circling high in the sky, and later a solitary golden eagle sweeping the sky in majestic circles. At the top of the highest pass, where the road just reached the snow line, we saw a couple of hinds on the slopes just above us. With time to spare we stopped a few minutes on each occasion and enjoyed watching these creatures — just as we enjoy watching geese (quite apart from the shooting).

At last we reached Glasgow where the van disgorged Keith and Ted with all their gear and three crates of game to catch the night train south. Their holiday was over, but I had promised myself a few more days and turned back north again towards my old haunts on the mainland.

****

The next three days tell a very different story. I first travelled up to a new secluded valley I had discovered some years ago. In summer it looked most promising goose country and when I had checked it later in winter I had found the flat valley bottom smothered with geese.

Next morning — being Sunday — I slipped out of my hotel before dawn and drove to the neck of the valley to see what came in at morning flight. It was a clear still dawn; perfect for observation; with a pale cloudless sky ranging from a soft pink on the horizon through orange and primrose to pale blue overhead. Not a goose could have flown into that valley without my seeing or hearing it, and no goose came. After breakfast I called at the farm where I had hoped to get some shooting, and they confirmed that there had been no geese for some days. So it was a case of the usual packet of sandwiches, a thermos, and moving on to other districts in the hope of finding something for the morrow. First to Sir James' estate but no sign of geese there; then on to the "Whiskey" territory with its famous sanctuary for pinkfeet, but again no sign of geese in all that broad valley, and so to the "Dark Estuary" itself where I stopped at the usual vantage point to search the long series of grass fields on the Laird's farms. Still no luck, and a call at the keeper's cottage brought sad news; no geese for the past fortnight and not even the sight or sound of one for the last week. Increased activity on the seawall and foreshore was blamed for this early departure of the geese, local gunners lining the estuary in increasing numbers both night and day and loosing off at everything in sight. The Laird himself confirmed all this. In fact, there seemed no sign of any geese all along the estuary, so I pushed on over the hills; first to "Mongi's" farm and that famous stretch of goose country, and then to the valley beyond. Still nothing to be seen or heard and I pushed on further north, exploring new ground that I knew often held geese, though I had never shot there. At last, with the failing light, I turned back and eventually reached my hotel tired and disappointed. Never before can I remember spending a whole day — and covering some 160 miles — in reconnaissance without finding a single bunch of geese on any of their favourite feeding areas. Even the sky shed a few large tears of snowflakes as I turned the van into the hotel yard.

So with no plans for the morrow I phoned Robert and George to see if they had any suggestions. Neither had anything very definite, but at least they were sufficiently encouraging to persuade me to stay on for at least one more day.

In the morning I was relieved to find the snow had gone and the countryside was wet and "black" again. The proprietor's wife gave me breakfast at 7.30 in my solitary glory, and I was on the road in time to check that there was again no sign of a flight into the secluded valley. I followed different roads this time, to cover fresh ground, and did at least see a few distant skeins high in the sky. One of these roads gave me the chance to search Scott's farm from across the moss, but still no sign of geese feeding.

And then, at last, on leaving this area, I noticed a skein of geese dropping into a field by an isolated farm on my right. More skeins followed, and the glasses at last revealed a "strong feed", with some 500-600 geese on the ground. They were almost certainly pinks, and very probably on Whiskey territory. I found my way to the farm, sought out the farmer (busy riddling potatoes in his barn) and found him sympathetic, but unwilling to give me permission to shoot without the approval of higher authority. By this time more geese had dropped into the field, and there were probably a good 1,000 on the field — all pinks except for two barnacles. So on to the estate office where I tackled the Whiskey factor; he also was sympathetic but said he would have to get the blessing of the Whiskey King himself — which he said he would try to do, and phone me. At least I had now found geese, and there was a ray of hope!

By now it was nearly mid-day, which just left time for another quick check on the Laird's land and round the estuary, and then to Robert and Shelagh's where I begged lunch. After lunch I set out to find George — some 20 miles away — who had recently moved up from Suffolk and was newly installed in a large mansion, with a considerable area of arable land above the house, and above that again some 2,500 acres of grouse moor — a very attractive property. It was said to hold a thousand or more greylags at times, but at this particular time there was no more than a vague report from the farm staff that a few geese had been using the stubbles. It was too late to check all this that afternoon, so I promised to come back next day and do a proper recce.

There was still no sign of geese as I returned to Robert's by a different route, and there I learned that the Whiskey King had firmly turned down my approach. Apparently he receives so many requests from people wanting to go after geese on his estate that he had adopted a rigid rule of saying "No" to everybody. And I must admit that however much I may be annoyed or critical when at the receiving end of this decision, I would probably take up the same attitude if I were in his enviable position. After dinner Robert nobly got busy on the phone again and came up with two names and addresses where there were reports of geese.

With such discouraging reports on the estuary geese and the prospect of a barrage of local gunners, I lacked the usual urge to go down to the foreshore for the morning flight. Instead I had breakfast with the family and set off at 9 a.m. for another day's search. I tried one of Robert's addresses first — an estate bordering the river well above the estuary. The house was deserted, so I had to find my own way about and made my way down to the river. There was no sign of geese using the bordering fields, but I found a few greylags on the shingle spits and islands of the river. But there was no chance of a shot; they lifted as soon as I appeared, so the only hope was to come back at dusk.

The next call was at Robert's second address, a farm well up in the hills and quite close to George, but on the opposite side of the valley. Here it was again a case of jam yesterday but none today. Geese were said to have been on the farm quite recently but there were certainly none on it now. I took a good walk round it, and also had a good look at George's fields a mile or more across the valley and was pretty sure there were no geese there either. But I had promised to call and I drove on, up to George's farm and up on to his grouse moor where I could look back on his fields below and check any dead ground not visible from across the valley. Again no joy. George came along in his Land Rover while I was eating my sandwiches and we exchanged condolences, and by then it was time I hurried back to the river in time for any evening flighting.

I took a couple of decoys with me and set them up in a grass field alongside the river and made myself as small as possible by the fence. Soon after 3 p.m. geese began to appear; high in the clear evening sky skein after skein appeared, making for their sleeping quarters ; some going south — presumably to the estuary, but others coming in the opposite direction and dropping into the river, but unfortunately about a mile below me, where I knew they were on a sanctuary estate. It was most interesting to note how these geese flew in at a great height and then came wheeling down in fairly tight circles to drop down by the river. Often I never saw them till they started circling down, and it was all rather suggestive of vultures appearing out of nowhere. There was no horizontal flying in ; no particular line of flight. In this way I estimated 1,000 greylags came down to roost by the river.

Only as the light began to fail was there some flighting up and down the river — as I had hoped, and it seemed that I might at last have a chance. But the geese kept close to the river and never ventured far over the fields. Only one single goose tempted me to try a shot, but it was barely in range and passed untouched. Duck also kept flighting in all directions, but I let them alone in the hope of a chance at geese. At last it was too dark to see any more; I collected the decoys and turned my back on the river. A sudden chill had descended on the fields and the grass crunched crisply under foot with the onset of frost as I plodded back to the van.

I had now decided that there was little point in pursuing the hunt any further. Three days of intensive searching had failed to produce any shootable geese; I might as well pack up and go home. Next morning on the road south I found quite a lot of geese! Some even on fields on either side of the main road. It looked as though while I was searching further north, the geese had in fact been concentrated to the south. But it was too late for second thoughts ; I carried on to Glasgow where I turned in the van — with 1,000 miles clocked up during the past 8 days, and that night took the train for London and home.

****

There are sad conclusions to be drawn from these last few days. The whole pattern of the movements and habits of the geese in this part of Scotland seem to have changed. No longer do they feed on the broad expanse of fields bordering the estuary, and this means that there is now little likelihood of the geese offering chances at morning and evening flight on the seawall, or out on the foreshore. Whatever geese still sleep in the estuary will rise to a safe height while over the mud or water and then flight 10 miles or more to remote inland farms, where they will be comparatively safe from the increasing numbers of shore gunners. I also suspect that the geese are increasingly adopting the habit of roosting on inland lochs, rather than on the tidal estuaries, especially those lochs on preserved and "keepered" estates. I can think of at least half a dozen such safe inland sanctuaries, and I am sure that the geese in their wisdom will find and adopt many more. At any rate, in spite of the increased persecution, the general opinion seems to be that the wild geese are increasing rather than decreasing in numbers. A recent "count", so I am told, showed 32,000 greylags and 20,000 pinkfeet in one county of Scotland alone! But the days of genuine wildfowling on and around the "Dark Estuary", as "BB" and I have known it in the past, are apparently over. To think that in those early days, at the end of the war and just after, we got all the wildfowling one could hope for within cycling distance of our H.Q.! Now it is a case of long range reconnaissance by car, and the sport we eventually obtain is better described as goose-shooting than wildfowling. Another calamity, which may prove only temporary, is that our long established H.Q. is no longer available. A family quarrel has arisen between Dan and his son, the hotel is said to be up for sale, and meanwhile it cannot cope with resident visitors. It is indeed the end of an era.

CHAPTER 27
OLD HAUNTS AND A NEW ISLAND
(1968 — 1969 Chun's Year)

I had been looking forward to a wildfowling trip in the winter of 1968/69 with more than the usual impatience. We had been obliged to cancel all plans the previous year because of the Foot and Mouth epidemic which ruled out of court any idea of wandering over other people's farm land. Thus it was two years since I had last pitted my wits and tested my skills against the cunning of the truly wild geese.

Unfortunately our wonderful "Island of Geese" was out of bounds to us this year as we could not obtain any suitable dates from the laird who controlled all the best goose areas. But Keith came up with another island and we fixed up to give it a trial for three days. Before that I would take my grandson Colin* for a few days in our old haunts — in spite of my pessimistic impressions of two years ago, and then Keith and Ted would join us to make a foursome for another few days before Chun had to return south to school.

At the eleventh hour complications set in. I retired to bed for Christmas and Boxing Day with a disorganised inside which made long distance motoring and dawn winter vigils seem most unlikely prospects in a week's time. To make prospects worse snow hit the east coast of England immediately after Christmas and cut off roads and villages in much of Norfolk.

However all was well in the end; my own troubles cleared up in time, the roads were opened the day before we were due to start, so on January 2nd Chun and I set out for the north. We made an easy day of it and spent the night with my sister in Newcastle.

Next day we crossed to the west coast and stopped at the Metal Bridge for lunch. Only Betty was at home; Martha and Jean were away for the day, and poor old Dick had passed away only a month or two ago. He had apparently had pleurisy a couple of years ago and had then started to go downhill. From the time that he could no longer fish he had seemed to lose interest in life. He was 75 when he died.

Betty told us she would soon be retiring herself and had bought the adjoining farm house. That indeed will mark the end of another era in another remarkable little world.

That evening we reached a small fishing hotel north of Dumfries ready for a day's pheasant shooting next day. This invitation had come out of the blue a few weeks earlier and fitted in perfectly with our dates. It proved a delightful day, bright and crisp, with some nine or ten drives out of blocks of conifer plantations. It was all fairly high ground with extensive views over the surrounding hills. Several roe deer were seen but the bag was almost entirely pheasants — 61 of them plus a few hares, rabbits and a woodcock. I was shooting well myself which always adds to the satisfaction! Chun walked as flank gun with the beaters and claimed four birds. That evening our host and his wife came and dined with us at the little hotel, and in the morning we were on the road again. The next call was on the Solway, to stay with John and Betty who had recently retired to a charming house, right on the coast. John had promised to organise a morning flight the following morning (Monday) and I thus found myself trudging through the darkness out on to a marsh that I had not set foot on for over thirty years! But it all seemed so familiar and

---

* Little Colin (6 ft. 2½ ins.) referred to in an earlier chapter by his nickname ''Chun'' to distinguish him from his father Big Colin (6 ft. 4 ins.).

Chun with Betty and John at their house on the Solway

quite unchanged; the first light of dawn beginning to show in the east over the bay, the lights of the town twinkling on the high ground to our right and the black mass of mountains on our left. The same deep drain running across the marsh with the cattle bridge of railway sleepers, and the same tempting flight of curlews coming in from the mudflats to feed on the fields. One big lot of pinks lifted and flew in, but they came high and just beyond me where I crouched in a gully. The extreme end of the V was possibly just in range and I couldn't resist trying both barrels — but with no success. We only saw two other small and distant lots, and then returned to the car and a hot breakfast awaiting us at the house.

But John and I enjoyed recalling nostalgic memories of this bay, which we had both known so well in the past. There was one occasion in particular when Tony and I had joined up with John and his brother Peter and a friend to make a fivesome. It was memorable for me because it was the first time I had shot geese over decoys and the results were impressive. Tony and I had gone out one morning with Bob McGuffie — the local fowler — who had three stuffed decoys. The others had gone down to the marsh, but Bob took us to a small but long grass field, running at right angles to the coast. The short landward end of the field was bounded by a deep ditch, which gave us perfect cover. Bob posted his decoys well out in the field — probably 100 yards in front of us (which seemed to me too far), and then we waited for the dawn. I can see that dawn still — clear and pale yellow-green, with a touch of orange and then red on the thin streaks of cloud near the horizon as the sun approached. And then — probably well over a mile away — one suddenly detected a thin black line against the pale background. The line swayed a little, and before long one could see it was a string of black dots, but from the first sight there was no doubt but that it was a skein of geese coming in from the sea. The skein came steadily on, heading straight for us, and when still a long way off one could see the wing beats cease and the long descending glide begin. It seemed they would land by the decoys — well out of range, and then Bob saved the situation with his ''whistle'' technique. When the skein was only a few yards above the decoys he let out a shrill whistle, and the geese immediately had second thoughts. The cupped wings started beating again; the downward glide was checked and the line of geese carried on to the end of the field, passing over the three of us in the boundary ditch.

In this way several skeins were drawn over us, and we all had our share of chances. I remember the total score was 11 — all greys — and I was from that moment converted to the use of decoys and the dawn wait for geese on their feeding grounds, as an alternative to the traditional type of dawn flighting on the coast.

John recalled another occasion in that area when he and I had been scouting round the fields and spotted a small party of greys on a patch of rough ground. A stalk seemed possible, and after getting permission from the local farmer I set out with the 8-bore. It was easy to approach in dead ground and reach a stone wall. The geese then seemed just in range, so I gently poked the gun over the wall and let fly. One goose fell to the double shot, and when we stepped it out we found it was 85 yards from the wall.

Bob McGuffie was quite a character. He wielded an ancient hammer gun with his one arm, and a little puff of smoke would squirt out sideways from one of the barrels where it was pitted right through. He addressed the geese with a cheerful form of endearing abuse. "Come on, you great grey beggars". "Look out, five of the baskets are coming in on your left" and so on.

But to return to 1969. After breakfast we took to the road again, and ran right through to our northern base, only stopping for a cup of tea with Jim and Nellie at Bridge of Allan. There was recent snow round Lanark and I was anxious to get through before things got worse. So we reached the "Dark Estuary" in time for supper with Robert and Shelagh and looked forward to several days of the old routine.

Next day — Tuesday — was a shocker. A thaw had set in, but brought rain and sleet. We did the usual dawn vigil on the coast but all the geese were far out on the water and very few came in on our side of the estuary. Neither of us fired a shot and we came back wet and cold. But a quick recce of the Laird's estate disclosed quite a few pinks moving on his grass fields. There's no time like the present with geese, so we called on the Laird and got permission to have a go at his geese next morning. After lunch we did a further recce of the estate that Simon introduced us to in January 1959. The Laird was away, but we found his son, and were immediately offered the chance of an evening flight along the river that very evening. So again I found myself on familiar ground — the same place where we had waited for the geese ten years ago. Chun and I took up position — and waited. The weather was still appalling — driving rain and a cold east wind. We saw a few geese on the move, but none came near us, and only when it was too dark to see did we hear geese moving about over the field, and sometimes landing at the other end of it. Eventually we gave up and made for base, extremely wet and somewhat tired and disappointed. But I had great hopes for the morrow.

Wednesday morning certainly proved kinder. It was at least dry (till nearly midday) and there was quite a bit of wind. We met the keeper at the farm where we had seen the geese and made our way over the large flat grass fields to a plantation of young conifers which gave us excellent cover. In due course geese began to arrive, but mostly passed high overhead obviously destined for further feeding grounds. For a long time nothing came to the decoys, but at last a lone pink-foot glided in and Chun dropped it with his second barrel — just before I added my own shot. These shots put up two parties of geese on fields further along, and these turned back into the wind and came towards us. One lot responded to the decoys and we got one goose out of it with our barrage of four shots. Later, another skein came in and I dropped one bird as they passed over the decoys. So we came back to lunch with three geese, well satisfied to have opened the scoring at last.

The rest of the day was spent in long range reconnaissance. We reached George for lunch, picked up two introductions and called on these, and a third from Robert, on our long circuit homewards. Two drew blank, but the third produced the offer of an evening flight (on Friday) along the river. Finally, as a last resort for the morrow, we 'phoned our long suffering friend next to "Mongi's farm" over the hills and got permission to try his fields next morning. We had seen geese on the field over his boundary burn, and hoped that with the help of decoys we might entice a few geese on to his adjoining field of potato stubble.

So on Thursday morning we set off over the hills again and made our way to the potato stubble. The boundary burn had several thorn bushes along the bank, so we had ready-made cover. For a long time we waited, with no sign of a flight to the field in front of us, though in time several lots of geese appeared high in the sky making for other distant feeding grounds. Now and again a single goose would come sailing out of the distance, its honking betraying its approach long before we spotted it high up in the sky. One of these — a pink — eventually circled down to join the decoys and on its last circuit of the field came near and low enough to offer a fair, though high, shot. My right barrel killed it stone dead in mid air and it fell close to the fence on my left. Later on a single grey came down to the decoys and this time Chun dropped the goose with a single shot. By now skeins were frequently in sight, but none seemed interested in our field or the decoys. We stayed on till nearly 11, by which time the clouds had disappeared and the sun was shining like a day in spring.

The usual afternoon recce produced nothing; the Laird's fields were bare of geese and though we tried some of the farms adjoining the Whiskey King's territory these also yielded no sign of geese. So as a last resort I 'phoned one of George's introductions and said we would try his land in the morning — as a "blind date" so to speak. Meanwhile Keith and Ted had arrived and decided to try our potato stubble under the moon — after hearing our report of the morning's encounter. In fact they spent the twelve hours from midnight to Friday midday on the farm; out in the field when moon and cloud conditions were suitable, and then snatching a few hours sleep before morning flight. All they got for their pains was a wigeon which disappeared while they slept, and a hard-hit goose which they never found.

Meanwhile Chun and I were off again on our "blind date" at dawn. This new farm had land running down to the river, and the most likely spot seemed to be a large loop in the river where any flighting geese would probably take a short cut across the loop. After trying various positions out on the open grass, we moved to a retaining bank which at least gave us a little cover, and seemed to cross the line of flight of the few early geese we saw. But very few geese appeared, and there was no regular flight along the river. One or two single geese, or pairs, nearly gave us chances, and then quite unexpectedly one of those single geese suddenly appeared as from nowhere, and came straight for us at shootable height. I only just saw it in time and got it with a single shot as it crossed the bank.

Returning to base we found Ted on the road by the potato stubble and turned back to collect Keith who had gone after his hit goose. We found him on the next farm — minus his goose — but with reports of geese dropping into a nearby field. Sure enough as we watched several skeins came over the farm and glided down to a potato stubble. Through glasses we could see that there must have been several hundred already there. So here at last was a "strong feed". We tackled the farmer — who had often given me permission in past years — and arranged to deal with the geese next morning. This left little time except for lunch, and a quick recce, before setting out again for the evening flight on the river which we had fixed up through George's good offices.

This evening flight proved a memorable one. Conditions were favourable; rough weather with rain and a strong wind, and the estate in question was next to a well known sanctuary estate and on the line of flight of geese returning to it for their evening roost. Only three guns had been allowed for us, so Keith and I shared one position by the bank of the river, while Chun and Ted had similar positions further downstream, several hundred yards apart.

As the light faded geese began to appear, but few skeins passed over us. At last I got a very high pink out of a small lot, and we could hear occasional shots from the other two. Then there was quite a pause and we began to think the flight was over. But suddenly we heard geese again in the sky in front of us and gradually a tremendous flight developed. Skein after skein came swinging down the river, some to the left over the river itself, some far out over the rough ground on our right, but a fair proportion slap over us, and of these quite a few were low enough to be in range. Keith and I took his gun in turns, and ended up with seven geese between us, with at least two down but lost. It was quite one of the most spectacular flights I have ever seen — with probably over 1,000 geese flighting in to their roost along the narrow corridor of the river valley. When it was all over we struggled back to the car, picking up Chun on the way, who had shot four himself. Three of these were accounted for by the remarkable feat of killing three geese with a right and left. I have several times shot two geese with one shot, and also brought off right and lefts, but to combine both achievements together is a thing I can only remember having done once (in January 1950), and it must be quite a rare occurrence. Ted was waiting for us by the car with two more geese, making the score for the evening 13. A red letter day.

Next morning we went out for the geese on the potato stubble. As we climbed over the hills we ran into mist and prospects seemed doubtful. Later in the morning a few geese were heard on the move, a few skeins appeared and flew round somewhat uncertainly, but none came to the decoys. They would be invisible beyond about 100 yards, and it looked doubtful whether this field was in fact the established "feed" it seemed yesterday. We had only a few desperate shots and came away empty handed.

For the evening we had arranged to try again the evening flight we had done on Tuesday. This time there were the four of us, but the Laird's son raised no objection, so we all turned up at his house about 4 p.m. David and a party were having a walk-round for pheasants on outlying parts of the estate and as we made our way down to the river we found them deploying to beat out a small gully of brambles and scrub. We were told to join the party as flank guns and towards the end of the beat a solitary cock pheasant broke cover and headed straight for Chun out on the right flank. I could share his relief that he successfully shot the bird — in full view of several guns, even though the cock was a runner and made back for cover where it was retrieved by one of the dogs. After that we left the syndicate to walk some bogs while the four of us moved down to the flat fields along the river and took up positions to await the geese. It was still misty, but not so thick — visibility perhaps 2-300 yards, and at least it was mild and dry. As usual in the failing light one heard geese long before one could see them, and before long one or two skeins appeared flighting along the valley. At last one of these passed over us and Ted and I each took a goose out of it. A little later Chun and I did the same with another skein — all lovely high shots with the goose cleanly killed. And then as we were packing up a couple of geese passed over Keith and he also got his goose. So we trudged back to the cars with 5 geese — all greylags — making a total bag of 24 geese for the week.

A total bag of 24 geese for the week. With Chun and Ted — and Fen

Driving back to base, and an evening meal with Keith and Ted at their pub, I realised that I had reached the end of my tether. I could hardly keep awake at the wheel, and I knew that I had reached the end of my reserves of energy — reserves which always seem miraculously re-generated at the start of a fowling trip, but which of course cannot last for ever. The red flag was showing and I knew I must call a halt at once. Fortunately it was Saturday night so I got back to my own quarters as soon as possible and slept the clock round till about 9.30 next morning. Keith had volunteered to put Chun on the early train south at the nearest main line station, and we had arranged to make our own departure by road at about 11. So there was a leisurely breakfast, collection of all our gear, the repacking of the car, and once again we were on the road heading for the second stage of our trip — a visit to Keith's new island.

We reached Jim and Nellie for lunch, and this gave me the opportunity of snatching another three hours sleep in the afternoon to make up for lost time and to "re-charge my batteries". We remained with them for the night and thus another long night's sleep and a late breakfast at 9.30 on Monday morning completed the recovery process as far as I was concerned.

A long day's driving took us westwards to the ferry and we reached our island in time for a quick recce before the light failed. Once again we faced new ground and uncertain prospects, though we knew the island held large numbers of geese, and there were reports of large bags. This time it was a case of organised goose-shooting on a preserved estate with two keepers and a Land Rover provided, and all linked up with accommodation at an imposing looking hotel. It all seemed rather formidable and very different from the free and easy wildfowling we have enjoyed in the past, but which is now getting so much more difficult to find.

The shooting was organised on a basis of six guns, so we found we were teamed up with three Lancashire Lads from Preston, who proved to be enthusiastic and expert fowlers who had served some ten years' apprenticeship on the Solway, but who had now given it up in disgust. They also proved to be expert shots.

In the morning the two keepers collected us at the hotel and took us down to the coast, Keith following in his car with Ted. Thanks to B.S.T. we had been fortified by a normal cooked hotel breakfast at 7.30 — a luxury I have never before known in over 30 years of fowling.

At the coast we were placed behind a scruffy thorn hedge, with a marshy grass field in front of us and beyond that the sheltered waters of the bay. There was plenty of goose talk out on the water, and we waited with the usual tingle of excitement as the time for flight approached. At last we heard a large mob of geese lift from the bay, and in a few moments we could see them heading straight for us. All six of us had chances and a regular fusilade broke out, with geese falling out of the skein all along the line. I got a single bird on the flank, and the others accounted for four more. A good start to the day.

A short pause for our packed lunch. Keith, Ted and the Bicycle Boys

After that we clambered into the two cars and spent the rest of a remarkable day searching the island for geese on the fields, and organising impromptu drives. No need to describe each drive, there must have been 8 or 9 of them, with a short pause for our packed lunch. But the general pattern was for the two cars to drive on past any gaggle of geese seen in a field and to drop off the guns safely out of sight. One of the keepers would then lead us on a long detour to bring us up to a wall or hedge, while the other keeper would drive back past the geese and in due course set off across the fields to put the geese up — and over us. The remarkable thing was the expert knowledge of the ground displayed by the keepers, and their equally expert forecasting of the way the geese would fly. Several drives were abortive through the geese taking alarm before we were in position, but I can only recollect one of the remaining drives when the geese failed to cross the line of guns. Another remarkable point was that in many cases we were 500 yards or more from the feeding geese, and yet they were still in range when they passed over us ; it is seldom one finds geese so confiding that they have not achieved a safe height in half that distance. Two drives deserve special mention. In the first case we were able to reach the stone wall bounding the actual field in which the geese were feeding. Through a chink in the stones I could see half-a-dozen of the distant geese, heads all down and feeding. Then, as the keeper came in sight, all heads were up ; and in a few seconds the geese were on the wing and coming straight towards us. The usual barrage met them, and the six of us brought down 10 geese. The

The six of us brought down 10 geese

day ended with a similar drive. On this occasion I stayed behind on the flank, and the skein came nowhere near me. But I watched it pass over the other five behind their stone wall, and this time the five guns accounted for eight geese. By the end of the day the total score was 34 — a figure which I found almost embarrassingly large. And I still think the dawn flight off the sea was the best and most authentic part of the whole day. Our own three guns fared comparatively poorly, and only accounted for a dozen of the geese.

The next day followed a similar pattern, but the geese were already more wary, and more difficult to find. Three of us waited for the dawn flight off the bay, but no geese came near enough to give us a fair chance. The other three guns, waiting with decoys on a grass field half a mile away were more lucky and shot several — 5 I think. After that we joined forces to take part in drives. Three were most successful and yielded 4-6 geese each ; one went astray on the golf course, and the final one of the day was an exciting anti-climax. We had located a large mob of geese well inland, and found we could get right up to the edge of the field by approaching up a burn in a gully. The field fell away to this burn and we began to line the gorse-covered bank of the burn close to the grazing geese just above us. But there was a small gap in the fringe of gorse along the top edge of the bank, and there must have been a sentry-goose keeping watch at

The two black labradors did a wonderful job of retrieving

Quite the most impressive retrieve from water I have ever seen

this gap. At any rate we were spotted and the whole 300 or more took off before we were all in position.

One of the earlier drives was specially memorable. The geese were on a field next to a loch,

127

and again there was a steep bank at the edge of the field where it fell away to the loch. We lined the bottom of this bank — along the edge of the loch, and in due course the geese came slap over the guns. Six geese fell, mostly in the loch behind us, and the two black labradors of the Lancashire Lads did a wonderful job of retrieving. The last goose must have been the best part of 100 yards out, but the dog swam out and retrieved it faultlessly — quite the most impressive retrieve from water I have ever seen. By this time Keith and Ted were pulling their weight. Keith — by a smart piece of re-loading — got three geese out of the drive, and during the day Ted had at least one right-and-left. Myself was unlucky in having few geese over me during the day, and missed my chances when they came. I shot no geese all day. The total score for the day came to 21.

On our third and final day the Lancashire Lads had to depart at midday, and so they only had time for the dawn flight. The keepers had heard of a new area where geese had been feeding for several days, so we all lined the hedge of the most likely field and set up our decoys behind us. A strong flight developed as the dawn broke, and I got a good long shot at a single goose. We all had a share of the shooting, but I am convinced that six guns at a morning flight to a field is too many.

One can assume that as each skein approaches two guns will normally have a reasonable chance of fair shots. The other four guns will experience some sense of frustration as the skein climbs out of range and other approaching geese sheer off. With only three guns — the ideal number in my opinion — the ratio of "participation to frustration" is 2 : 1, as against 1 : 2 in the other case! So it was this morning. Nevertheless the exercise yielded 5 geese.

After that Keith, Ted and I were left to fill in the rest of the day with the same routine of search, find and drive. But the geese were still more elusive, both to find and to drive. We had one classic drive when the geese were driven through a saddle in the cliffs between the fields and the sea. But we shot badly and only Keith and I got one each, instead of the 5 or 6 we should have had between the three of us.

Then we found a tremendous concentration of geese well inland, and just above the scene of yesterday's anti-climax. We got fairly close to them behind a hedge, and then the whole 1,000 odd were put over us. This time we did a little better and collected four. The geese settled again a mile or so further on; we managed to drive them again, but this time they climbed higher and were out of shot. We followed them up yet again and came up with them a couple of miles further on. This time they just rose on the wind and never gave us the slightest chance.

We finished the day by driving a small long loch for wigeon. There were several hundred of them, but they all rose high in the wind and were out of range by the time they reached us at the far end. So ended the three days; the score of geese on this third day was 12, making 67 shot by the six guns in the three days.

Obviously the island has great possibilities, provided the shooting is controlled and limited to what the goose population in a limited area can stand. But Keith and I much prefer our original "Island of Geese", where the scenery is wilder, the shooting more natural and the accommodation simple and homely.

The remarkable thing about this new island is the expertise of the keepers, who know their ground so well and can arrange drives throughout the day so that geese almost invariably pass over the hidden guns — sometimes 4-500 yards away. Elsewhere there is usually a long gap between dawn and evening flight when there is nothing to do but make long range reconnaissance by car in the hope of finding new geese and planning the morrow's operations.

Here we were hard at it all day, moving into position and waiting for the geese to be put over us, then into the cars and repeating a similar process perhaps several miles away.

But this also meant that all the reconnaissance and planning were done for us, and this detracted somewhat from my own satisfaction with the results. I like to find my own geese, plan the method of dealing with them and then put the plan into operation — probably next day.

On this island the sport is more akin to pheasant or grouse shooting; it is goose-shooting rather than wildfowling.

On the Friday morning we were up early and catching the early ferry for our long drives home. Fortunately the weather was mild, though the hills across to Scotch Corner were white with snow. Rather than risk being held up by ice or fog I pressed on and got home to Catfield that evening — 440 miles in 10 hours non-stop.

CHAPTER 28
"MACANUDO"
(1969 — 1970 Luis' Year)

This winter we had booked the same period of goose-shooting as had proved so successful last year — on our new island. Four days' shooting were allowed — January 12th to 15th, so we had to leave Catfield on Saturday, January 10th, in order to catch our ferry on the Sunday.

This year, instead of Ted, the party was to include two business friends of mine from Spain, who I knew were keen on shooting and whom I had often asked to spend some time with us at Catfield in the shooting season. But, of course, general open invitations are not often taken up, so this year I offered them firm dates, firstly for a few days at Catfield, and then on to Scotland for our usual wildfowling trip.

To our great delight they accepted, but unfortunately they arrived during our coldest spell of the year, so that all our duck had departed, and we were only able to provide a very rough day with the pheasants, a few woodcock, and a couple of afternoons with the pigeons in the birch wood.

Worse still, the cold weather, on top of a tiring day's travel from Spain, which landed them at Catfield at 2.45 a.m. on the morning of the pheasant shoot, brought on a recurrence of the older man's heart trouble, and we had to leave him behind at Catfield till he was fit enough to return to Spain.

So Keith and I set off with the son — Luis — on a long tiring drive to Dumfriesshire, with mist on the road most of the way, and 366 miles on the clock by the time we stopped for the night. Next day worse was to come. Keith and I were both caught in a radar trap in a 30 m.p.h. limit — on a quiet sabbath morning in Scotland with the minimum of traffic about and no-one's person or property at risk.

Arrived at last on our island we found our companions of last season were again to complete the party of 6 guns, and had in fact already arrived. This year we re-christened them "The Bicycle Boys" as two of them were apparently engaged in the cycle trade in Preston. Our quarters also had changed. The sumptuous hotel had closed in January, and they had passed us on to a more modest establishment on the sea front which was really more appropriate for the occasion.

Next morning — Monday — the hunt started in earnest, and we were down in some grass fields near the coast awaiting the morning flight. We were some 3 or 4 fields inland from the edge of the bay where we met the morning flight last year. With a fresh wind off the land it was advisable not to wait too near the coast, or our first shots would have alerted all the geese still in the bay. The flight proved rather disappointing; only a few skeins came in to our fields, but thanks to a massive display of silhouette decoys put out by the Bicycle Boys, and their usual good marksmanship we collected 11 geese between us, of which Keith and Luis accounted for 3.

After that began the usual sequence of drives, most of them producing several geese, but with a few abortive ones in the middle of the day. Personally, I was shooting badly and after four fruitless long shots at the morning flight, I missed easy right and lefts at two drives after lunch. Only at the end of the day did my fortune and skill recover, and I ended up with 3 geese out of 4 shots at the last two drives. Keith and Luis, however, were in good form, and thanks to their contributions I think we accounted for half the total bag for the day — 42 greylags.

One incident in the day stands out. We had lined up between a bunch of geese and the head of Goose Bay, waiting for the geese to be put up and driven over us. The field where we waited had no cover except for a break in the ground where the field dropped steeply to a lower level. So we all crawled up to the crest of this small escarpment, and lay or knelt on the ground out of sight of the geese above us and in front of us. Just before the main drive started a single goose came flying in from the bay behind us. Luis saw it in time, and with the elegance of a matador rolled over on to his back and shot the goose from where he lay. In spite of the report the main body of geese came slap over us shortly afterwards, and we collected several more — I had one on the extreme right flank.

On the second day we divided forces for the morning flight, Keith, Luis and I going to the flat fields near the golflinks and putting out our 4 decoys behind us. The flight was disappointing, but a couple of geese came in early to Luis, and he got one while I got the other as it swung back to the coast over me. We got 2 more later but the flight soon eased off and we set out to join the others. We then had several excellent drives. At one a large pack of geese were moved off some grass fields in the centre of the island, and came over the whole line of us waiting behind a stone wall on the edge of a patch of moor. We collected 8 geese that time, each of us getting at least one. Later we stood in a plantation of young conifers and I got a very satisfying right and left, though we never found one of them in the dense undergrowth. Still later we found geese back on the fields at the head of Goose Bay : this time we lined the rough ground at the head of the beach, and again we all had geese over us and I got another right and left, both birds falling in the sea behind me. The second was a long way out, but the Bicycle Boys' retriever did another excellent job and brought the goose in. The total for the day was 38, and for once I think I did my share with 7 geese claimed.

A retrieve from Goose Bay

MACANUDO!

Goose Bay — after a drive

The third day opened with a fair amount of wind, and we had great hopes of a better morning flight. Our three guns went to Goose Bay and lay up behind a good thorn hedge two fields inland while the Bicycle Boys waited on higher ground to the left of the bay. But again the flight was disappointing; few skeins appeared on the **move**, though some early geese came in low and dropped into the fields in front of us. At last Keith went round on the flank to put them up, and a large bunch came straight for me, giving me an easy right and left. The drives during the middle of the day were not so successful; the geese were getting more wary, they were rising steeply on the wind, and were usually flying high and fast by the time they reached us. But we usually managed to collect one or two at each drive. To finish the day we tried driving a long narrow inland loch for duck. There was a causeway running across the centre of the loch, and we stood on this and waited for the keeper to start moving the duck at the far end. Several came over — at enormous height, and then in the dusk we heard two lots of geese come into the loch — to roost. In due course these too were put up and came over the causeway. Luis got his usual two, and I added a third — the others had no luck. Only 2 duck were shot but only 1 retrieved. Bag for the day — 15 geese and 1 duck.

On our fourth and last morning, Keith and I took Luis to try morning flight at the wigeon loch. This was another long narrow inland loch which always held hundreds of wigeon in the daytime, usually resting in large packs on the grassy slopes of the fields running down to the loch. It had always seemed to us that these duck must disperse over the island at night to feed, and must return at first light to their resting quarters. So we spread out along the side of the loch, and even as I sought my way to a suitable hedge for cover, I heard geese and a small skein swung round over me. For once I was caught unprepared — with an empty gun! But more geese could be heard, obviously roosting on the loch, and when the other two started shooting at the returning wigeon the geese took off and came towards my end of the loch. There was still little light, but just enough to see them and shoot, and I managed to drop one of them with the first shot.

Later on from time to time more geese could be heard on the move, and twice the distant shots from the other two were followed by dull thuds. In fact a good deal of shooting was going on, and it seemed that Keith and Luis were better placed for the wigeon than I. By the time the flight was over and it was fully daylight we found we had got a goose each and 17 wigeon between us.

We then set out to find the other three and to start our usual search for possible drives. After

131

their hammering over the past three days the geese were not so easy to find, but at last we found a nice lot on several grass fields overlooking Goose Bay.

Goose Bay is one of the most attractive parts of the island; admittedly due in some part to the fact that it always seems to hold geese! Shaped like a broad rather flat U the two sides slope up to high ground, but the head of the bay (the bottom of the U) ends in a shallow sandy beach running up to a strip of rough ground with a sandy track, and after that a wide deep flat valley. The valley runs back for the best part of a mile, and consists of large fields much liked by the geese. The geese we now found were on the higher ground on the left of the bay, and at first sight seemed to offer an easy drive. They would surely fly out to the bay when disturbed, and we had only to take up position between them and the coast. But further study showed that this would be extremely difficult, if not impossible. The slope of the rising ground was slightly concave, so that the geese looked down on everything between them and the bay. So it was more than doubtful if we could ever get into position unobserved. And then, as we watched and deliberated, four geese rose from the grazing gaggles and flew out over the bay. When safely over the water they swung righthanded towards the head of the bay and crossed the coast again to seek new grazing in the fields behind. But the keeper was quick to seize on this lead: he was convinced the main body of geese would follow the same "flight plan" when disturbed. So we drove on, parked the cars at a safe distance from operations, and lined the stone wall enclosing the first field from the beach-head. From there we could watch the whole operation. Half-left, and half a mile away on the sloping fields we could just make out the distant geese — a motley pattern of grey in the dull green grass. Meanwhile, the keeper had driven back past the geese and had set out on the usual long detour to bring him up behind them. It was some time before the quiet countryside erupted into action, and then at last a grey cloud of geese rose from the distant fields and headed out over the bay — exactly as anticipated. And sure enough, when safely over the water they started to swing round and head for the land again; and there we were, precisely on their course. Although the bay must be a good half mile wide and we could only cover about 200 yards, the keeper had placed us on exactly the right stretch of the beach to intercept the flight. On came the geese, flying at quite a low height over the safety of the water, so that as they reached land again they offered very fair shots. Luis got his usual right and left again, while Keith and I each got one. After that a couple of more difficult drives only produced one more goose before lunch, which we took on the shore of Goose Bay.

Another retrieve from Goose Bay

MACANUDO!

On the shore of Goose Bay. D. S. A. McD. — the Bicycle Boys — Luis

After lunch Keith left us; he had promised to look up a friend further north, so had to be driven back to our hotel to collect his car, pack his gear, and catch the last ferry to the mainland before sunset. By the time I had found the Bicycle Boys again they were just preparing for another big drive, and though we had another wonderful display of geese over us I completely failed to connect, though the others got several between them. Continuing the hunt the next find was a massive concentration of geese on some grass fields on high land above a line of cliffs. These must have been coastal cliffs ages ago, but the sea had since receded leaving a broad expanse of rough marshy ground at the foot of the cliffs before this met the present shore and the open sea beyond.

The set-up was exactly the same as that of the last drive on our first day last year — a drive which I missed, but which yielded 8 geese to the other five guns. This time I was determined to take part. So we all trooped off to the cliff-top, a safe half mile or so from the distant geese. But the prospect which awaited us at the edge of the cliff filled me with despair. I had assumed we should make our way along the top of the cliff under cover of the stone wall that bounded the fields, but apparently this was considered impracticable. The plan was to slither down to the foot of the cliff, make our way along the rough ground at the foot and then clamber up the cliff again when we had reached a point opposite the geese. Alas, my days of cliff-climbing are past, and I remained at the top with the keeper while we watched the others make their way along the foot of the cliff. Eventually they disappeared from sight round a projecting crag, and the keeper then set off on his long inland trek. By the time he got behind the geese he knew the guns would have got into position. I reckoned I had a good ten minutes to wait — so why not see how near I could get, working along the cliff top, between the stone wall and the edge of the cliff. It did not prove particularly difficult. At some points there were tricky patches to negotiate where dips in the ground or bends in the wall threatened to expose me to the watchful eyes of the geese, but a little care and a resort to hands and knees served to overcome these danger spots, and in the end I must have gained a good 200 yards. By now the geese were in the next field and my companions could not be much further along on my left. So I chose a firm stance behind the wall, found a chink in the stones through which I could keep an eye on the distant geese, and laid out a couple of spare cartridges on the wall.

There was still much time to spare; the geese were all busy grazing, heads down. Then at

133

last I saw all the heads go up — like umbrella handles, showing that the keeper had come into view on the inland side of them. As far as I was concerned everything now depended on how the geese behaved when they lifted. There was a steady wind off the land, so the geese were bound to take off inland — towards the keeper. They would then swing round to make their way out to sea. If they swung left-handed there was not a hope that any of them would come near me, but if they swung right-handed then there was a fair chance that some of those on the widest circle would pass over me where I waited far out on the right flank.

As the geese rose I saw there was indeed hope; they lifted half-right and in a few seconds it was clear they were swinging right-handed. With every succeeding moment it became even more certain that some of them must come my way. As always, my sense of excitement and climax became intense. There was just time to open the gun and check — for the n'th time — that it was loaded, a glance to see my spare cartridges were still on the ledge of stone, and then the whole long line of geese were overhead. They were at a good height, and with the wind now behind them there would only be about a second when any particular bird offered a fair shot. I picked a goose coming just left of me, gave it a long lead, and saw it crumple to the shot. I swung on to a second bird but already it was too far and I missed. But a glance inland showed that more geese were still coming; I just had time to reload and another wave of stragglers were over me. Again I picked a goose over my left shoulder, shot it, and again missed with the left barrel. Meanwhile, a fusillade had broken out on my left, and then when all the geese had departed and were far away out over the sea, figures appeared along the top of the cliff from behind the stone wall. Luis with his usual competence had got a right and left, and so had Bicycle Bob further along; the other two on the extreme left had no luck. Ironically enough the two left guns had found themselves nearest to the geese, and could see them (through the wall) within 30 or 40 yards. But in taking off into the wind and then swinging right-handed they had crossed the clifftop well to the right and hardly offered a fair shot.

Waiting for the others to rejoin me I looked down over the edge of the cliff to see if I could spot my two geese. There, far below and a long way back, lay two grey bundles on the marsh; so similar had been the two shots that the birds lay within a few yards of each other. So we came back to the farmyard and the cars with six more geese.

There was only time for one more drive that afternoon and it was not half so spectacular. We stood below the geese who flew into the wind and therefore came over at a great height. I tried two long shots without success, but Luis on my right brought down a goose from a terrific height — with his last cartridge fired at the last drive on the last day: truly a fitting finale to a sparkling performance throughout the four days. This brought our score for this last day to 23 geese — an unexpectedly high figure, and our bag for the whole trip to 118 geese and 19 duck.

The number of geese looks uncomfortably large, but with 6 guns it averages just under five geese per day per gun; not an excessive number in itself, and less than we have often achieved under freelance conditions on the mainland, though admittedly we do not often maintain such a score for four days running.

But the outstanding feature of this trip was the company and performance of our friend from Spain. Advance intelligence had satisfied us that he was an experienced and expert shot, but no-one could say how he would react to our type of winter shooting. Long days from before dawn to dusk, a good deal of walking, a lot of waiting in ditches or behind walls, and comparatively little actual shooting. A few shots perhaps at morning flight, but for the rest of the day it was seldom that one had the chance to get off more than two shots at the driven skeins.

Our accommodation was simple, the food plain, and the beds hard (by Luis' standards). All this in the depth of winter in Scotland. We hesitated to think what Luis was used to with his large-scale partridge shooting in the warmth of a Spanish autumn, and with the support of what we imagined must be something like a feudal organisation. But we had no need to have felt qualms. Luis entered into the spirit of our sport with enthusiasm, and apparently found no difficulty in adapting his skill to the challenge of wildgeese. Using an ordinary game gun with 2½ inch cartridges and BB shot he started knocking geese out of the sky from the first morning, and established a reputation for "right-and-lefts" which none of us could match. He must have shot far more geese than anyone else in the party — probably well over 30, and thanks to his contribution our trio more than held their own with the redoubtable Bicycle Boys. As to his personal company, I can only record that very early in the proceedings I said to him — "Luis, I am not treating you as a guest: you are one of us".

And so back to Catfield: the early ferry, the long slog home, and home again within the week. It had truly been "macanudo"! *

*"Macanudo"— a colloquial and expressive Spanish word from the Argentine signifying that the matter in question is fine — excellent — superb. American equivalent — "swell". Trendy English equivalent — "fab" (fabulous).

CHAPTER 29
BACK TO THE OLD ROUTINE
(1970 — 1971)

A good deal of heart-searching took place before we made up our minds about this winter's expedition. I was greatly tempted to return to our new island, where we would be assured of plenty of geese, many encounters with them, and no doubt a considerable bag to show for our efforts. But these attractions were offset by other considerations. In the first place both Keith and I missed the satisfaction of working out our own plans; too much was in the hands of the keepers, who organised each day's operations and masterminded each manoeuvre: it was all made too easy for us. And even the size of the bag was becoming an embarrassment. Some years ago I read a report of a party of guns who slew over 100 geese at one single morning flight. This was on a large preserved estate which I know, and I can well imagine how such a thing took place. I well remember my feelings of disgust that any party of sportsmen could allow a morning's shoot to extend to such extremes, and my sense of contempt for the correspondent who considered such an achievement a matter to write and boast about. But last year our party of 6 guns collected over 100 geese, not at one morning flight it is true, but as the accumulated reward for continuous effort that extended through all the hours of daylight of four pretty strenuous days. Nevertheless we were not too happy about it all, and for the first time we were hard pressed to dispose of the 30 odd geese which we brought home as our share.

Another feature which detracted somewhat from our uninhibited enjoyment of the trip, was the fact that we had to team up with another party of 3 guns, making 6 in all. Six is, in any case, too many for a wildfowling trip, and if three of them are not of one's own choosing the disadvantage is all the greater, however congenial one's companions may prove.

And finally the question of cost had become more serious; not easily to be brushed aside. For the past two years the estate in question had quoted a fee (per gun per day) which included hotel accommodation as well as the shooting, and the services of two keepers with their Land Rovers. This year the fee had been increased but was to exclude any accommodation, so that our brief holiday would be anything but cheap! What a contrast to the "good old days". Before the war, a weekend's fowling would cost me £1. 5s. 0d. for accommodation and meals, and immediately after the war the rooms that "BB" and I took with "Auntie Tares" cost us 8/-d. per day each, all meals included, and the use of our own large dining-cum-sitting room. Nowadays, accommodation at quite modest country hotels, in the heart of winter, costs anything between £2 and £3 for bed and breakfast alone.

So in the end we turned our backs on the temptations of the island and decided to work the mainland again; and as conditions are now so uncertain in our old haunts we arranged to try a new area in the far north.

Ted was to make the third member of the party, and as both he and Keith could only spare a bare week of holiday, they arranged to travel north by sleeper on one Saturday and return the same way .the following weekend. I was to take the car up by easy stages and meet them off their train on the Sunday morning.

Meanwhile, the usual Christmas hazards developed. A streaming cold went through the household and overtook me a few days before zero hour on January 5th, and at the same time freezing fog and icy roads spread across the country. This was all very irritating and no doubt increased the restlessness I always feel shortly before setting forth on my annual northbound migration. It seems to me that this is another case where human beings often acquire some similarity — in appearance or character — to another species of the animal kingdom in which they are particularly interested. We all know the fishmonger with pop eyes, pallid complexion and sloping shoulders, who begins to look like the large codfish on his slab; or the naturalist with the long neck and beaklike nose who reminds one irresistibly of the bittern on which he is an acknowledged authority. So, I fear, my restlessness matches that of the grey geese as they approach, each autumn, the moment of final decision that launches them on their marathon flight from Greenland or Iceland to Scotland.

The family started making discouraging noises — "You can't set out with the roads like this", and "You're not fit to travel with a cold like that", and when one faintly protested that there was no need to take a decision till the last minute, there came muttered remarks to the effect that "You can't do anything with him; he's so obstinate" or "Leave him alone, he's got goose fever".

So the Obstinate One waited till the last minute, found his cold much better, and was assured by the A.A. that although there was freezing fog and icy patches all up the east side of England to Scotch Corner, it would soon clear. And clear it did; very little trouble by Dereham, only slight mist by King's Lynn and clear sunshine by Newark — sunshine that shone on a fairyland of bright hoar frost covering every branch of every tree and hedge in dazzling white tracery. So an easy run brought me to my first staging post — with Betty in Newcastle. Next day was easier and shorter still — to Jim and Nellie, with a call in Edinburgh to find Peter and Elaine's new flat. Peter, of course, was out at work, but I was lucky to find Elaine at home and luckier still to be persuaded to stay for lunch.

With time in hand to reach my ultimate destination, I had always hoped to fit in one or two sorties on the way north, and so a session on the telephone at Jim's produced a couple of promising prospects for the next two days. But first of all Jim had arranged a morning in the Carse of Forth for the next day, and so I found myself as dawn was breaking, somewhere very near the fields where we had waited for the pinkfeet under the moon many years ago. In fact, I could well have been on the same farm — even on the same large grass field. But this time few geese were in the Moss and we only saw three skeins coming out — very high and quite out of range — so we packed up at about 10 a.m. and went home.

After lunch I took to the road again, and made my way to David to try the evening flight along his valley. A new problem faced me; the river was in spate and it was impossible to reach the usual stand by the river wall as the adjoining field was flooded, and in places under several feet of water. But the next field seemed more promising, and proved to be a potato stubble, trampled flat with the innumerable paddle marks of geese! So it was by the edge of this field I waited as the light began to fade. Geese could be heard up and down the valley, and skeins were soon on the move, though mostly going away further upstream. At last a bunch came straight over me, and I picked the leader. He showed no sign of being even touched, and I fired again at another bird in the skein. Again no result, and I was cursing my incompetence when I realised that a goose was in fact falling out of the sky! Obviously I was not giving enough lead to my shots, and had killed a bird further back in the V! Anyhow, it was a cheering start to the trip — a goose with the first two shots. A little later a single bird came in low to the field and gave me an easy shot. That was all — and quite enough for the hard slog up the hill to David's house where I had left the car. After a rest, a drink and a chat, on to my third staging post by the Dark Estuary.

Next morning I had been allowed a flight on the Laird's estate. I picked up the under-keeper at 8.15 and together we made our way to that wonderful stretch of grass fields alongside the estuary. Even in the dark we could see that the fields were smothered with fresh goose droppings, the white ends showing up like faint daisies on the grass. We chose the corner of a plantation of young conifers as the best cover to use, and crouched down between the small trees; the decoys placed out on the grass in front of us. As daylight brightened geese began to move, but they seemed very unsettled and took little notice of the decoys. A single pink came in at last and offered an easy shot, but though I hit it hard with both barrels it carried on and we could not see if or where it fell in the poor light. It was, however, picked up next day. It was clear to me that the presence of the keeper and his yellow labrador wasn't helping the problem of concealment, and at last I tactfully persuaded him to set out and move any geese that had settled in distant fields. In the end this resulted in some 300 geese joining up in a large mob and settling near the decoys — but just too far out. So they moved on again unscathed by my two shots. The keeper soon returned and reported that geese were strongly attracted to a field of winter wheat two farms further on. So it was a case of up-sticks, into the car and away to this other farm where we re-set the decoys on the wheat, and again lay up in a plantation of conifers. Sure enough a bunch of pinks came along and eventually settled well out of range on the adjoining ploughed field. With them were a couple of dark-necked light-breasted geese, which I could only think must be brents. Then a smaller lot of greys circled in and landed just beyond the decoys on the wheat. They were barely in range, but as I waited they began grazing towards me. After a while — and not knowing where the keeper was or when he might appear — I decided it was a case of "now or never". So with a couple of BB cartridges I took the first shot "sitting" and the second as they rose. One huge greylag was left dead on the ground, and the distance I found was only 58 yards so I might well have got a second. By now it was midday, leaving just time for a brief call on the Laird and a report on the morning's events, and then back to base for lunch.

In the afternoon I drove back to David's for another evening flight down by the river, but though many geese were again on the move, most waited till it was too dark for me to see them before coming in to the potato field, and I hardly fired a shot.

Next morning I was on the road again and reached our final destination in the far north in time for a quick recce of the district by car. It looked attractive; a bay on one side reputed to hold 6-700 pinks, an inland loch said to hold 1,200 greylags, and another estuary on the far side of the peninsular which certainly used to hold geese, and which also has a reputation for duck. I had not been in these parts for over 30 years, and now spent much of my spare time seeking the scene of that memorable stalk with my brother Tony in 1937/38 ("Just in Case"). I found it at last and re-lived again that exciting morning with nostalgic enjoyment.

Keith and Ted arrived next morning, and on our way back to the hotel from the station I showed them a large concentration of Whooper Swans I had found yesterday in a field alongside one of the roads. I had counted 177 of them, and for the next two days we often heard their musical "whooping" as they flew over the bay. After lunch we did another extended recce by car, taking the hotel "guide" with us, but found little to encourage us. One small party of geese on the farm where the hotel had the shooting rights; a few skeins of greys dropping into the inland loch at dusk, and nothing moving under the moon later that night.

The following day did little to revive our hopes. We waited for the geese at dawn on the hotel farm but none came, nor did we see any on the move except for one small lot. In the afternoon we tried the rough shooting attached to the hotel, of which they claimed to have several thousand acres; all we saw were two pheasants and a hare, and managed to reduce the pheasants by 50%! In the evening we drove across to the other firth and tried for a duck on the coast, but none of us saw anything. I was becoming convinced that the area had been overshot, and that in any case most of the geese had left the district. We decided to give it one more chance, but that if prospects did not improve next morning we would pack up and leave.

So at dawn again we were out to await the geese, this time on the foreshore of the bay. I dropped Keith and Ted to make their way to the mouth of the river, and took myself further on to the seawall at the head of the bay. I was hardly in position when I heard two double shots from the direction of the rivermouth, and hoped it was Keith and Ted in action. For myself, I saw no sign of geese except for one very high skein, but when I collected the other two at 10 a.m. I was pleasantly surprised to see them waving a goose as they came across the field from the shore. Apparently they had stumbled on a party of greys at the mouth of the river and managed to down one as they jumped. But this was not enough to keep us any longer; after lunch we packed our gear and headed south to our old familiar hunting grounds. After finding accommodation for the boys at a hotel (which proved expensive and unsuitable) I made my way to Robert and Shelagh's who had insisted I should stay with them on my next visit.

So, next morning, it was back to the old routine — dawn flight on the Dark Estuary. There sounded plenty of goosetalk out in front of us as we reached the edge of the mud, but when the geese began to move they either flew up river or away to the other side of the firth. One very high skein did come in right over me — far out of range — and then another lot came in at possible height, but exactly between Keith and myself, so that they were just beyond reach for either of us. By 11 it was no use waiting any longer and we tramped back to the car with clean guns. A regular paperchase of spent cartridge cases along the seawall confirmed the reports of excessive shooting in the district, and the sprawl of empty beer tins, cigarette packets and other junk at the end of the road where their cars are parked, gave a depressing indication of the litter-louts who now try their hand at wildfowling.

Keith and Ted dropped me off at Robert's for lunch (and then a spell of Egyptian P.T.) while they went over the hills to recce further afield. We joined up again in the afternoon and this time I left them down on the coast for the evening flight while I went on to see the Laird and beg another morning's assault on his grass fields. The Laird was laid up with some indisposition but Patrick nobly offered all facilities, and I at once went on to contact the keepers to warn them of the morrow's encounter. So although the day had been a blank one, prospects now looked better again, and were further improved when Keith similarly arranged a repeat visit to David for the morrow's evening flight.

In the morning we divided our forces as usual on this extensive stretch of goose fields. I made for the same plantation of young firs as I had used last week, not expecting too much of it on this return visit. Keith moved further on to the corner of the young wood where Patrick shot his first goose ten years ago. Ted went off with the keeper to some cover further upriver. It was dull, still and overcast as the light began to appear and the geese began moving up from the estuary soon after 9. Large and numerous skeins came swinging along the grass fields, but mostly high up and in no apparent hurry to settle. At last two skeins came low enough to give me a goose out of each. Then the geese started dropping into a distant ploughed field, and before long some 200 must have collected there. I felt sure the keeper must have seen this, and would take steps to move the geese who were of no use to anyone where they were; and if they flew out to the shore there was a strong chance they would pass over either me or Keith. Sure enough, after a tantalising wait the whole mob rose like a grey cloud, and headed straight for me. It was very like the cliff-top drive on our last day last year. As the long line passed over me I stood up and took the first bird slightly to my left front, and the second over my left shoulder. There was just time to reload and take a third goose out of the second line. In the lull that followed I went over to Keith and persuaded him to change places with me, as he seemed to be having no sport. No sooner were we both settled in our new hides than a skein came over me and gave me another goose, and before long Keith got two from my old position. When the flight eased off we packed up and rejoined Ted who had had few chances and no success, though plenty of geese had passed his way. We fell to speculating how many geese we had seen that morning — at least 1,000; though if there were no duplication of the same skeins passing and repassing it could well be 3,000, and they were all pinks. It had certainly been a grand sight and the shooting also had been satisfying; all at high birds in full flight. My own six geese had only cost me ten cartridges so I was particularly pleased with myself.

In the afternoon we sped over the hills again in the hope of finding something for the morrow, and also to contact a new farm we had heard about, but nothing hopeful turned up. By then it was time to press on to David's for another evening flight at the potato field.

When we arrived the field already held a hundred or more geese. These departed as we approached, and then we waited for the light to fail and for the geese to return. Presently a tremendous evening flight developed, skein after skein moving up and down the valley; some circling our field and a few hesitating at the sight of our decoys, but the geese were more wary, flew higher and offered very few chances. In the end Keith got three and I managed to shoot two out of late skeins that came in rather lower with the last of the daylight. Ted again was out of luck. As we staggered up the hill to the car with all our gear, decoys and dead geese, we could hear geese coming back to the field and settling in it, and we were tempted to stay on and try our luck under the moon. But the cloud cover was rather too thick and we reckoned we had already had a full day and had taken sufficient toll of the geese. As in the morning we must have been in the thick of anything between 1,000 and 3,000 geese, depending on the degree of duplication: this time they were all greys. What a splendid day it had been!

BACK TO THE OLD ROUTINE

The morrow did not look so promising. With nothing prepared and no discovery of any geese on accessible farms the other two decided to take their chance over the hills — on the well-proved flight line along the burn that flows past Mongi's farm. I could not raise sufficient enthusiasm to join them, and chose instead a lie-in and a leisurely breakfast. They returned mid-morning with news of few geese seen and nothing in the bag except a lone mallard.

So we came to our last outing and yet another evening flight at David's potato field. I found a good thick thorn bush by the river and waited for the flight to start. We could hardly expect it to be so impressive as the previous night, but a good lot of geese were still in the valley, and there was plenty of movement between about 5 and 6 p.m. At last a skein came over me and though I thought at first that I had missed, I saw a goose peel off from the formation and glide away to the left. A few moments later it suddenly collapsed and fell to earth, but far across the river. A little later exactly the same happened to a single bird, and I realised I must change my position. A wild goose is too noble a quarry to be left to the crows and gulls, and in any case one hates leaving shot game — even if one is confident they are dead. So I moved a good 100 yards from the river and went back to the edge of the potato field. There was now not much activity, though an occasional shot still came from Keith or Ted. I began to think it was all over, and then a couple of shots from the others heralded the arrival of another skein and the possibility that it might come on to me. I was doubtful whether I should be able to see it, and then I just caught sight of half a dozen dark blobs out in front of me — fairly far out but not too high. I aimed well in front of what seemed the nearest blob, and as I swung on to a second one I could just see the first blob falling. A few seconds later a reassuring smack told me the goose had hit a patch of flood water.

This seemed a very satisfactory moment at which to end the evening — and the whole trip. I made my way to the others at the far end of the field, found they had collected another two geese, and so we all trudged up the hill once more, back to the car, the usual refreshment and a spell of relaxation at the house, and then the homeward journey. Keith and Ted took the night sleeper to London, while I took the car — with its load of geese — home via the usual stages. It had certainly been a good trip with a reasonable but not excessive bag, and every goose well earned and well shot. The far north had been disappointing, but our old haunts better than we had expected.

One incident is worth recording. On one of the mild clear days of the trip we were standing on the coast watching a skein of about 30 geese flying out over the bay. They flew on, high and steady, right across the water to the far side and then over the ridge of the distant peninsular towards the open sea beyond. I could see them till they disappeared over the ridge and dropped behind the crest. Checking with the map afterwards it was very nearly six miles from the point where we stood to the highest contour of the peninsular. So one can see a skein of geese with the naked eye for a distance of certainly 5 miles in conditions of good visibility!

It would be interesting to know what the corresponding distance is for the sound of geese in flight — in still air. I'm sure it must be several miles.

What incredible organs of perception are the human eye and ear.

140

CHAPTER 30
TWO LUCKY RETRIEVES
(1971 — 1972 Peter's Year)

Keith and I found that the middle of December suited us both for our annual shooting holiday on the trail of the wild geese. Our choice of dates was fortunate, in that we just missed the spell of mist and fog which affected most of the country earlier in the month, and which would have made travelling most unpleasant.

At the last minute Keith could not get away at the weekend, and the third member of our party dropped out, so I took the car up north on my own and arrived at the centre of operations on Sunday, December 12th.

Our friend the local Laird had already offered us a morning on his goose farms, so I called on his keeper that evening to glean the latest information. It was not encouraging. There were very few geese about, though there had been plenty until a week or two ago. It appears the large flocks of pinkfeet here changed their habits. They used to disappear for a few weeks in the New Year and return later: now they move away before Christmas and return in the New Year. So last season — in January — we found plenty; this season we could expect very few in December. Anyhow, I arranged to put this all to the test on Tuesday morning.

Next day — Monday — I was down on the coast to see what the estuary held. A clear bright dawn enabled me to see anything coming inland over several miles of the coast. And I only saw three skeins: two that came slap over me at "Goose's Graveyard" but at a safe two gunshots high, and a third that came in a good mile to my left. So there was nothing left but to spend the rest of the day on the usual long-range reconnaissance — to find geese and lay plans for the future.

First to the Laird's ground to see if there were in fact any geese there at all. All I could find was one small lot of greys in one of the usual grass fields. Then over the hills to the area of Mongi's farm, which seldom fails to produce geese. But not a sign could I find, either on the ground or on the move in the sky. A call at the farm confirmed that there had been no geese about for the past fortnight.

Still further on in the next valley I at last found geese, but mostly on preserved estates where visiting fowlers are not welcomed. But there is one small property in this area where I knew I would be allowed access, and it seemed worth inspecting. It borders the river and includes a few small flat fields which might attract geese. Sure enough, as I reached these fields down a farm track I almost walked on to a bunch of greylags. They were feeding on a potato stubble, and the next field was the same, with a drainage ditch running between them down to the river. This was promising, and I mentally reserved this place for dawn on Wednesday morning.

The next area to inspect was 20 miles away in a completely different area, so it was a case of a brief call at base for lunch and then off again to inspect the distant valley. A call on the local shooting tenant and his gamekeeper secured access to a long stretch of the valley on one

141

side of the river, and an inspection from the road disclosed several parties of greylags on various grass fields all along the valley. This looked more promising, and should provide a good evening flight down by the river later in the week. For the present — and with an hour or so of daylight left — I decided to try another stretch of the river and see if I could intercept any geese as they took a short cut across one of its bends.

A roadway ran down to a farm on the very bank of the river, and in a grass field on the left was a little party of 5 greylags. The field was undulating and halfway down to the farmyard I found myself in dead ground with the geese out of sight behind some rising ground. A stalk looked possible! Leaving the car out of sight I came up the blind side of the rise, and as I topped the crest there were the geese out in front of me. It looked a long shot and a remote chance, but with no-one to criticise or reproach me I could not resist the temptation. I aimed just above the head of the nearest goose as it lifted into the wind, and it fell back to the ground stone dead. I was so surprised I didn't even fire my second barrel. Stepping out the distance as I went forward to collect the goose, I made it exactly 70 yards, and the goose had stopped at least two pellets; one in the head and one in the body. I was using No. 3 shot, and this incident made me wonder whether I should modify my-views on shot sizes and forget all about BB in future.

By now it was time to take up a position by the river. It was another grass field which filled the bend in the river, and a few geese were grazing on the far (inland) side of it, with more on the field beyond, and still larger concentrations collecting in fields on the other side of the valley. Presently a skein came swinging down the valley and crossed the river just in front of me. A long high shot brought a goose down with a thump out on the field. Then a single goose came flying back in the opposite direction and I had to take him early before he got too close to the river. He came down alright but only winged, and before I could get within range of him he picked himself up and scrambled half flying half running over the bank and into the river. This looked pretty hopeless: I lost sight of him swimming upstream, but there is always a chance that a wounded goose, if left to itself, will make for the bank or shore. So I followed up along the riverbank, into the next field, and sure enough after a couple of hundred yards the goose fluttered out of some rough ground. But again he made the river before I could catch up with him. There was only one answer — a shot to finish him off in the water. So there was my goose, floating slowly downstream, only a few yards from the bank, but quite out of reach. The water was deep under the nearside bank and I would have been up to my neck with the first step. Nor was I prepared to swim for it! I could only follow the goose downstream hoping it might drift into the bank, and all the time looking out for a long stick with which to reach it if it came much closer. In desperation I pressed on ahead of the goose, searching for a branch amongst all the patches of flotsam lining the edge of the water. And at last I found it, a lovely knarled branch about 7 feet long, barkless and worn smooth with continual pounding by the river. I seized it thankfully and turned back to see how the goose was faring. At first I could see no sign of it, and then I saw it close in under the bank. In a moment the stick held it firmly against the little cliff, and by lying flat on my stomach I could reach the goose and haul it out on to the grass. What a lucky retrieve!

After that I returned to my stand behind a bush, and presently another skein came along and offered another chance very much like the first one. Again I got a goose with my shot, dead and safe out in the field. The light had now nearly gone so I packed up and made my way back to the car. A discouraging morning had turned into a most interesting and successful evening, with four geese in the boot of the car.

That night my nephew Peter arrived from the south to spend Tuesday with me. I collected him from his hotel at 6.30 next morning, and handed him over to the Laird's gamekeeper, who in turn took him to a potato stubble that the geese had been working. For myself I chose the next farm where I had seen a few greys on the grass field. I had a couple of decoys to place out on the grass, and took cover in a plantation of fir trees (the same stand that Keith had used last year, and which Patrick and I had shared 10 years earlier when the trees were only shoulder high).

Very few geese were to be seen or heard, but as the dawn broke numerous hares became active in the grass field around my plantation. They all seemed paired up, and began indulging in playful chasing and circling all over the field. Several times one or two of them would lope up to within a few yards of me where I waited in the corner of the wood. I stood perfectly still, and though they obviously saw me they showed no alarm till I moved or made a noise.

At last a few geese turned up, but would not come near the wood. One lot landed well beyond the decoys and I had to fire a shot to move them lest they attracted later arrivals beyond my reach. Then a skein of greys dropped into a field of winter wheat on the other side of the wood, and a second lot soon joined them. They were quite unapproachable, grazing safely at least 100 yards from any fence or ditch. The only chance lay in the fact that my plantation lay between them and the coast. If I could alarm them without showing myself they would probably swing back to the estuary and might pass close enough to offer a chance. So I fired a shot up through the fir trees and quickly reloaded. The geese lifted into the wind and at once swung round towards the coast. They seemed just in range so I took a shot at the nearest bird. He came tumbling down, but only winged like the goose last night. He landed out on the grass and at once made for the fence enclosing the plantation, then started to work his way along it. I could not possibly catch up with him through the jungle on the inside of the fence, so precious moments were lost while I negotiated the barbed wire fence and got out on to the grass.

By then there was no sign of the goose! The post and wire fence had a run of small-mesh wire netting along the bottom 2 or 3 feet — no doubt to keep out hares and rabbits when the trees were young; so I could not see how the goose could have got into the plantation. So he must be legging it across the grass field, heading for the river. But the field was flat and close grazed with no cover for a goose to hide in, and a quick cast round the field drew blank. So I was forced to the conclusion that the goose must somehow have got into the plantation. In that case I had a problem on my hands — to find a wounded goose in a dense 2 acre block of young fir trees. It was now full daylight, the morning flight, such as it was, was over; I could now concentrate on a methodical search of the plantation. Fortunately the dense canopy overhead suppressed practically all other vegetation under the trees, and by walking across the planted lines one could see several yards to right and left down each line in turn. And so at last I found my goose. He had reached the very centre of the wood, and there expired, his wings outstretched. He looked remarkably large in such unusual surroundings, and his clean grey plumage shone out bright and clear, and very pale, against the dark carpet of pine needles.

Apart from the usual satisfaction of recovering a wounded bird, I was glad that I had at least spared this one the indignity of providing a meal for the first passing fox. Another lucky retrieve!

Peter, alas, had no luck in his potato field; no geese came over and he never had a chance of a shot. But his turn was to come that evening.

It was 10.30 a.m. when we got back for breakfast and before we could organise any other excursion it was time for an early lunch at 12.30 p.m. and then we were on our way to the distant valley that had produced such pleasant results for me the previous evening. This time we went to the well-proved stand a mile further up the river, where we have experienced so many excellent flights over the years. It is curious how the flight line of the geese up and down the valley seems to concentrate on this gap of a mere 200 yards between a line of trees on the "inland" side, and the old riverbank on the other. Yet the floor of the valley must itself be nearly a mile wide at this point. One can only suppose the geese follow certain landmarks, and these lead them inevitably along a narrow flight path.

By now the weather was worsening; storm clouds were sweeping up from the west and the wind was freshening to half a gale — all very promising. I left Peter in the centre of the gap, where he found some cover amongst clumps of rushes, and took up my own stand by the old river wall. Quite early a huge mob of 1,000 or more geese lifted from the fields across the river and swung past on their way to their roost on some inland loch. Then there was a pause and the real flight only got underway as the light began to fade. Skein after skein came up the valley, battling into the wind and keeping at a reasonable height. Peter was in the thick of it, and was getting plenty of shooting. Out on his right I did not get so much, and I seemed to be shooting as badly on this occasion as I had shot well 24 hours previously. In the end I had collected 2 geese, and when I joined Peter I found he had got 8 with at least another one to find. (In fact we found 2 more of Peter's next day.) Altogether it was quite one of the best evening flights I have ever experienced, and I know Peter set off on his homeward journey with every reason to be satisfied with his day's goose shooting.

When I got back to my own base that evening Keith had already arrived to take Peter's place, and to stay with me for the rest of the week.

Next morning we set out for the two potato fields down by the other river. It was nearly 20 miles away, and we left it rather late, for even as we set up our decoys we could hear geese on the move. We scrambled for the cover of the ditch and had hardly reached it when a skein loomed into view. Keith dropped a goose with his first shot and then we both had several chances over the next hour. I was shooting badly again, and only managed to get one, but Keith fared better, and collected three. It was a promising and spectacular flight with parties of geese leaving the river and setting forth for their feeding grounds to all points of the compass. Most of them went out over high ground in front of us, but enough came our way to provide an exciting and profitable morning.

For the evening we decided to repeat the previous day's programme. It isn't often one can repeat with success a previous day's morning or evening flight, but there were so many geese in this other valley, and they seemed so strongly drawn to a regular pattern in their evening flight, that we decided to lie in wait for them again. In the event conditions repeated themselves with great similarity. Strong winds developed, storm clouds raced across the sky, and the same mob of 1,000 geese lifted early from across the river and made off for the safety of their loch. Keith and I covered the same gap on the line of flight, and in due course a wonderful flight developed. This time I had my full share of the shooting and seemed to have recovered my form. After getting two single birds out of early skeins I had a good right and left at a pair of geese, and a little later a large skein came along and gave me another right and left. That made my quota of 6 for the evening, and though I was sorely tempted to wait for more, I resolutely unloaded my gun and put it away in its canvas cover. I moved along to Keith to see how he was getting on, and with the last of the light another skein came battling along and Keith got one out of it, making his fourth for the evening.

That marked the end of the first part of our trip. With 31 geese in three shooting days it far exceeded our expectations — now, with the car already packed with all our gear we moved on to a completely new area and reached our little hotel in time for a welcome evening meal.

A long stretch of the coastal strip and much of the higher land behind belonged to one estate, and we had been allowed three days shooting over it — for geese only.

We met the keeper at 7 a.m. next morning and he directed us to a field on the coastal strip where geese had been feeding on a potato stubble. We put out our decoys in the field, lined a wall on the downwind side, and awaited the dawn and the arrival of the geese. One small lot came in early on and Keith got one of them, but several skeins rose high into the wind and went streaming over the hills to distant feeding grounds. At last a skein of a dozen or so came skimming over the ground in front of us — like a covey of huge partridges in line abreast. With instinctive caution they lifted high to clear the wall between them and the potato field, but not high enough.

I was feeling very pleased with my right and left only to find that Keith had also fired at — and claimed — the second bird. So it was 1½ each for the morning!

For the rest of the day we toured the countryside trying to find other "feeds", and at last found a large concentration on a grass field up on the high ground. But the keeper said we could not go after them — others had the rough shooting rights there. This was extremely frustrating; we had been given to understand we should have the run of the whole estate, and had chosen our dates so as not to clash with the owner's pheasant shoots. To find oneself in competition with another party on the same ground, after the same game, and at the same time, was quite inexcusable, and we took a very poor view of the confusion which allowed such a state of affairs to arise.

That evening, on the phone, I left the factor in no doubt as to our views.

Next morning, with so few geese working the low ground, we tried to intercept the skeins which flighted over the hills to more distant fields. There were apparently well established flight lines where the geese passed over gaps or saddles in the range of hills. The keeper produced a Land Rover and took us up to one of these gaps, where we waited hopefully. There was still a strong wind — a chill piercing one, and with a 10/10 covering of cloud conditions looked promising.

But only a few small skeins attempted this particular passage of the hills. Two or three managed to make it and battled their way over the crest — but well to my left. Others struggled along for a while and then gave up as they met the full force of the wind and swung back to the estuary. It was curious to be able to look down on formations of flying geese struggling upwards towards me; their light shoulders (they were greylags) looking almost white against the dark ploughed fields below them.

So we returned to breakfast empty handed and with clean guns — to find a message from the factor offering us an evening flight at a duckpond up in the hills.

This was indeed a generous gesture, and some compensation for the confusion over the goose shooting. We accepted readily, and after spending the rest of the day in a fruitless search for accessible geese we met at the duck pond at 3.30 p.m. It proved a grand flight; mallard and teal hurtling in at great height and speed, and offering very tricky shooting. We ended up with 15 mallard, 5 teal and a shoveller, most of which fell to Keith, though the few successful shots I had were real screamers and made up in quality for what I missed in quantity.

We had already decided there was little point in staying on for our last and third day. The car was already packed, so we set our faces homewards after the flight; reached Newcastle that night and had an easy run home on Saturday with fine weather and dry roads.

CHAPTER 31
CRUELTY IN SHOOTING

Shooting, like other field sports, is continually subject to the attacks and criticisms of the "anti" brigade.

In spite of the general dismissal of this opposition as the rather hysterical reaction of a crank minority, one should not ignore it, nor belittle its possible effect on large numbers of people who have no first hand experience of field sports in question.

Moreover, I am sure that for their own peace of mind most shooting men must have searched their own consciences and satisfied themselves that their own particular sport is an acceptable form of recreation. Certainly I have often pondered over the issues and arguments involved, and I can only say that I still set out for a day's shooting with a clear conscience and with the same anticipation of pleasure as I did in my earliest days, when a boy's mind was not even aware of these higher moral questions. So let us try and sort out the issues and arguments.

In the first place, there is the extreme view that mankind should not take the life of humbler creatures, but this of course is such a complete refusal to accept the basic facts of man's existence on earth that it need not be taken seriously. Man is, in fact, by nature and evolution carnivorous and his normal and natural diet includes the meat of lesser creatures. He is, in fact, the supreme predator on earth and preys — for food — on the beasts of the field, the fowls of the air and the fishes of the sea. He must, of necessity, take the lives of those creatures he requires for food.

Rather more plausible, at first sight, is the argument that man should at least not kill for sport. This issue has obvious emotional overtones. The sports concerned are "smeared" with the description of "Blood Sports", and the image sometimes suggested is of bloodthirsty sadists glorying in the slaughter of helpless beasts and birds, and enjoying any spectacle of pain or distress that arises. I would be the first to admit that there is a streak of cruelty in many of us; a touch of original sin perhaps. It seems to show up in childhood when little boys in particular are sometimes guilty of very unpleasant behaviour towards kittens, small birds and other lesser creatures. But we seem to grow out of it with age and education and the example of our elders, and in adult life the British character is more noted for its excessive sentimentality towards animals.

How then is this to be reconciled with the tremendous following of shooting as a sport — and even more so of fishing — where the end result is a dead bird or fish?

I am quite sure that the answer lies in a very strong "hunting" instinct that persists in us, and which is a relic of the time when man simply had to go out and seek his meat by catching a beast, bird or fish.

Now, under the organisation of modern civilisation man's requirements of meat are provided for him by a specialist section of the community — the livestock farmers, who breed, rear and slaughter in their countless thousands the special breeds of animals and birds that they have domesticated and improved for that purpose over the centuries. And the great majority of us are therefore left with a basic instinct very largely thwarted. No wonder so many of us take deliberate steps to find some outlet for it. Those steps take us to the fields of shooting and fishing.

Here we are fortunate (in this and many other countries) in finding a natural population of game birds and game fish which provide a natural outlet for our hunting instincts, a challenge to our skills, and at the same time produce a small but most attractive supplement to our basic meat diet of beef, mutton, pork and poultry.

Even the conservationist camp now agrees that these wild creatures provide a natural harvest that can be "cropped", and in many cases needs to be cropped, if they are to be preserved in a well-balanced countryside. In the same way most shooting men would now agree with conservationists and support any further restrictive regulations that may be shown to be necessary to protect any particular species that is in danger of extinction or even serious decline. One must not take out of the kitty more than its natural increase will stand, or if you do, then you must take steps to put something back.

So one comes to the point that if the natural population of wild game calls for some form of controlled cropping, what better method could possibly be devised than the present long-established and well regulated methods of shooting and fishing.

Let me make another observation. Over the years, and in the course of travel to most of the main pastoral countries of the world, I have had occasion to go through some of the largest commercial slaughtering establishments - the "frigorificos" of South America, and similar abattoirs in New Zealand and South Africa, as well as smaller units in Britain. These factories, where death is dealt out to sheep, cattle and pigs on a cold blooded production-line scale, are places that always fill me with nausea and a great disquiet. This is not to allege that those places are run on inhuman or cruel lines, though I believe that some methods of killing (e.g. ritual slaughter) leave much to be desired. But in any case, the crowded transport, the penning, waiting, and then goading along the crushes to the point of execution, with the sight and sounds and smell of death just ahead; these do not make for an easy conscience.

By comparison, I think of a stag on a Scottish hill, suddenly and instantaneously shot by a hidden stalker who has possibly spent the best part of a day manoeuvring himself into a position within range. The skill, the excitement, and the sudden climax for both man and beast; this seems to me a far more acceptable way of taking a beast's life than the use of knife or pole-axe on a captive animal in a factory building.

And in the same way I cannot help comparing the sudden death of a game bird, killed in the full freedom of flight, with the fate of those lorry loads of broilers one sees travelling along the roads in their wire-netting cages. Again, I'm sure that in most cases the birds are despatched as humanely as possible — but I'd rather end my days as a pheasant or a wildgoose than as a broiler chicken.

The other line of attack on shooting and most other field sports, is based on the charge of cruelty, and this is much more difficult to deal with. In the first place there is room for argument as to what constitutes cruelty — it is not a straight issue like life or death. And secondly, how can one assess the degree to which birds and beasts — and lesser creatures — are sensitive to physical injury which, by our human standards, would be regarded as cruel. However, I do not think that shooting men should avoid the issue either by maintaining that cruelty never occurs or by claiming that their victims are insensitive to any apparent cruelty. What satisfies my own conscience is the knowledge that cruelty is not deliberately inflicted, and further that it only occurs in a small minority of cases. None of us likes to wound our quarry, still less to leave an injured bird unretrieved, and the accepted practice of shooting men is to go to considerable trouble to find these less fortunate victims and to complete as quickly as possible what their marksmanship failed to achieve. If these cases were the rule rather than the exception, then the balance in support of shooting would be harder to justify. For in my view the whole issue is one of balance; of weighing the advantages against the disadvantages, the good against the bad. In the case of shooting there is so much that is attractive, enjoyable, natural and healthy that I accept the small element of cruelty that is sometimes inevitable.

CRUELTY IN SHOOTING

And it is a small element; of that I am convinced. When reasonably conducted with normally competent marksmen, shooting ensures that the great majority of game birds meet a mercifully instantaneous death. A few have to endure a few seconds or even minutes between shot and final despatch, though in my experience the overwhelming majority of shot birds are dead by the time they are picked up, even if they were not killed outright in the air. There remain the still smaller minority of "runners" and "swimmers" who take some time to find, or who may evade capture altogether. It is often assumed that all these creatures crawl away to die a lingering and painful death; I am not at all convinced that this is so. Wing damage is probably the main cause of these lost birds, and though inability to fly is a serious enough matter, it is not necessarily a fatal handicap. If a bird is not also injured in a vital organ, then it will be able to find food and to continue its existence on a two-dimensional basis (instead of three!). The main danger will lie in its increased vulnerability to other predators, such as foxes.

But of all field sports, what about fishing? Every fish caught on hook and line must surely suffer cruelty. It cannot be other than painful and terrifying to be "caught" by a sharp hook in your mouth, and then to be hauled ashore, either immediately by brute force, or after a period of being "played" by the angler until you are thoroughly exhausted. Why is there not a greater outcry against the sport of fishing? Is it because it has such a tremendous following, or is it because the unfortunate fish is a silent creature. Can one contemplate the different attitude that would prevail if fish screamed like a wounded hare as they were hauled out of the water.

By comparison shooting must surely be the most humane of all the field sports. In spite of its rather bloodthirsty image due to the emotional impact of firearms, shooting does at least ensure that its quarry, in the great majority of cases, meets an instantaneous death in the midst of its normal life and freedom.

One final comment; why, oh why must the anti-sport brigade be so aggressive and intolerant in pursuing their campaign. There is much talk of this age being that of the Permissive Society, but there is nothing permissive about the attitude of those who happen to find something distasteful in field sports. Certainly they are entitled to their views, and to express them in the normal media of the press and radio, or in debate, but many of us are getting rather tired of the present popular but childlike habit of protesting by way of demonstrations — e.g. at Hunt Meets, and we resent still more the efforts to interfere with our recreation by restrictive legislation.

After all, those who hunt or shoot or fish cause no interference with other peoples' daily lives; we do not upset their work or their rest; we make no demands on the police or other public services. We merely seek to find recreation and sport with others similarly minded in the more remote places of these crowded islands.

Let the spoil-sports mind their own business, and leave us to enjoy our sport.

CHAPTER 32
GUNS AND GEAR

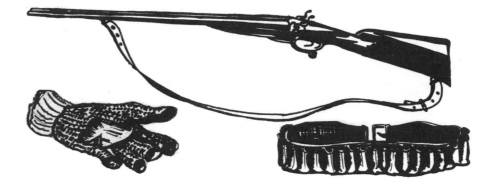

Those who write about wildfowling usually devote some attention to a discussion on guns and ammunition, and offer their advice on the question of clothing and accessories. One has only to read what many others have already written to realise that there is a considerable choice in the matter of cartridges, shot-loads and shot sizes, and an infinite variety in the range of clothing that can be worn. In fact, all this is usually confirmed when one comes across other fowlers in the field. Quite possibly no two in a casual party will be carrying the same type of gun; they will probably all be using different loads of cartridges, while in the matter of dress they will look as varied a lot of ruffians as you are likely to meet anywhere.

And yet there are, of course, several basic principles that hold good for everyone; the same objectives to be achieved, and these can be simply described as : —

1. To get within range of your quarry. (This has been described as 90% of wild-fowling).
2. To have a weapon with which you can shoot your quarry when you have achieved 1.
3. To remain reasonably warm and dry yourself throughout the process, and to return alive to your base at the end of the day.

Guns

A suitable gun is obviously the most important item of any fowler's kit, and the whole subject of the sporting gun is a fascinating study in itself. Volumes have been written about it. A good quality shot-gun is, to my mind, a wonderful example of hand-craftsmanship, a beautiful combination of wood and metal perfectly designed for its purpose. The perfect fit and finish, the slender graceful lines and, above all, the "feel" and balance of the weapon when handled; all these perhaps explain why so many of us become deeply attached to our favourite weapon. And to think that this slender assembly of some 6 to 7 lbs. of steel and walnut is going to control an internal explosion which will generate a pressure of up to 4 tons to the square inch; all within a few inches of your face!

For wildfowling, of course, one will not take a "best" London-made game gun, worth several hundred pounds. The inevitable rough handling combined with the hazards of saltwater, mud and sand call for a more rugged weapon. So what should one take? The first thing to bear in mind is that the majority of shots at wildgeese are taken at long range, say over 40 yards, for the simple reason that it is exceedingly difficult for the fowler to get within that distance of geese, and it is only under exceptional conditions of moonlight, storm or snow that the geese themselves will fly within that distance of the man on the ground. But to kill a goose (or any other bird) at over 40 yards range requires a large heavy pellet that will retain its velocity and striking energy at these extreme ranges. So the first conclusion is that for normal wildfowling on the coast one should keep to the larger sizes of shot, and I believe myself that this means the three sizes BB, 1 and 3 in the standard range available from I.C.I.

The next point is that with these large shot one only gets a comparatively small number of pellets in a standard game-load cartridge for a 12 bore gun. The actual statistics per oz. of shot being: —

BB   —   70 pellets
No. 1   —   100 pellets
No. 3   —   140 pellets

(a normal game load for Grand Prix cartridges is 1¹⁄₁₆ ounces.). By comparison 1 oz. of No. 6 shot gives you 270 pellets. So in order to counteract the small number of pellets when using large sized shot the obvious solution is to use a larger gun, which will fire a heavier charge of shot. And in order to improve still further the thin pattern of large pellets, the gun should be fully choked — at least in the left barrel.

So to anyone who is hoping to do a fair amount of wildfowling, and who is prepared to equip himself with a special gun for the purpose, I would say — invest in an 8-bore, double-barrelled, and with the left barrel full choke. (I am not dogmatic about the right barrel: there are times when one gets shots at closer ranges, and a more open pattern might then be better. My own gun is fully choked in both barrels, and I have never felt the need to bore out the right one).

There are, of course, 4-bore guns, and I expect there may still be some in use. But I doubt whether a double-barrelled 4-bore would be a practical proposition to lug around the marshes all day, and I would certainly rather have two potential shots in an 8-bore, than only one in a single-barrelled 4-bore. A further snag is that 4-bore cartridges are apparently no longer freely available : they would have to be loaded specially or home-loaded, and the cost would begin to look serious.

A double-barrelled 8-bore will weigh about 12 lbs., and is a tiresome weapon to carry in the crook of your arm or over your shoulder, but is not too bad if fitted with a leather sling which you can clip to rings on the butt and on the underside of the barrels.

And remember that unless it is "nitro-proved" you will not be able to buy cartridges off the peg, but will have to have them specially loaded with black powder. The standard "nitro" cartridge for 8-bores is 3¼ inches in length, and holds 2 oz. of shot — practically double the normal 12-bore game load of 1¹⁄₁₆ ounces. My own gun will take 3¾ inch cases, and is proved for 2½ oz. of shot, so I am not now really able to use it to its maximum capacity, unless of course I could get cartridges specially loaded.

One snag about 8-bores should be mentioned. They are really too heavy and unwieldy for shooting under the moon, when you may have birds in sight and range for a matter of seconds only. Their place is on the coast and the sea wall in daylight, where you see the skeins coming and are usually able to take deliberate aim. Also I am rather diffident about using an 8-bore inland. One is then usually with one or two companions, waiting for geese to drop in to their feeding grounds, or to be driven off them over you. An 8-bore in such close company with 12-bores seems rather out of place — it is a gun for the estuary not the fields.

So if you have an 8-bore or not, you will also need a smaller weapon for shooting inland, and at night, and for this the obvious choice is the 12-bore with 3 inch chambers (instead of the normal 2½ inch). This will be a little heavier than a standard game gun, but very similar in its handling. The usual load for this gun used to be 1⅜ ounces of shot, but I.C.I. have now brought out a "Magnum 3" cartridge which holds 1⅝ ounces of shot. There is a snag about this, in that many 3 inch guns are only proved for 1½ oz. of shot, and to fire a heavier charge it is recommended that the gun must be proved for the higher charge and pressure (4 tons per square inch instead of 3½ tons). This is an unfortunate position, as the 3 inch wildfowl gun has for long been known as a "Magnum 12-bore" or "3 inch Magnum", and anyone would naturally assume that a 3 inch **Magnum Cartridge** would be suitable for use in a 3 inch **Magnum Gun** — but this is not necessarily so. I found I had to have my own 3 inch gun re-proved to take the new magnum cartridge, and this in itself, with the cost of preparing the gun for proof, set me back by over £9.

(As a matter of interest, a 3 inch gun proved for 1½ oz. of shot will safely fire the magnum 2¾ inch cartridge, as this only contains the bare 1½ oz. The loss of pattern is measured by the difference between 114 and 105 BB pellets for the 3 inch and 2¾ inch cases respectively!)

As with an 8-bore I would always like to see the left-barrel of a 3 inch 12-bore fully choked in order to maintain an effective pattern for the longest possible range. The degree of choke for the right barrel is more arguable. If the gun is also going to be used for other forms of rough shooting, say against pigeons, then a more open pattern will be useful, and in any case provides you with a more flexible weapon. Indeed, there is no reason why a 3 inch gun should not be used for normal game shooting, though in that case it is advisable to use normal 2½ inch cartridges (larger cartridges will cause raised eyebrows).

I prefer not to have ejectors on a wildfowl gun. An ejector is another piece of mechanism that can go wrong, and which may suffer from saltwater or dirt. One seldom has the good fortune to have geese offering shots in such quick succession that an ejector is helpful. It is usually a case of a skein coming in range and the chance of two shots; then all the time in the world before the next chance.

And finally, another good reason why one should equip oneself with a 3 inch 12-bore proved for magnum cartridges. With such a gun one can safely fire any standard 12-bore cartridge that comes to hand. If you run out of cartridges or a particular size of shot and have to borrow from someone else, then you can rest assured that your gun will safely fire whatever is available and not burst and take your left hand with it.

So arm yourself with a double 8-bore if you can; have a 3 inch 12-bore as your second string, but if you can only run to one gun for wildfowling then settle for the 3 inch 12-bore, proved for 1⅝ ounces . and fully choked in at least the left barrel.

After the 3 inch 12-bore one can always fall back on the standard 2½ inch game gun, and don't let the absence of a bigger gun discourage you from making a start. Plenty of geese are shot with game guns and normal game loads, and it is as well to remember that a BB shot will travel just as fast and hit just as hard, whether fired from an 8-bore, a 3 inch 12-bore or an ordinary game gun. The main difference is simply that one gets a thinner pattern and a shortening of the effective range as one comes down the scale. The idea that some guns "hit harder" than others, or that big guns hit harder than small guns is simply not true. Where guns can vary is in the evenness of patterns with different shot sizes; only practical target tests will reveal for certain any suspected weaknesses of this type.

But behind all these comparisons of statistics there is always the one overriding and variable factor of the competence of the man behind the gun! All one can say is that whatever the standard of marksmanship of the man himself, he should do that much better with a large gun than a small one, using of course the appropriate type of cartridge, size of shot and degree of choke. One should also mention fit of gun, for no-one can perform at their best with a badly fitting gun. When checking the fit of a gun, don't go to your gunsmith in a summer suit. You will be wearing much thicker clothing out on the marsh in winter, and this may mean an appreciably shorter stock than you would have on a game gun.

There are two other standard types of gun not already mentioned; the 10-bore and the 12-bore with 2¾ inch chambers. I can see no use for the 10-bore; it is merely a larger and heavier gun than a 12-bore, but unless one has a model with extra long chambers and proved accordingly, there is no advantage over the 3 inch 12-bore in the charge of shot. In fact, the only standard 10-bore cartridges listed by I.C.I. fire **less** than 1½ oz. of shot: i.e. less than a 12-bore magnum cartridge. Similarly, the 2¾ inch 12-bore is merely a larger variety of a 12-bore without going so far as the 3 inch variety. If one is going to have a 12-bore of extra capacity one might as well go the whole hog.

Cartridges

The choice of cartridges is limited to what the gun will safely fire, and the golden rule is to use the maximum load of **shot** for which the gun is proved. Don't be tempted by "high velocity" loads; this usually means more powder at the expense of shot, and the increase in velocity is of no significance in the long shots taken at geese. The big pellets hold their velocity and their striking energy quite adequately without any extra "push". In fact, the second golden rule is that "Pattern gives out before Penetration". So if in doubt go for a smaller size of shot than a larger. BB is the traditional shot size for geese, but I only reserve it for my left barrel; in my right barrel I always use No. 3 shot, and there is no doubt that I have shot more geese with No. 3 shot than with BB. However, I am sure that this is partly due to the fact that one's first shot is usually taken at a skein in steady level flight, whereas for the following shot the geese have "stood on their tails" and shot upwards, probably swinging left or right as well, and are inevitably several yards further away. Nevertheless, for many years now I have stuck to my own routine of No. 3 in the right and BB in the left barrel — for both 8-bore and 12-bore.

If I had to confine myself to one shot size I think I would compromise on No. 1 shot for the 8-bore, but No. 3 for the 12-bore, and if I had to go out after geese with an ordinary game gun I would prefer No. 4 shot in the right barrel but something larger in the left in the hope of the occasional lucky shot at long range.

To appreciate the statistical comparison between the various cartridges and loads, the following table is taken from the figures in I.C.I.'s Shooter's Year Book (1970).

Gun	Chamber Length	Maximum Shot Charge	No. of pellets per charge			
			BB	No. 1	No. 3	No. 6
8-bore	3¼ inch	2 oz.	140	**200**	280	540
12-bore	3 inch	1⅝ oz. ("Magnum")	114	162	**228**	439
		Weight of individual pellet in grains	6.25	4.38	3.12	1.62

By comparison the corresponding figures for normal 2½ inch game guns using either "Maximum" cartridges or the more usual "Grand Prix" are: —

12-bore game gun	2½ inch	1³⁄₁₆ oz. ("Maximum")	83	119	166	321
	2½ inch	1¹⁄₁₆ oz. ("Grand Prix")	74	106	149	287

Some enthusiasts load their own cartridges, and if one has a gun with an unusual chamber length or proof charge, then there may be a good reason for this D.I.Y. activity, apart from the inherent interest in the practice. There may also be a case for the special loading service offered by some gunmakers for the same reasons. Personally I prefer to rely on the standard loads offered by I.C.I. Ammunition filling seems an obvious operation for large scale factory production, and I cannot believe that any other method of production can produce such a standard uniform and reliable product.

Of all recent developments the use of plastic waterproof cartridge cases is surely the most important and useful, especially for wildfowlers. To be able to retrieve dropped cartridges from the wet mud or from a rain-soaked pocket and find they are still serviceable is a great boon. I only hope this practice will be extended to all cartridges very quickly.

How should one carry one's cartridges? The usual solution, and one which I followed for many seasons, is to wear a cartridge belt. But I have come to the conclusion that one's waist is not the part of one's body best designed for supporting a load. The obvious place for carrying a load is the cross-bar of your shoulders. Your cartridges are much more comfortable and much readier to hand carried loose in the waterproof pockets of your shooting jacket, which in turn spreads the load over the whole area of your shoulders. Your pockets will easily hold enough cartridges for any normal day's shooting (3's in the right, BB's in the left), but if you think you may be in for an exceptional day (or night) take a spare supply in an ordinary game bag, and if your game bag is not completely weatherproof, tie your spare cartridges first in a light polythene bag.

Clothing

The choice of the most suitable clothing for a wildfowling trip is largely a matter of personal taste, as the appearance of any group of fowlers will testify, and as is confirmed by what has already been written on the subject. Knickerbockers, Norfolk jackets, deerstalkers, yachting caps, balaclavas, oilskins and string vests — all these have their supporters, but personally I would have none of them. The main essentials are : —

1. To keep yourself dry.
2. To keep yourself warm.
3. To keep yourself light (in weight).
4. To keep yourself free in action.

1 and 2 are obvious, but in achieving these essentials it is no use encumbering yourself with so much thick and heavy clothing that it is an ordeal to cope with the creeks and gulleys on the saltings, or that you cannot readily swing your gun into action.

The most important garment is your outer one; this must be absolutely weatherproof; not merely "showerproof" or "water-resistant". There are various excellent jackets now available: they are not cheap, but they are sound and should last for years. With proper flaps to the pockets they hold your supply of cartridges dry and readily to hand. For many years I have used Barbour's jackets and have no wish to search further. Under the jacket it is simply a question of how many layers of insulating clothing you need, dependent on your circulation and your sensitivity to cold. Three layers is normally enough for me: first a thin woollen shirt or vest, then a second layer of wool in the form of a light close-woven pullover with high neck (or polo neck) and long sleeves. The third layer can be of any material, but still fairly light. An important function of this last garment under your outer jacket is to provide pockets for all the minor clobber you will want to take with you. Two side pockets and two breast pockets on a bush-type drill jacket will take your flask, a 35 mm camera, your spectacles (if required), your smokes, and perhaps a packet of sandwiches and some slabs of chocolate, if you are going to be out all day. Somewhere amongst all this, or perhaps in your trousers, will be the minor impedimenta — compass, whistle, cartridge extractor, goose-call, wallet with important documents (? shooting permit), car keys, etc., etc. At night there should also be a torch.

Lower down, the other equally important article of clothing will be your rubber boots. Wellingtons are not usually adequate; both inland as well as out on the coast you will often have to stand in water at least up to your knees, or cross streams and gullies. Long three-quarter length rubber boots are really essential. Full length fisherman's waders might be even better, but I have never tried them; I have an idea they might be more difficult to get out of in an emergency.

There remains one snag, and I still haven't found the perfect answer. There is a vulnerable gap between the top of your boots and the bottom of your jacket. This leaves a belt that is exposed to direct soaking, and also leads to rain running off your jacket down inside your rubber boots. The only practical solution I know is to wear waterproof over-trousers from the waist to the knee, but this is a clumsy restrictive arrangement, and unless it is clear that there is going to be heavy continuous rain, I prefer to stick to my usual pair of light drill trousers, and rely on a change when I get back to base. One great advantage of long rubber boots is that you can kneel in them without getting wet — and crawl to a stalk. And if they do get water inside, the old trick of filling them with crushed balls of newspaper, heated in an oven, will usually restore them to wearable condition overnight.

As for headgear, the choice is legion. I don't like balaclavas because they impede your hearing. A peak in front is most desirable; it helps you to hide the white moon of your face till the last second by merely keeping your head well down. I like a well fitting ordinary cap as well as anything, and have in fact had the same one for over 30 years! It is true that a cap lets rain water run down on to your collar, but driving rain will always reach your neck, and the best protection is a light absorbent scarf tied fairly tightly round your neck. In any case, one should always have a complete change of all your under layers of clothing, so that one dry set is always available each morning while the other set is being dried.

There remain your hands — another difficult problem. Some people can shoot in gloves, with perhaps only the trigger finger of the right hand free. For myself I don't feel I have a sufficiently close and intimate control of my weapon unless the fingers of both hands are in contact with it. So I keep to knitted woollen mittens, and have some difficulty in keeping my hands warm. Alternate spells in each trouser pocket, or inside my jacket under the armpits are the only means of alleviation. If my trigger finger should become completely numb the consequences are disconcerting. The finger does not feel the resistance of the trigger as it seeks to make contact, and invariably the gun is fired before I am ready — with most frustrating results.

Dogs

It is a great pity that there is not greater scope for gun-dogs in wildfowling. One of the great pleasures in shooting, especially of the rougher varieties, is in working a gun dog, and developing that partnership between dog and master which does so much to widen the interest in shooting. The dog literally brings into the sport an additional sense which we humans are quite unable to exploit — the sense of smell. On the other hand, dogs cannot compete with humans in long range use of sight and sound. They seem uninterested in anything beyond their immediate vicinity — say about 100 yards — although we know they have very keen hearing and presumably normal long sight. By contrast we mortals can see, and recognise as such, skeins of geese at a distance of several miles on a clear crisp day, and can hear and recognise their calls at about a mile. But with scent it is a different story, and I never cease to be amazed at the extraordinary powers of perception which exist in a dog's nose.

In wildfowling, however, there is no need for the hunting and flushing assistance of dogs, and there is seldom any call for the mere finding of the game when shot. Most geese are shot over the wide open spaces of the saltings, or on the large inland fields where they feed, and there is little difficulty in spotting such a large bird as a goose on open ground. But, of course, there are other occasions: the dense reed beds that border the upper reaches of some estuaries make it extremely difficult to find a bird that falls at any appreciable distance, and even inland a shot goose may reach a nearby patch of rough ground.

But the main value of a dog in goose shooting is in retrieving an inaccessible bird — and that usually means a bird that drops into the sea or loch, or on the wrong side of a creek or gully on the coast, or an unfordable stream inland. On such occasions a dog is invaluable, and I would be the first to remember thankfully the number of geese found and retrieved for me by dogs.

Yet, on balance, I find that dogs have a small and occasional role to play, and with the problems of travel and feeding, and accommodation in strange quarters, I prefer to be free of the obligations which their company imposes. I have only taken my dog on two or three fowling trips, and I have felt that it was really not fair on him.

Of course it is a very different matter for the man who is fortunate enough to live within daily travelling distance of his fowling grounds. In such circumstances a dog can go with his master on many expeditions as he would for any other day's shooting.

Incidentally, the specification for a fowler's dog is that it should be a three-way cross between a greyhound, a bulldog and a retriever, so that it can reach your bird before other dogs, hang on to it against all-comers, and bring it back to you.

One "doggy" story is worth recording, about my own springer spaniel, Jock, who shared twelve years of a very full life with us, both indoors and out in the countryside. Jock simply lived for shooting, and the mere opening of the gun cupboard threw him into ecstacies of anticipation. But he had very strong views on certain matters. If I shot a bird and sent him after it, he would find it, bring it back to me and hand it over without complaint. But if **he** found something on his own; a pheasant or rabbit squatting in the undergrowth, or even a moorhen or hedgehog, then nothing on earth — short of brute force — would induce him to part with his prize. His little mind had clearly worked out the canine equivalent of "render unto Caesar............". Anything I shot he would gladly render to me, but what he acquired on his own was his for keeps, and why on earth should he give it up to anyone else. I wonder if this is a wellknown habit in gun dogs; I have never come across it elsewhere.

Binoculars

I regard binoculars as a most important piece of equipment in fowling, though by no means essential. It is simply that they add greatly to one's enjoyment of the scene. There is so much to watch on a wildfowl estuary; not only the quarry itself but other birds, and nearly always at a considerable distance. Inland they are of very great help in searching the countryside for feeding geese, and I know of several vantage points overlooking broad valleys or carses where a few minutes spying with a glass will make good literally several square miles of goose country. On other occasions they are a nuisance, and have to be left behind like dogs. You can hardly do a difficult stalk with a pair of glasses swinging from your neck and dragging in the mud. Unfortunately, the better the glasses the larger and heavier they become, but I would suggest that the normal 8 x 30 is well worth having, and is small enough to carry in some pockets.

Glasses are probably at their greatest value under conditions of poor light — such as one has at the early stages of dawn flighting, or when shooting under the moon, when they will pick out a fallen bird lying in the next field or out on the mud that you would not otherwise know was there. So "Twilight Performance" is of even greater importance than magnification. "T.P." depends chiefly on the size of the objective lens — the large lens at the opposite end to the eyepiece — as a large objective clearly "collects" more light into the system than a small one.

So a 7 x 50 glass is really preferable to an 8 x 30 (the first figure denotes the magnification, the second the diameter of the objective lens in mm). Better still are glasses with magnifications of 8, 10 or more, so long as the objective lens remains of at least 50 mm. Manufacturers may say that a magnification of 15 is more than can be coped with unless a tripod is used, but I find my 15 x 60 quite practical, though it is certainly on the large size. Vital statistics for binoculars, as given for those of one of the leading makes are : —

Model	7 x 50	8 x 30	8 x 50	10 x 50	15 x 60
Magnification	7	8	8	10	15
Diameter of objective lens	50	30	50	50	60
Twilight Performance	18.7	15.5	20.0	22.4	30.0
Weight	35 oz.	18-23 oz.	38 oz.	37 oz.	45 oz.

Dangers and Precautions

Wildfowling involves its followers in certain risks which do not normally apply to other forms of shooting. Curiously enough the ones which are most easily avoided are those which appear most spectacular and lead to the press headlines, about wildfowlers lost and drowned. If anyone chooses to go mudlarking out on the vast open spaces of the Wash, the Solway or Morecambe Bay, then they are asking for trouble unless they take obvious and sensible precautions.

The usual causes of disaster are : —
1. being cut off by the tide,
2. being lost in fog,
3. getting stuck in quicksands.

There is no need to suffer the first of these fates if you study your tide-tables and make sure that you only go far out on the mudflats and sandbanks on a falling tide, and retrace your steps back to the seawall before the tide starts to flow again and fill all the creeks and gulleys you have to cross. The second risk is rather more difficult to insure against, but the use of a compass is your main hope. Personally I have never ventured further out in foggy conditions than a sure return route can be relied upon to bring me back — a groyne or breakwater, or the course of a well-known creek. But it is an eerie feeling to be out on the mud with nothing in sight in any direction, no sounds, no sun or moon or stars, and no wind. It is very easy to lose completely all sense of direction, and to end up by walking out to sea instead of towards the land.

I once had a small example of this in a different context and a different sense. I had shot a goose from the seawall and it dropped in the dense reed-bed bordering the estuary. I set off through the reeds, which were well above my head and tried to hold a straight course on the line I had marked. The next thing I knew I was back on dry land, having traversed a wide semi-circle out and back again!

As for quicksands, I have no first-hand experience of them, but others have described their dangers and the technique for rolling out of them. "BB" gives a terrifying description of a fowler caught in a quicksand in "Tides Ending". But all these hazards, when the ultimate enemy is the sea, can be avoided by common sense and discretion.

The one serious risk which we are all liable to incur sometime or other, and which is so dangerous because it is insidious, is the plugged gun barrel. It is so easy when creeping along a deep gutter in the mud, or even when merely waiting for morning flight in the shelter of a creek, to let the muzzle of your gun touch the bank. It is easier still when doing a stalk on hands and knees, or flat on your stomach. I am told that a mere one-inch plug of snow in a barrel will cause a burst, and a burst may well take part of your hand with it. That is why I always carry my gun in a canvas cover for as long as possible, and after I have taken it out I open the breech at every appropriate occasion, take out the cartridges and make sure the barrels are clear. This habit soon becomes part of the similar habit of breaking the gun (to see it is unloaded) every time it is laid down, put in a car or taken into a building.

There is a reverse precaution, which has nothing to do with safety, and that is to check that your gun is loaded whenever you have time to do so, before an obvious chance is coming your way. In the excitement of getting a goose down, and perhaps rushing out to collect it, you can easily leave your gun with spent cartridges in it; and then if more geese come along you grab your weapon and point it impotently at the departing skein. I know because I have done it!

Another golden rule: always take a loaded gun with you when going out after a wounded goose. If the bird still has its head up anything is possible. If it has only been stunned or shocked it may very well be sufficiently recovered to take to the air again. Or even if it can only walk it may well reach a boundary ditch or a creek before you catch up with it, and then swim to safety. So be ready to shoot as soon as you get within range — if you do.

CHAPTER 33

GEESE FOR THE TABLE

It is hardly surprising that there is a good deal of ignorance about the edible qualities of wild geese. They are not normally displayed for sale in poulterer's shops (in fact their sale is now prohibited by law), and comparatively few people ever get the chance of tasting a wild goose. I have often been met with such remarks as "Why do you shoot wild geese?" "You can't possibly eat them, can you?" or "They must be terribly fishy". I suppose that with the popular association of geese with the Wash and the Solway, they are assumed to be sea-birds, feeding on seafood, and therefore oily and fishy. But, of course, this is far from the truth. Geese only frequent our estuaries and bays for sanctuary; chiefly for passing the night in safety, but also for the purpose of getting sand or gravel to help their digestive processes. The open spaces round our coasts serve as their bases from which they set out each morning to seek their feeding grounds inland. And of course they are increasingly using various inland stretches of water — lakes and lochs — for the same purpose, because of the increasing harassing they are suffering on the open coast.

But their main food supply — while in this country — consists of the same basic material as that which produces our beef and mutton — grass. Early in the season the geese will also glean the unbroken stubbles for grain, and later on the pinkfeet in particular will seek the fields from which the potato crop has been lifted. These fields will always hold a number of small potatoes left in the ground, and these in due course turn rotten and soft with the arrival of frost. Both geese and duck love these mushy potatoes. Still later, as the herbage in the grass fields dies down, the geese will seek fields of winter wheat and feed on the young green shoots. And if the wheat follows a crop of potatoes, then there is a two-course meal awaiting them, and some of our most exciting and profitable mornings have been waiting for geese to flight into such fields at dawn.

So the flesh of wild geese is perfectly sound and wholesome. It is dark and closely grained, and as can be expected from such a tough and muscular bird, there is not a suspicion of fat about it. The first essential, therefore, is to hang a goose long enough, otherwise it will certainly be tough. We have a rule never to touch a goose under three weeks, and one year we kept one for 12 weeks. This seemed to justify a letter to "The Field", and the following appeared in their issue of April 9th, 1959.

"I am beginning to wonder what are the hanging limits for game in this country. I am not thinking of cold storage or deep-freeze cabinets, but of ordinary hanging in a game larder at current outdoor temperatures.

I would have said that for normal game birds the usual period of hanging would range from about five days in the warmth of early September to three weeks at the end of the season in January. Large birds such as wild geese seem to require much longer hanging. Many years' experience has taught me that a goose should never be touched for at least three weeks after it is shot, but I have not yet discovered the maximum period it will withstand!

Some years ago I brought home several geese and proceeded to eat one a week until the last was eight weeks old.

This winter I brought home three for the larder and owing to various complications it was eight weeks before we ate the first. A second followed at the next week-end and the third was destined for the third week-end. But on examination this third bird was found to be one that had smashed itself rather badly on falling on to hard frozen ground, and it was quite unpresentable for the table. It was then I remembered there was still a goose in the larder that had been killed before Christmas. It was a pinioned one that had escaped from its pen; my dog had come across it and in a moment of misplaced enthusiasm had retrieved it. Although it showed no external damage the dog had obviously nipped it, and the bird was dead in a few hours. I cannot be more certain of the date than that it was before December 23rd (when we went away for Christmas). We ate it on March 20th — and it was delicious. That means it had hung for over twelve weeks!

Of course, not having been shot the bird would have suffered no destructive damage to its innards, and admittedly there was some fairly cold weather at the beginning of January.

I should add that I have in no way suffered from these well-hung meals — except in the rude remarks of my friends who promised to visit me in hospital".

Hang a goose by its head, preferably in a fly-proof game larder, but otherwise in an unheated well-ventilated outhouse or garage. But look out for flies: I have known a goose to become fly-blown in Scotland in November, before we could get it home. Leave it unplucked and "un-drawn" while hanging, and remember that if you want to prolong the keeping period by putting the goose in deep-freeze, it must be put in **after** the normal hanging: in other words it must be ready for eating when it comes out of deep freeze. We leave our geese still unplucked and un-drawn in deep freeze, though others say that birds should be plucked and drawn before changing to deep freeze.

After deep freeze thaw slowly at normal unheated room temperature — a goose may take 48 hours — then pluck, draw and cook.

The usual method of cooking, as for all types of fowl, is of course to roast. But there are other methods, and for the benefit of those who may be faced with a plucked wildgoose for the first time, or who have hitherto not had much success with this admittedly difficult bird, I will suggest three possible recipes. These are methods which we have evolved over the years. Margaret is the expert who has been preparing game and wildfowl for the table for almost as many years as I have been shooting them!

So here are **"Margaret's Recipes for Wild Geese"**.

1. **Roast Wildgoose**

Take your plucked and drawn goose (after at least 3 weeks' hanging) wash it and then dry it. Stuff it with an ordinary sage and onion stuffing. Place the bird in a roasting tin, rub the breast with margarine and cover with greaseproof paper or foil. Add ¼ lb. of dripping to the tin. Then place in a moderate oven (top right of a 4-oven Aga) and roast for 1 hour. Then transfer to a cooler oven (top left) for a further 1½ hours. Baste well and frequently.

To prepare a gravy pour off and discard the fat from the top of the roasting tin. To the remaining liquid add flour, browning, condiments and water to obtain a suitable consistency; serve separately in a sauce-boat.

Serve also a sharp fruit jelly — redcurrant, crabapple, quince, japonica or even orange sauce as for duck.

Carve the breast lengthwise like a saddle of mutton, starting alongside the keel, but you will find the legs and wings hardly worth struggling with — though they can be used in the next two recipes.

2. **Salmi of Wild Goose**

This begins where the first recipe ends — with a roast goose.

When cold carve all the meat off the bird, cutting it into small slices — about the size of a sardine. Place in a deep oven dish or casserole.

Prepare a sauce as follows : —

In a saucepan place a fried sliced Onion, 2 oz. of margarine, 1 oz. of flour, a piece of carrot, a bunch of herbs and about ½ pint of stock. Simmer for half an hour, then pour the mixture — through a strainer — over the meat in the dish. Add some redcurrant jelly and cook all together in a moderate oven (top right) for 1 hour.

Just before serving add a good dollop of port (or port-type) wine — about a small cupful.

3. **Wild Goose Pâté**

Start with the raw goose — washed and dried. Disjoint it and cut the carcase into several pieces. Put all into a saucepan and add just enough water to cover the pieces. Add a bunch of herbs, 6 peppercorns, 6 cloves and one small onion. Cook all together in a moderate oven (top right) until the meat is tender — usually about 2 hours.

Take out the pieces and remove all the meat from the bones and carcase. Put all this meat through a fine mincer. Place the minced meat in a fresh saucepan, add 3 oz. of margarine, grate half a nutmeg into it and add sufficient of the original stewing liquid from the first saucepan to give the paste a suitably soft consistency ; it will probably need about half a pint. Heat all together on top of the oven for about ¼ hour, with regular stirring. Then press into round shallow jars and when cold seal with a layer of melted butter. The finished pâté should be firm, but just soft enough to spread, and can be eaten on bread, biscuits, or best of all on hot buttered toast. It seems to keep indefinitely in an ordinary fridge.

Remember that wildgeese are not really very large birds. The largest of the more common varieties — the Greylag — will provide four portions if the breast only is carved. If the whole bird is utilised as in the second recipe it should make a meal for six. The other varieties of geese, being smaller, will not go so far. The following table gives in round figures the weights of the three most common species "as shot" : —

Weight in lbs. (complete bird)

	Small	Average	Large
Greylag	5½	7½	9½
Pinkfooted	4	6	8
Whitefronted	4	5	6

The yield of edible meat is only about a fifth of the original live weight, so an average goose will only produce from 1 to 1½ lbs. of meat.

As for flavour I do not think there is any consistent difference in taste or texture between the different varieties, and I certainly could not identify a species from its taste. I imagine that any variation is more likely to be due to age, condition and the principal recent food of the bird, rather than to its species.

CHAPTER 34
THE FLIGHT OVER DECOYS
(1953-1954 — Tom's Year)

December 9th, 1953

I got away to a late start this year. "BB" and Tom had set out from the Midlands on December 5th, whereas I had not been able to leave home till the 9th. So they had four days shooting before I arrived, and had already collected several geese by the time I joined them on the night of the 10th.

My own reunion with "BB" and Tom reminded me of the daily reunion of the gaggles in the "Dark Estuary" — a lot of chat and discussion! What was the news? What had they been doing? Were there many geese about? Where were they feeding? It appeared there were plenty of geese, but they didn't seem to be using many of their usual fields. However, they had located a nice lot that day feeding on the famous field where we had finished up with such a grand morning at the end of last year's trip. Everything was laid on for an ambush over decoys in the morning.

This was great news and exciting. I turned in early, but though I was tired after two long days driving, my mind was busy with active imaginings of what the morning might hold for us.

December 11th.

As usual the first night of the trip was a restless one with short snatches of sleep. At last I switched the light on — 5.30 a.m. and turned over for a final doze. Next moment — so it seemed — the light was on again and "BB's" head was round the door to tell us to get up, and it was 6.30. How easily one slipped into the old routine — pulling on one's clothes, staggering downstairs, gulping a mouthful of tea from the overnight flask and then out into the black night to collect guns, decoys and the final outer layer of clothing from our "bothy". We were at the farmyard soon after seven, and then had the long walk across the open fields to the oat stubble. In the dark we chose the best hides we could find in the boundary ditch, and proceeded to improve them with branches cut from the overhanging trees and handfuls of dead grass to thicken the screen. 35 yards out in the field we placed our decoys — a formidable array of eight — four "greys" in one group, and four "pinks" in another. It was a mild cloudy morning with quite a bit of haze, and at about 7.45 the first party of greys arrived, circled the field, but then passed on. Presently more lots began to come in from the coast, and before long some skeins came low enough to offer us shots. But the shooting was poor: I think we were all too excited and inclined to be "trigger-happy".

At last I opened the scoring, and then for three hours we had another of those wonderful flights one dreams about. Geese were continually coming in; the sky was seldom devoid of them, and we never even had time to gather together for our picnic breakfast till about 11. And even after that we stayed on till midday as further skeins continued to appear — some from the coast, but others from inland where they had no doubt been disturbed from other fields. The slight haze added to the excitement, as time and time again one heard geese before one spotted them, and then a bunch of a dozen or so would glide into view a

160

quarter of a mile away and three gunshots high. In our hides we would crouch motionless while the skeins circled warily round the field. Some would obviously spot something amiss and would then press on to other feeding grounds, but many were irresistibly attracted to the decoys, and gradually circled lower and lower, till they dropped their paddles, cupped their wings and glided towards the stuffed decoys.

Even then it was seldom that we got more than one bird out of a skein. They probably only just came near enough to the ditch at one point, so that very often only one of us had a fair shot, and even then none of us ever managed to get a right and left.

Our total score was 18, of which only three were greys. One of these greys and one of the pinks seemed to be only slightly wounded in the wing, so we kept them alive, tied their legs and brought them back to our quarters. If they survived I hoped to take them home. That evening one of them was already pecking at a dish of mixed corn!

December 12th.

We had decided to go down for the morning flight off the coast. The morning was clear but dull with slight rain; the most promising feature was a fairly strong breeze. But it proved insufficient to keep the geese low. We made our way out through the reeds in the darkness and listened to the continuous clamour of goose-talk out on the water. At about 8 they started to come in, but mostly far too high, and the greater number passed far to one side of us.

I had two lots high over to my left and of the second lot (a pair) I hit one very hard. He started to fall, then recovered and turned back to the water. I gave him the second barrel as he glided down, but he reached the mud a quarter of a mile out and sat still. A little later I could see through the glasses that his head was down — so no doubt he was dead.

"BB" also had several shots, and I saw him bring down a grey and nearly get a right and a left when he hit a second bird hard with his left barrel. Later we had a hunt for "BB's" fallen bird and only found it after a long methodical search together in the tall reeds. Back at the car we met our companion who also got a goose. So it only remained for me to retrieve mine. Although only a quarter of a mile out there was a deep creek between the shore and the mud bank, and it would have meant a 3-4 mile walk to go back inland, cross the creek at the first bridge and come back down the other side and out on to the mud bank. So I asked the others to take me by car to the bridge, then go back and have their breakfast, and call for me in an hour's time. Even so it was a strenuous walk. Inland the ground was waterlogged and a quagmire, and the long trek out over the mud was the usual laborious squelchy process. I stripped down to a shirt and two pullovers and did the trip in just over the hour. So I got my goose — but missed my breakfast!

Next we took a sandwich lunch and explored inland to find where the geese were feeding. But they seemed very elusive; we found no big lots and saw few geese on the move. We called on several farmers and searched some new areas but returned with no very clear ideas as to where we should go next week. Back on the coast we were just in time for evening flight but again had no luck. Some huge skeins of pinks came out very late — and very high; a wonderful sight in the dull winter sky. They were hardly visible till nearly overhead, but their high-pitched chorus preceded them from afar. One skein of about 300 came out almost directly over my head; it had only two birds in one leg of the V — the other leg had the best part of 300 — a long weaving line snaking out to the safety of the open water.

December 13th.

The usual Sabbath — of recuperation and reconnaissance. We found no big lots, but a small party on a "combined" stubble, where last year we decoyed them in the snow. We decided to try it again next morning if the weather proved suitable. Our two pricked birds seemed reasonably well and taking both food and water in their coop.

December 14th.

It was mild and raining slightly when we got up at 6, and we decided to go ahead with our plans for decoying the geese inland. The slight mist and low layer of dull cloud made a late dawn, and it was 8.15 before we heard the first geese. It was one of those mornings when one nearly always heard geese before one could see them. The first few lots passed on without taking any notice of our decoys and then a large skein of about 40 pinks came in strong and straight from the North and glided down to the decoys with no hesitation or circling. They passed right across our front as they prepared to land and gave us all shots. But only two birds fell — one a winged bird in the next field and another that gradually collapsed and was found dead in another field half a mile away. There was some doubt as to who accounted for these birds, but I was perfectly convinced in my own mind that they were both mine!

After that several more big lots of pinks passed by overhead, and sent us all into the depths of our hides, but only two more skeins came right in to the decoys. One lot got away unscathed, but "BB" got a grey out of the last lot.

In the afternoon we went down to the coast for the evening flight, but the geese all came out late and high: none of us had a shot though we all heard them high above us as they crossed the seawall. The winged bird from the morning seemed otherwise unhurt, so it joined the other two in the coop.

December 15th.

It seemed fine and clear when we ventured out this morning, with the promise of a bright dawn — not very encouraging. We had decided to go down to the coast again; this time a mile or so further along than on Saturday. As was to be expected the geese all came in high but "BB" had several lots over him, and although he tried a few long shots he brought nothing down.

Presently a small lot of pinks passed over me high to my left and rather rashly I fired and, missing with my first shot, I fired again, against my better judgement. To my enormous surprise the goose crumpled and dropped like a stone. I reckoned it fell at least 100 yards away in dense reeds, in the heart of "Goose's Graveyard" — that maze of reeds and creeks from which so few fallen geese are ever retrieved. The flight was not yet over so the only thing to do was to mark the line very carefully with a series of broken reeds in line, and leave the search till later.

Presently I had another lot over me and dropped a pinkfoot quite close, where it was very easy to find. Then as the flight eased off I tackled the search for the earlier bird. The first problem was the creek, but after following it inland I found a narrow point where I could jump it. I had left a branch stuck in the mud on the near bank to mark the line, and I was thus able to pick up the line again on the far bank. My distant mark was a tree on the seawall a mile away, but this was not easy to hold in view, as much of the reed bed was eight feet high. I ploughed on for perhaps 150 yards till I was sure I had overshot the distance, but still no sign of the bird. Then I started back on the parallel track, 3-4 yards to the downwind side, as one could only hope to see a goose if it was within a yard or two; it was hopeless trying to cover too wide a strip at a time. And thus I found it — just visible in the tangled mass of old reeds. Like the other, it was a pink.

After lunch a tour up the valley disclosed a small lot of about 40 geese using a new field on a new farm. But the farmer was away from home and we had to leave the geese — only for the time being we hoped.

There only remained the inland farm of yesterday's expedition; so off we drove again — and to our surprise found the field already covered again with 200-300 geese. But we decided to leave them for another dawn expedition tomorrow. Hurrying back we were just in time for evening flight on the coast. We had spotted quite a few geese on a huge grass field bordering the seawall, and took up our positions on the bank — between the geese and the water. Sure enough at about 4.30 they started to lift, first several small parties — then the main body of about 100. The latter came straight over "BB" and he got the leader with his first shot. Neither Tom nor I had a chance. I had been watching these geese through my glasses and I had noticed that there was an albino amongst them — the first I have ever seen. This one must have been a greylag as the skein that came out were greylags — by their calls, and by the evidence of the one that "BB" shot.

December 16th.

The usual peep through the window at 6.30 showed mist — and we were in some doubt whether we should go inland for our planned ambush. If visibility were too low the geese might not be able to find their distant fields; in fact they might not even be able to cross the hills. But the mist was slight and we decided to keep to our plans. We soon drove out of the mist as we climbed the road over the hills, and when we reached our field it was a cold clear crisp morning. First of all we tried lying out in the field; each of us under a few armfuls of the loose "combined" straw with the decoys a dozen or so yards in front of us. Very soon skeins began arriving; we would hear the distant talk of flying geese, and presently a skein would swoop over our field at a great height — but usually show no interest in the field or in our decoys. It was most disappointing. Eventually four greylags came along and circled with obvious intent to land. At last they came in range, but only just, and "BB" and I both held our fire, as we thought they would circle again and give us all a surer chance. But the birds were clearly suspicious and flew on elsewhere. By now we had realised that all these skeins were dropping to a field half a mile away. So I left my hard and uncomfortable position on the frosty ground, and set out to put the geese up in the hope that some would then come back to our field where "BB" and Tom were still lying under their straw. It was now broad daylight, and I soon found the geese — a couple of hundred of them — scattered over a large sloping pasture. They rose with a roar of wings before I reached their field, but moved off still further away. I rejoined the others and we took the chance of a bite and a drink of hot tea from our picnic basket. By this time we were all rather cold and stiff, and decided to abandon the prone position for the greater comfort of Monday's hides.

We replaced the decoys accordingly and waited developments. A few further skeins appeared from time to time but still they showed no interest in our ambush. Why this should be we could not make out; possibly they will not feed on a combined stubble while it is covered with hoar frost and the straw is all frozen to the ground in chunks. Anyhow, they all started to settle again in the same grass field as they chose earlier on. We decided therefore that if the geese would not come to us we must try and go to the geese. Our glasses showed that the burn flowing at our feet flowed also past the field where the geese were. Whether it offered deep enough cover or not we could not tell, but it seemed the only hope. "BB" and I set off up the burn, with the idea of getting right up to the geese if we found them within range of the burn (an unlikely prospect), or failing that, of getting as close as we could to them and waiting for Tom to put them up over us.

Tom, meanwhile, set off on a long detour to bring him up to the opposite side of the goose field. "BB" and I found we had a fairly easy stalk; the burn was nowhere above our knees, the bottom was fairly firm and the banks were just high enough to keep us out of sight, provided we bent double. There was one farm bridge of railway sleepers to negotiate (underneath) and two post and wire sheep fences running across the burn which we had to squeeze through sideways between the lowest wires. But such a stalk — in heavy clothes and bent double — is always exhausting and we eventually arrived opposite the geese sweating and panting. A peep showed the geese to be out of range in the middle of the field, so we settled down to wait. But not for long — in a few minutes a couple of shots rang out from Tom, who had reached the far side. A roar of wings and cackling broke out in front; and "BB" and I pressed ourselves into the bank of the burn. In a few moments the leading line of geese appeared over the rim of the bank and we straightened up to take our shots. They seemed absolute sitters — the best part of 200 pinkfooted geese came straight for our burn, and the line crossed immediately above us at what seemed an easy range, and yet only one bird fell — to my second barrel! Why my first bird didn't fall I cannot imagine and "BB" was equally amazed at his double miss. But this sort of thing is always happening with wildfowling. In the first place wild geese can take an awful lot of punishment, and secondly they are always higher up than they seem — due to their size.

We returned to our hides for another hour or two, but again with no luck.

A little later a single bird came along, but instead of coming to the decoys it went and settled in the next field — just out of sight in dead ground. Clearly it must have been a pricked bird. This time "BB" went off to try and get behind it and push it across the burn lower down. Tom and I moved down the burn to intercept it, and almost before we knew what was happening the goose came into sight, flying straight for us. Tom was the nearer and needed no help from me in dropping it.

Soon after that we packed up and came home for tea; we had been out for over 9 hours, with only a sandwich and a thermos of tea for both breakfast and lunch, so we were ready both for the tea and the hot fire that was awaiting us.

December 17th.

This was one of our most strenuous days: we were out from 7 a.m. until midnight with only brief rests after lunch and tea. Dawn found us on the coast as usual, but it was another still morning, fairly clear with a soft pearly haze and hoar frost on the reeds. The flight was a poor one — only a few skeins came our way, and mostly high in the calm air. I had two lots nearly over me — near enough to tempt me to try long shots which had no effect. Tom and "BB" were more lucky, and each got a goose. There was nothing to tempt us to stay on late so we got back in time for a proper breakfast at 10. An hour later we started on our rounds again — to all the more likely fields, but found them all empty of geese.

In desperation we tried the scene of Friday's ambush, and to our amazement found geese back there again — about 50 of them. Although they were stalkable we decided to leave them till the morning — for another ambush.

Towards the end of our search we tried a large stubble where we had seen a few geese earlier in the week (where I had sat out under the moon in November 1951). A spy with the glasses showed two small parties of geese on the very far side; it was hard to see them through the haze, and the light was failing rapidly, so we planned a drive on the spot. "BB" and Tom were to work round the outside of the field, get between the geese and the sea, and in 20 minutes I would walk across the field and put the geese up. In due course I started off; the geese now practically lost in the gloom. As I got nearer they showed no sign of moving — or even of showing alarm, and it wasn't until I was about 100 yards from them that I could see through the glasses that they were not geese but clumps of thistles!

Finally, we went down to the coast for a couple of hours before midnight, in the hope that a few geese would be on the move under the moon. At such times they sometimes fly up and down on the edge of the mud in small parties, and if you can find some cover in a creek or in the edge of the reeds they may offer a chance. I took Tom out by my favourite track and left him by a small creek. I took myself some quarter of a mile to the left and edged out towards the mud. Geese were calling out in front of us on the flowing tide but I heard no sign of them in the air. Somewhere on my left four shots rang out and I could hear a large body of geese taking to the air and disappearing out to sea. Then a dim form loomed up on the very edge of the water to my left. As it came nearer it looked like a man — but it seemed to be moving quite silently and smoothly — whereas progress through the mud is a laborious, squelchy and jerky business. After a few more seconds I could see that it was a man in a gunning punt creeping stealthily along on the edge of the tide. As he passed me 30 yards away I stood up and waved — lest he might mistake my head for something that was worth a chance shot! He flashed a torch in return and we exchanged greetings. He had not had a shot yet — nor had I — did I know my way back to dry land? It was a dangerous place and there were some deep holes behind me. Yes — I reassured him — I knew this stretch of coast and would get back all right. By this time the water was up to my knees, and I did in fact move back above the level of the rising tide. And so he passed on, silently and eerily, sitting in the stern of his long low grey punt, looking and listening ahead, and pushing her along with strokes of his double-ended paddle. He soon dissolved into the pearly greyness of the distance, and Tom on my right never even saw him pass.

Soon after, a whistle from "BB" on the seawall told us he had had enough, and I repeated the signal to Tom in case he hadn't heard it. In a few moments the two of us joined forces and retraced our steps back through the reed beds to dry land. None of us had had a shot; the mist was probably too thick for the geese, though there was enough light for us to have seen any geese in range.

We got home by midnight, and I realised I had had my long waders on for 17 hours without a break!

December 18th.

Our last day, and a complete change in the weather. The frost had disappeared during the small hours and the haze had increased to a fairly thick mist. It seemed doubtful whether the geese would find the field where we had planned to ambush them at dawn flight, but on the other hand a mist on the coast always increased one's chances there. So we hurried down to the seawall once again and struck out through the reeds towards the edge of the mud. At least five other gunners were also out on this same stretch of coast; it seemed quite a crowd!

The firth sounded full of geese, but the mist made a late dawn and it was quite half an hour later than usual before the first geese risked the daily gauntlet of the flight to their feeding grounds. All was very still and damp — the reeds no longer crisp and powdered with drops of hoar frost, but soft and brown with condensed mist on the end of every down-bent tip. Apart from the reeds, mud, sea and sky formed one soft grey dome, enclosing everything.

Every now and then one could tell by the change in tone of the "goose talk" that a party had taken wing and one was left straining to hear whether they were heading towards one or not.

The first lot I saw slipped in low to my left, but just too far for a shot. Then a party of about ten suddenly came flying along the coast just in front of me. I saw them just in time, crouched down in the reeds, and then stood up and let fly. The first shot dropped a goose with a thud in the shorter reeds in front of me, but I missed the second. Presently Tom on my right winged a goose coming in the opposite direction, but it reached the mud and made off into the mist. Tom and his dog set out after it and must have followed it for nearly half a mile down a creek — the goose repeatedly diving and the dog having to climb out on to the mud and wait for its next appearance. I followed them nearly out of sight with my glasses and hoped neither of them would get into trouble. But the dog won in the end and a very exhausted pair regained the cover of the reeds.

Just as they were passing me again another lot of geese came flying along, and again I killed with my first shot but missed with my second. After that the flight eased off and we foregathered on the seawall. "BB" had had no luck this time, so we just had our three geese.

On the way home to lunch — it was now after 11 — we called at the farm of the proposed ambush so as to see if the geese had in fact found their field. As we drew near it was clear that they had — we could hear geese in the air over the field, obviously circling to land. The mist was still thick so "BB" and Tom went off to one flank where there was a deep ditch on the boundary which might lead them up to a stalk. I went off to the other flank (seawards) in the hope that I also might find a stalk possible, or failing that, I would be on the right side of the field for any geese put off and making back to the coast. Before I had gone very far I stumbled on to a pack of about 100 sitting right out in the field, and of course they went straight out to sea. By the time I had reached the seaward ditch "BB" and Tom on the inland side 500 yards away had similarly put up a smaller pack of geese. I heard them rise and knew they were bound to head my way. I flattened myself in the shallow ditch and very soon the waving line of geese appeared out of the mist. By the time they crossed my ditch they were a good height and just to my left, and I reckoned only the extreme end of the nearest leg of the V was in range. I stood up, picked one of the last of the V and fired well ahead of him. He staggered and started to fall — and then recovered. The very last bird was the target for my second barrel; I fired still further ahead and well above him, and he crumpled up and fell like a stone. I remember thinking what a long time it took him to reach the ground — and realised what a long shot it must have been.

THE FLIGHT OVER DECOYS

I had my 8-bore out that morning; I don't think I would even have fired with the 12-bore. But I had been using No. 3 shot in my first barrel, and BB in my second. I have little doubt that BB in the right barrel would have brought the first goose down.

By now it was time for lunch, but we hurried back to the field immediately afterwards, complete with decoys, in the hope that the geese might come back again to finish their feed, as they could have hardly had more than 2-3 hours feeding that morning. We took up position in our usual hides in the hedge, and within a few minutes a single grey glided silently in to the four grey decoys. Fortunately "BB" spotted him in time and dropped him with a single shot. Though we waited another couple of hours and heard geese several times somewhere up in the mist, no more came to the field, and we eventually packed up at four, pretty well wet through with the continual mist and drizzle.

But it was a good end to the holiday. Five geese in the day, all three of us scoring and "BB" and I ending up with a clean kill with our last shot of the trip.

December 19th.

The usual winding up of the trip; sorting out our gear, packing, stowing the vans and dividing up the bag. The total score was 39 geese for the fortnight, though I had only been there for seven shooting days — the others had had four more days. My own contribution had been 13 geese.

During the night the drizzle had increased to rain, and had washed the skies clear. Even the clouds had departed and the sun was rising over the distant hills in a clear sky. Every detail of our "goose country" stood out in sharp outline and clear colour, and even as we loaded up the vans the skeins were streaming into the fields. We could see them two miles away as they first left the mudflats, and followed them all the way till they either dropped into a field in sight, or more often carried on over the hills till they disappeared from view. Two small lots passed directly above us — almost in range — as though bidding us a triumphant farewell at having survived the fortnight's harrying and seeing us about to depart.

Never mind; perhaps we shall meet again!

CHAPTER 35
VALLEY OF GEESE
(1972-1973 — Andrew's Year)

I had hoped to arrange a week's wildfowling this season when the state of the moon would provide opportunities for one or two shoots "under the moon". These opportunities are most likely for a few days after the full moon when there is a distinct dark period between daylight and moon-rise, but still enough moon later to provide light for the geese to flight back to their feeding grounds, and for the waiting gunners to see them.

But the November moon clashed with other engagements at home, and the December moon was too near Christmas. So I settled for the week of December 11th-16th.

My nephew Andrew was to join me this year — one of the few remaining nephews who have not yet tried wildfowling with me. Keith couldn't complete the trio as he had used up his few remaining days of holiday on a deer-stalking trip. So I asked John — from the Solway — to come in his place, but he was only able to join us for the last three days.

I took the car up north in easy stages, and allowed a whole day (Sunday) for reconnaissance and laying plans.

It was after breakfast on Sunday morning that I saw the first geese — from Jim and Nollie's dining room window; two skeins flying high to the west. This seemed to break the last tenuous link with home, family, farm and my normal pattern of life in Norfolk. From now on, and for the next six days, I should hardly see a newspaper, never listen to the wireless (except possibly for weather reports), cope with no correspondence, struggle with no forms.

I had hardly left the main road before I found several hundred greylags on a grass field. But they were on forbidden land, and there was no point in lingering, so I pushed on along minor roads in the foothills and found plenty more geese. This was all new territory to me and still a long way from our H.Q. for the week, so there was nothing to do but to note the area and the farms on my map for future reference, and press on to more familiar ground.

And so, for the rest of the day, I visited and inspected all the well-proved areas that have held geese in the past, and where I knew I would be allowed access.

Jimmy's territory produced hundreds of geese, many spread over a series of grass fields at one end of the valley, with another large concentration on a field of turnips at the other end. Then and there it seemed to merit the title of Valley of Geese. Twenty miles further on I checked with a farmer whose fields usually provided both morning and evening flighting. Then on to that wide expanse of "goose country" of which Mongi's farm is the heart and centre. A few geese here, but enough to offer prospects for a dawn ambush. Finally, a careful search of the four goose farms on the Laird's estate. I could see nothing on the first; a small handful of geese on the second; but on the third a cheering sight awaited me — at least 500 pinks feeding on a large potato stubble close to the farmhouse. On the fourth and last farm only a handful of geese again. But the potato field posed problems. It was large and flat, and afforded absolutely no cover, only post-and-wire fences on its boundaries. It seemed we would do better by intercepting the geese on their morning flight to this field by waiting for them in the plantations on the next farm. Back at the Big Hoose I reported my arrival to the family. The Laird, alas, was no longer there to greet me. He had died a few months earlier while on a fishing holiday in the Western Isles; struck down with a heart attack at the very moment he had a fish on his line. (What a way, and what a moment, in which a fisherman should be summoned to the Happier Hunting Grounds!). Patrick and his elder brother said they would come out with us in the morning, but as there would be four of us we would divide up into two pairs, the brothers going to the first farm (which they said the geese had been using) leaving Andrew and myself free to go to one of the others.

A final call at the local hotel found Andrew safely arrived from England, so I left him to unpack and settle in, with instructions to be ready on the doorstep at 6.30 a.m. next morning.

And so at last to Robert and Shelagh who had again insisted on putting me up. I found I had covered over 100 miles in the day's reconnaissance and had made at least half a dozen calls on landowners, tenants and farmers, but it was time and distance well spent as I felt assured we should soon find ourselves getting to terms with the geese, especially in that well-proved Valley of Geese that had so seldom failed us, and which this year seemed to hold an exceptional concentration of geese.

Monday December 11th.

I collected Andrew as arranged, and together we made our way across the grass fields to the young plantation where I had taken cover two seasons ago, and where I had then shot 5 pinks. We put a batch of decoys out on the grass and awaited the dawn. At last a few skeins began to move, but all passed far out over the grass and seemed to show no interest in the decoys. Some lots even came flying along in the opposite direction.

I thought I would try and divert the passing skeins towards Andrew by moving out on to the grass field and openly showing myself. And the first thing that happened was the sudden appearance of a single goose flying straight towards me. I froze against the nearest fencing post; the goose came on, and at the last moment I straightened up and took him well in front. He fell with a thump almost at my feet.

I then moved further across the field till I reached the far side. There I was in line with "Patrick's Wood", and as the skeins were still flying wide of me I moved up under cover of the plantation and hoped to get a shot at any geese flying close enough to the wood. In the east the dawn was brightening in a patch of clear sky, and it was easy to see the skeins a mile or more away as they came in from the firth. At last I saw one coming straight towards the wood. I kept an eye on it from behind the corner of the wood, and sure enough it duly passed close along the side of the timber and offered an easy shot as it reached my corner. I got a goose with my first shot but missed with the second.

A little later I saw another skein heading for the wood, and obviously going to fly *over* the trees. So I quickly moved along so as to cover a gunshot to either side, and in a few seconds a lovely V of geese sailed into view over the tops of the fir trees — and slap over me. Again, I got a goose with the right barrel but missed with the left. After that the flight eased off, and I returned to Andrew who had had few chances and no luck.

Back to a late but welcome breakfast at the hotel, and then with a packet of sandwiches and the usual thermos of coffee we set out on a brief tour of reconnaissance before heading for the distant valley which held so many geese, and where I had planned to await the evening flight.

By now the wind had got up, storm clouds were gathering, and it looked as if we were in for a real wild night — just as we were last year. I placed Andrew in what I shall always now think of as "Peter's Post", and took station myself on his right, close to the old river wall. Early on, before the light began to fade, a small skein slipped in on my right and dropped on to the area of rough marsh and grass between the river wall and the present course of the river. It looked as though they could be within shot of the wall, and that a stalk might be possible. And so it proved: I made my way along the bottom of the bank, and when I got opposite the geese I peeped over and found them only about 40 yards out. But I only got one with the double shot.

Presently the flight got under way, and we both had several chances as the geese came battling up the valley. I got three more myself, and at last Andrew got his first goose. By the time it was all over I was suffering from neglect of my own advice on clothing. I was wearing an old jacket whose zip-front wouldn't work; I had not bothered to put on waterproof overtrousers, and in wading out to retrieve a goose from a patch of water I had stumbled and filled my left wader.

By the time I got back to base and a change of clothes, the only dry garment I was wearing was my right sock.

Tuesday December 12th.

This morning I took Andrew to the other river and the farm that Keith and I found to have such good possibilities at morning flight. Our two potato fields were corn stubbles this year, so we didn't expect geese to come to them for feed at this late stage of the season, but there should be skeins passing that way to other feeding grounds on the uplands. We took up our positions in the ditch running down to the river between the two fields, and set out our decoys well behind us to try and keep any geese on the right flight path.

A mild morning with a clear sky to the east enabled us to see the geese moving out from their roost from the very beginning of daylight, and before long a most impressive flight developed — very much as last year — with skeins flying out to all points of the compass. As before, a fair number came our way and gave us both several chances. There were no special incidents to report, but at the end of the flight we found we had collected six geese between us.

In the afternoon we set out again in good time, chiefly in order to recce the Valley of Geese for next morning's battle, which I planned to stage on the grass fields which I had found so full of geese last Sunday. But alas, there were no geese to be seen — except a dead one lying in one of the fields. On retrieving it another one was found nearby, and as they were freshly expired it was clear they must have flown into some electric power cables immediat ly above them. So there was probably a normal flight from the valley to the fields that morning, and since then something had disturbed and moved the geese. We could only hope for the best; but it was a little disturbing.

Meanwhile, we moved on further down the valley to the bend in the river, which provided me with my first "lucky retrieve" last year. This time the flight was even better, geese moving in all directions and giving both of us many exciting moments.

At one shot I misjudged my timing, and the goose landed with an almighty splash in the river. But it was only a few feet out and a fairly strong crosswind blew it to the bank before it had travelled more than a score of yards downstream. By the end of the main flight I had shot my quota of six geese and Andrew and I began to load up our spoils and make our way back to the car.

And then came temptation. Andrew was nobly carrying all the geese — festooned round his shoulders, while I was trudging along beside him carrying only my gun — still loaded. Suddenly a few squawks in the sky above us broke into an agitated chorus as both geese and man recognised each other at the same moment in the failing light. Instinctively the safety-catch was pushed off, the gun leapt to the shoulder, and a couple of geese fell dead on to the grass. What a satisfying end to a long and interesting day!

Wednesday December 13th.

This was the morning booked for an assault on the geese on the series of grass fields noted last Sunday. An early start brought us to the farmyard just before 7 a.m., and we then set out up the track past the buildings where lights were blazing in the milking parlour and two of the staff were coping with the morning milking. There were four or five of these grass fields, stretching along the country road, with the farm at the eastern end. I had never shot on these fields before, nor had I ever had the opportunity of observing how the geese flew in to them at dawn, or in what direction they departed at dusk.

I had a strong hunch that many, if not all, of them would fly up from the valley below, where I suspected they spent the night, though there were also at least three large sheets of inland water which I knew offered nightly sanctuary to literally thousands of geese, and which were within easy flighting distance of our fields. So geese might appear from various directions.

The first field — nearest to the farm — didn't look very promising. It was very large and offered poor cover, and anyhow was too close to the farm. The fence along the top side was the usual bare post-and-wire affair, though the boundary between this first field and the second was a stone wall. But stone walls are of limited use for cover; they are alright for geese coming straight towards you, but to birds coming in from behind or from the flank your huddled body will stick out like the proverbial sore thumb.

VALLEY OF GEESE

So we struggled along the top fence and reviewed the second field. This was smaller, and the next cross fence — between it and the third field — was a lovely straggling thorn hedge, reinforced of course with the usual post-and-wire to make it stockproof. The thorns were neglected and untrimmed, with gaps here and there along the whole length. One could stand in a gap and merge with the bushes on either side as occasion demanded, and escape detection from almost any point of the compass.

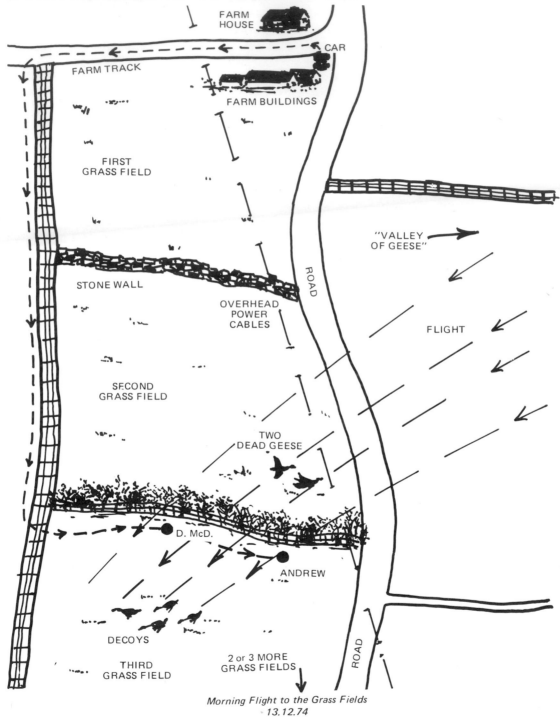

Morning Flight to the Grass Fields
13.12.74

170

This seemed the ideal place to await the geese, if only they would flight over the hedge, or we could persuade them to do so. Time was now pressing, the light was getting stronger, and we did not dare to waste more precious minutes exploring the next two or three fields. So we set up a group of four decoys in the *third* field — behind us and above us, and took up position behind the hedge. Even as I looked for a suitable gap, and before I had even loaded my gun, three geese sailed over the hedge a few feet above me, looking enormous in the faint light. It was a good job I couldn't fire: if I had hit one I must surely have blown it to pieces.

Then, as the light increased, a steady flight of skeins came flying up from the valley on our right, crossing the road where it ran along the bottom of the field in front of us, and then flying diagonally up the field till they crossed our hedge. I am sure our decoys must have helped to attract them to this flight pattern — a pattern which brought them over either Andrew or myself, or sometimes between the two of us so that we both had a chance at the same skein.

Before long I had shot my quota of six geese, and conscious of my over-indulgence the previous night I unloaded my gun and moved down to confer with Andrew. He seemed to be having difficulty in connecting with the geese so I suggested he borrowed my gun for a change, while I went off and searched for a goose that I thought might have dropped out of an early skein on to a field above us. And while thus searching (with no success) I saw two more skeins fly up from the valley past Andrew, and each time he got a goose.

Soon after that all further movement ceased and we packed up and returned to base for our usual late breakfast at about 10 a.m.

That evening we were due to change our headquarters to a hotel on the other side of the firth, so after an early lunch we bade farewell to the long-suffering Robert and Shelagh and set out to reconnoitre the new territory. We met one of the keepers on the estate in question, and with him carried out a wide-ranging tour of inspection. A few lots of geese were discovered on various fields bordering the coast, and a fairly large concentration on a big field up in the hills. But the latter looked difficult — poor access and inadequate cover, so we finally settled for a smaller lot of about 100 spread over two grass fields down by the coast. At least there was an excellent deep drainage ditch running the length of both fields. So we arranged to meet on the road at 7 a.m. next morning and made our way to our new quarters. There we found John newly arrived from the Solway, and as it was then too late to embark on any evening expedition we spent a quiet evening unpacking, dining and exploring the resources of the bar.

Thursday December 14th

Back at the grass fields before dawn we found the drainage ditch afforded excellent cover; it might have been designed to a wildfowler's specification! Deep but narrow, it tapered to a mere foot or so at the base, with a few inches of water on a hard bottom. So one could move along it freely and change one's position if the need arose. The ditch ran parallel to the coast, on the landward side of the two fields, so the problem would be to get the geese to come within range of the ditch. The decoys were therefore placed well out in the next field behind us. John took up his position on the right (eastern) end of the line. Andrew was in the middle, while I was out on the left, which I imagined would be the long-stop position as the geese were expected to fly in from the east. But we were wrong; a few skeins started to appear from the west, but all kept well out over the fields and took no notice of the decoys. Then a skein came along rather nearer, but still out of range, and when at the end of the line swung over the ditch in response to the decoys. They flew in a wide semi-circle over the field behind us, and then came back over the ditch exactly where I was crouched. By now they were lower and seemed to be in range, so as they passed overhead I straightened out and let fly. I had the satisfaction of seeing two geese tumble out of the sky and fall dead on the grass behind me.

Later a single bird came along flying east to west. Again I had all the luck. It was too wide for John and also for Andrew, but by the time it was opposite me it was nearer and offered a fair chance. It crumpled to my shot but was obviously not killed, as it fell struggling on a broken wing. Fearing I should have a rough time retrieving it I gave it the second barrel just before it reached the ground. This time the BB pellets finished the job cleanly, and the goose never stirred after hitting the ground.

Picking it up later I found it lay 65 yards from where I had stood in the ditch.

The flight — such as it was — now eased off. Mist was rising from the firth beyond the grass fields and blotting out the trees on the far boundary. It was probable that most of the geese would be mist-bound out in the firth and would wait for the weather to clear before flying inland.

So we returned to our base, with just the three geese; did a brief recce between breakfast and lunch to find something for the morrow, and then relaxed till it was time to set out for the evening flight in the Valley of Geese.

This we decided to try at the bend in the river where Andrew and I had such good sport on Tuesday evening. It was a bit soon to return to this same place again, but there seemed so many geese in the valley and they moved so freely at dusk that another onslaught was too tempting to be ignored. In the event the geese behaved much as before, with flighting across the river in both directions, along the river and over the loop of the field. We spread out 100 yards apart and each of us had some shooting and contributed to the bag — a total of six between us.

Andrew and John in the Valley of Geese

Friday December 15th

It was a potato field we tried for the dawn flight. We had seen a fair number on this field close to the firth when we did our recce yesterday, and there seemed good cover on one side of it in another deep ditch. But the flight was most disappointing; very few geese appeared, and mostly flying high in the clear still sky. Only one lot landed near the decoys but they were too far out, and hardly any of the other arrivals offered fair shots. In the end we came home empty-handed — our first blank morning.

It was just as bad in the evening when we went to the scene of Tuesday morning's successful flight. As the light failed mist rose from the river and blanketed the valley, so that we hardly saw or heard a goose. In fact, I do not think any one of us as much as fired a shot. So a blank evening followed a blank morning, making a completely goose-less day.

Back at our base we found Peter had arrived; to take John's place next day, as John had at the last minute got tickets for the All-Blacks Rugby Match at Edinburgh.

Saturday December 16

John had decided that he could manage the dawn flight and still get to the rugger match, provided he did not stay on too long at the flight. So with four guns we agreed to divide our forces and operate as two pairs. Andrew and Peter were to meet the local keeper, who would take them by Land Rover to a grass field up in the hills where we had seen greylags feeding. John and I would try our luck at a potato field in the distant Valley of Geese where I had seen greylags feeding.

The potato field was quite small; not much more than five acres, and ran down towards the valley with a short bank and good cover at the lower end. Yesterday's mist still persisted but not too thickly, and we could just make out the features of the valley below us as the light increased. An early bunch of four geese flew in between John and myself, and offered easy shots. Yet only one goose fell. A little later five more flew in over the decoys and landed beyond them. They were too far to justify a shot, so we left them, hoping they would attract later arrivals. Nothing happened for some time, and John came along to discuss tactics with me. The geese probably heard our voices, though I doubt if they could have seen us. Anyhow they were clearly restless, and in a few moments took off to fly back to the valley. And they came straight past where John and I stood amongst some brambles and bushes. Again we fired all four barrels, and again only one goose fell! John and I will never understand how we failed to collect eight geese from those two encounters.

Soon after that John had to depart, but not before we had collected three more geese from various small parties. I stayed on for the best part of another hour, but had no more shooting, though I missed an easy chance when a skein came gliding in silently from a flank and took me completely by surprise.

Back at the hotel I found the other two finishing their breakfast but having seen nothing up in the hills, the geese no doubt being again mist-bound in the firth.

For our final flight we paid yet another visit to the Valley of Geese. There was still a huge concentration of geese in the district, and as the light failed skein after skein came flying in from their feeding grounds to drop in to an area across the river, where it seemed they must be collecting for the night. It was hard to estimate their numbers, but they must have been well over 1000. Occasionally large groups of them would take off and start flying about in large and small skeins, and it was on such occasions that we all had a few chances as some of the geese crossed to our side of the river.

An early couple came straight for me and I got the first, though missed the second. Then five came flying along the river and I saw one of them sheer off from the others and keep well over the field. As soon as he appeared over the bushes on the bank I dropped him safely on the field.

We stayed on in this field under the moon till about 6.30. The sky was mostly covered with layers of mist or thin cloud, and with the moon a few days past the first quarter there was enough light to shoot.

A few skeins kept moving about and we all had a few more shots, but only Peter thought he had a goose down though we were unable to find it.

And so at last the week came to an end. Peter returned to Edinburgh that night, while Andrew and I waited till next morning before setting out on our longer journeys to England.

* * * * * *

Looking back on it there is no doubt that this has been one of the most enjoyable and successful of our many wildfowling holidays. Its main feature was the consistent success which rewarded every one of our sorties, with the single exception of one completely blank day on Friday. My one day's long-range reconnaissance on the previous Sunday had paid off handsomely. I had assured myself that there were plenty of geese in the five distinct areas that I hoped to work and especially in the Valley of Geese. From Monday morning onwards there was a ready choice of venues, and no time had to be wasted in further reconnaissance to new areas and the tracing of owners or tenants.

The weather also was kind to begin with; rough weather at the beginning of the week, but no appreciable frost and no snow. Later the waxing moon with clear skies and subsequent mists upset the normal pattern of flighting and reduced our bags.

The bags themselves were not excessive; nine was the maximum and two the minimum; so that each time we went out we experienced all the thrill of seeing and hearing geese, and the mounting tension and waiting for them to approach. And then we all usually had a number of those brief opportunities when one has the chance of placing the seal of success on the morning's — or evening's — objective. What more can one ask?

For the sake of the record the week's bag was made up as follows:

	Morning Flight	Evening Flight	Total
Monday	3	5	8
Tuesday	6	9	15
Wednesday	8	("Half-Day")	8
Thursday	3	6	9
Friday	—	—	—
Saturday	5	2	7
	25	22	47

The only fly in the ointment, and a matter of some embarrassment to me, was the disproportionate number of geese that fell to my own gun. It was no use protesting too much, but I cannot help thinking that my companions must have suspected I knew exactly where the geese would fly, and that I placed myself in the best positions accordingly.

Of course, exactly the opposite is the truth. With a novice on my hands I placed Andrew where I thought he would get most shooting and where on previous occasions the highest scores had in fact been made. Thus on the first morning I placed him where I had shot five geese two years ago — this time he got none. That evening I placed him where Peter shot 10 geese last year — this year Andrew got one and I got five. Next morning he stood where Keith got three (to my one); this time I got five and Andrew got one! And so it went on. On several other occasions I was the only one who had a fair chance of a shot. It seemed that the "radio-location" which "BB" accused me of possessing in 1943/44 was working overtime and drawing the approaching skeins to my particular position in the line.

But there was another factor, and Andrew would be the first to admit that he had some difficulty in adjusting his shooting skill to the unaccustomed speed range and size of these large targets. John also, an experienced fowler, seemed out of practice when he arrived for the second half of the week, and hardly contributed what I expected of him. But what does all this matter? I am sure they enjoyed themselves and had plenty of shooting even if it was not always translated into dead geese in the boot of the car.

Andrew in particular was a tower of strength in other directions. He nobly appointed himself Chief Gun-Bearer and Goose Carrier, and rigged up a sling to carry dead geese, made up of a pulp sack and lengths of binder twine which would have delighted the heart of Heath Robinson himself. To see him struggling across the fields with nine geese draped all round his person was to suggest a wildfowler's version of Orion the Hunter returning from a mythical hunt.

CHAPTER 36

THE LITTLE LOCH

(1973-1974 — Robert's Year)

This year I managed to fix the dates of my usual winter shooting holiday so that the moon would be in the right phase for any moonlight shooting. The week of November 12th-17th followed immediately after the full moon on the 10th, and so should be just right.

But before that I would take up the chance of spending two days in a new area where I had not shot for many years, and where I had now been offered facilities by an estate which normally held large numbers of geese.

So after an easy drive North I arrived at this new area in good time on Thursday afternoon, so that I could inspect the lay of the land in daylight and meet the keeper to fix details for the next morning. Peter was to join me for these two days, so that evening we arranged over the phone to meet at a certain road junction at 5.30 a.m.

I was staying with a friend some distance away, and I could not help smiling next morning as I crept out of the house at 5 a.m. with a suitcase, and wondered what any curious neighbours would think as I exchanged apparent tender farewells with a lady (my hostess) in her dressing gown at a lighted upstairs window. In fact Sonja was calling out harsh words to me for forgetting the picnic case she had filled overnight with hot coffee and sandwiches.

Out on the open road a car closed up behind me with its headlights dipped. It never tried to pass me, nor fall back, and I felt sure it must be Peter. And so it was; we drew up together at the pre-arranged rendezvous, swallowed the coffee and moved on to join the keeper at 5.45 a.m.

The estate contains a large area of rough undrained land — a typical Scottish "Moss" — covered with heather, rough tussocks of grass, bushy scrub and a certain amount of birch. In the heart of this marshy jungle are several open pools, the largest of which — perhaps two acres in extent — provides a roost for hundreds of geese.

We took our cars down a rough farm road, and then over several upland fields till we reached the edge of the Moss. Then it was a case of a 20 minute walk through the Moss to the pool.

Meanwhile, the keeper had prepared us with bad news: the several thousand geese recently in the area had practically all disappeared in the last few days.

As we approached the pool a small party of perhaps 50-60 geese rose from the far end and made off with a clamour of alarm. Peter and I took up our positions in two hides at the edge of the pool and awaited developments — with not much hope. A few duck could be expected, returning to the pool after their night's feeding, but I could see little hope of geese appearing.

So I waited, with a game cartridge and No. 6 shot in the right barrel, and a 3 in. magnum with No. 3 shot in the left.

A few teal came along, in ones, twos and threes, and between us we shot four.

And then suddenly, out of nowhere, a single goose appeared on my left, flying back to the pool. It crossed in front of me over the water in easy range, and I shot it with the game cartridge. Peter's dog soon retrieved it from the pool.

A little later another single goose appeared from the right, passing in front of Peter but apparently too far out from him. Then it turned and passed over the Moss between the two of us. It seemed to be just in range, but only for the heavier charge and shot, so I gave it the left barrel and it fell safe and dead in the heather. They were both pink-footed geese, and the only two we saw all day, escept for the small mob that disappeared on our arrival, and two or three skeins flying over the distant hills.

There was nothing we could do in the rest of the day, except make a long recce of the district by car, but in the evening we were taken to a small flight pond and got three mallard.

There was equally no point in going out after geese next day (Saturday), so I took the opportunity of taking my car to the nearest town and getting a new universal joint fitted to the propeller shaft. The original was beginning to break up and was causing an alarming and dangerous vibration in the transmission.

In the evening we again went out to a flight pond, joining up with a shooting party that had been out all day after pheasants. There were three such ponds and we split up into groups of two or three guns to each pond. It was a calm clear night with a full moon, and therefore not promising for evening flighting. I was told that my pond had produced 30 duck last time it was shot. This night we got four!

Peter had a pleasant surprise at his pond. In the midst of the flight a small party of geese flew in, and Peter was able to shoot one — another pinkfoot.

After that a drink and chat with the Laird in the Big Hoose, and then the road again; Peter to his own distant home, myself back to my hostess of the upstairs flat.

As far as goose-shooting was concerned the past two days had been most disappointing, though we were extremely lucky to collect three geese. But there were other compensations. In the Moss I saw the greatest concentration of glow-worms I have ever come across; dozens, if not scores, of them in patches of the ground, sparkling like reflected stars in the darkness of the ground as we trudged through the Moss. We also saw roe deer in the Moss. In the middle of the day we saw two Harriers, which I could not recognise at the distance, but which the keeper assured us would be Hen Harriers. And then we had pointed out to us a small wood where a pair of Ospreys had nested and safely reared three chicks this very year.

Next morning (Sunday) I set out on a wide-ranging tour of reconnaissance following very closely the route I had taken last year. The Valley of Geese was full of geese, and so was the area where Eric allowed us to shoot. But there were no geese on Mongi's farm, nor anywhere else in that surrounding stretch of wide open country. Nor were there any geese on the Laird's estate — a surprising and disappointing discovery. The goose farms on the other side of the water were also bare! I sat in my car at midday on a country road high up in the hills, eating my lunch and watching and listening for geese. But not a sign reached me; the fields were empty and only a few small parties of geese were resting out on the calm waters of the estuary.

Finally I reached Robert and Shelagh for supper after 140 miles of extensive reconnaissance.

The plan was that Robert would be my companion for the next two or three days, till Keith could join me later in the week. Robert himself had suggested this at the end of my trip last year. The suggestion surprised me and intrigued me more than somewhat. For Robert — for the past 15 years or more — has owned one of the best "goose farms" in Scotland! From his house on the side of the hill he can look down on several large square fields which used to be mainly under grass, and which were favourite grazing areas for hundreds of geese. I myself have watched 500 geese circling down on to his fields. Beyond Robert's own fields were other grass fields also favoured by the geese, while on the left were similar fields belonging to a farmer who never let anyone shoot on his land.

It was a tremendous area for geese, and I hesitate to think how many times we have waited for the geese to come to these fields at dawn, or how many geese we have claimed from the two accessible farms. Robert used to say that his farm was one of the collecting areas for the geese in spring, where they would assemble in ever increasing numbers and mobilise themselves into suitable formations before setting forth on their long migration back to Iceland. After several false starts and a certain amount of practice "circuits and bumps" they would eventually depart for the North about the first week in April.

And Robert had never shot a goose! Not that he is anti-field sports; he goes out pheasant shooting and fishes for salmon, so I can only think it must be a case of familiarity breeding — not contempt, but indifference. At any rate, he had now decided to try his hand at the game.

176

THE LITTLE LOCH

Monday November 12th.

Our best prospects for a morning flight seemed to be on the farm where Eric allows us to shoot. For the past few years this farm has always produced a few geese for us, and it deserves a few words of description.

Eric is the shooting tenant of a small estate which comprises a mixed farm of cereals, potatoes and livestock, and several blocks of woodland. On one side the farm lands drop down to the river valley, and along this valley the geese will frequently flight at dawn and dusk as they leave or return to their distant inland roost. There is also a little loch on the farm, and we have often noticed that at morning flight many of the geese will fly over this loch, or just to the left or right of it, as they swing away from the valley and head for their feeding grounds on some distant upland farm. From our point of view the loch provides ideal cover as it is surrounded by a belt of scrub timber — elders and birches. One has only to stand behind this wood and wait for a sight of approaching geese through the bare branches of the trees, and then take them as they sweep into view in the open sky above. Moreover, one can move freely along the outside of the wood — still under cover — if one finds the geese are mostly passing to left or right. So the Little Loch has a special place of affection in our list of promising sites for dawn flighting.

This Monday morning, however, Robert said he had business to attend to (and for an unworthy moment I wondered whether his resolution was failing!), but he promised to join me for an evening flight, and I therefore fixed a rendezvous with him at 3.30 p.m. on the road to the Valley of Geese.

So I had to set out by myself and reached the Little Loch in good time. Promptly at 7 a.m. the first geese started to move, but it was some time before any came near me. Then a couple of skeins gave me fair chances and I took a goose out of each. I missed a few later chances and then packed up at 8 a.m. On the way back I called at our friend next to Mongi's farm, and found that though there were no geese on the home farm there were plenty on some grass fields of his a mile further on. This sounded promising for a morning ambush with decoys, later in the week.

And so back to base for a late breakfast. The middle of the day was spent in further reconnaissance, and after lunch I did a tour of the area. There were no geese on the grass fields where Andrew and I had such a good morning last year, but I found a small party of greys on the field where John and I had waited for them on our last morning. This year the potatoes had been followed by a corn crop with an undersown ley and it was the young shoots of the new grass that the geese were finding attractive. A small stream made its way down to the valley below, cutting a narrow but fairly deep gully along the edge of the field. It looked as if the geese were just within range of this gully. So I set off on an "instant stalk". It proved quite easy; I could walk along the bed of the stream, and only had to bend double at a few shallow stretches. Eventually, after a few cautious peeps I found myself opposite the geese, and decided they *were* in range. So I bobbed up and took the usual double shot — the first one as their heads all went up, and the second as they jumped.

But only one goose was left behind. After that I waited behind the hedge at the far end of the field on the chance that geese might start to come back to the field. A single goose did turn up after some time, and I dropped it with a single shot. By then it was time to pack up and go and meet Robert.

We made our way to a stretch of the river that could usually be relied upon to produce a good evening flight. A large bunch of geese moved off early, away from us, and then there was such a long pause that I feared the geese were not flighting along this part of the valley. But in the end, with the last of the light, a terrific flight developed, with skein after skein swinging along the valley, but mostly over the river where, of course, it would be hopeless to shoot them, as they would be carried away by the current and lost.

I did in fact shoot one goose which I lost in this way, due to my own misjudgement. Robert was better placed and had several skeins approaching from the fields, and he safely downed two — two geese shot on his first outing! So at last we returned to our cars — with six geese to hang up from our first day's efforts.

Tuesday November 13th

We decided to go and deal with some geese I had discovered yesterday feeding on a large stubble field. They were on the farm where I had taken Chun on a "blind date" five years ago, and they seemed vulnerable to the usual dawn ambush with decoys. We found a few bushes for cover on the river wall and

177

set our decoys 50 yards out in the field. But conditions were unfavourable; very little wind and a clear bright dawn. Plenty of geese were on the move, but those that came our way passed high overhead, and took little interest in the decoys. A few seemed just in range and I did try one shot, but I left it too late and the goose fell in the river and was swept away on a journey to the North Sea. At last a small party of geese did circle round and land near the decoys, and I got one as they took off again. A little later a single goose made one of those remarkable sudden appearances; one moment an empty sky and the next a goose flying past in comfortable range. I dropped it safely on the edge of the river. Robert had a few shots but no luck.

As we left the scene of battle we found a farm worker had been collecting loads with a tractor and trailer in the next field, and this had no doubt discouraged the geese from our ambush.

On our way back to a late breakfast we called on the keeper of a nearby estate where Robert had obtained permission for us to have an evening flight further down the same river. This was just to show us how to get the car down to the river wall, and where we should get the best chance of some shooting. We arranged to come back that same evening.

So at 3.15 we set forth again and got down to the river bank in good time for the evening flight. Even as we waited a continual stream of geese started collecting in an area across the river in front of us. We could not see them over the far river wall, but I should not have been surprised if there were not at least 1,000 of them. Behind us we knew there were also many parties of geese further up the valley.

And then, at about 5, the flighting started, and a most exciting hour followed. Skeins appeared from all directions, some flying along the river (where it was useless to shoot them) but others crossing at all sorts of angles — some from behind, some from across the river in front. The dusk was full of the clamour of geese, and there was hardly a moment when one was not watching an approaching skein and wondering whether it would offer a safe shot.

After a couple of right and lefts, and two singles, I stopped shooting and went along to see how Robert had got on, 200 yards further along. He had got a couple, but lost a third in the river.

And so we started for home, with a long slow haul up the rough farm track, through the farmyard and up to the country road. We stopped in the nearby town; Robert to buy a packet of nails for his coffin and I to make a telephone call about the morrow. Then trouble started; the car would not start. There seemed no kick in the battery, or else the self-starter was faulty. With the help of some passers-by who pushed the car, it at last started as I let in the clutch, and we managed to get home, but only just. The headlights were getting dimmer and dimmer, and I then noticed that there was no charge going into the battery. No doubt our long slow climb from the river, with headlights blazing, had drained the last of the energy out of the battery, and when I turned to go up the steep drive to Robert's house the engine lost revs, stalled, and of course remained dead. So there we left it for the night, and phoned the local garage to come and cope with it first thing in the morning.

To add to my disgrace, I was so exhausted by the past week's activities that I fell asleep in my chair after dinner!

Wednesday November 14th

With my car out of action I was secretly rather glad to be immobilised myself and looked forward to a quiet morning in the house. My own batteries were getting run down and I needed a rest to re-charge them. In fact, I seriously thought of taking a complete rest for the whole day.

The trouble with the car was soon diagnosed — a worn and stretched belt that no longer drove the dynamo. It would be a simple matter to fit a new belt, but enquiries of the nearest four main agents in Scotland produced no belt, and in desperation I phoned Keith in Norwich and urged him to get me one from Mann Egerton and bring it with him.

So I rested in the house and enjoyed the television programme of the Royal Wedding. How splendidly the British do these things: we all agreed that no other country can stage such a display of pageantry with such smooth efficiency and dignity. What an answer to those miserable anti-royalists whose outlook appears to be based on envy, hatred, malice and all uncharitableness.

My anticipation of a quiet afternoon's rest on my bed was rudely shattered at lunchtime by Robert's "Where shall we go this evening?" I could think of nothing better than a return visit to the Valley of Geese, so we set out again — in Robert's car — for the same reach of the valley that we had visited on Monday.

No need to describe the flight in detail; it was another excellent one, and we struggled back to the car with eight geese, three to me and no less than five to Robert.

On the way home I collected a hire car from the garage to use on the morrow, till my own was repaired.

Thursday November 15th

I woke just before 5 and realised in some panic that I must have overslept my alarm clock, and that Keith would be just about to step out of his overnight sleeper and find no-one to meet him. So it was a case of pulling on my clothes as quickly as possible and hastening to the distant station.

Keith was there, already kitted up and ready for the fray. I told him we would go to the Little Loch; I had not had many shots there on Monday, and plenty of geese had flighted past the loch with no interference from me. But first we had to leave the all-important dynamo belt at the garage, where the foreman would find it when he turned up for work.

We reached the Little Loch just before 7, and were still discussing our dispositions when four geese slipped quietly past us. Keith had just loaded and was ready for them, and we both thought we saw a goose peel off from the others in the darkness. (Later in full daylight we found the goose out in the middle of the field).

Presently I got a good high single bird, and eventually we returned to the car with four geese.

Keith had been in his Norwich office at 4 p.m. the previous evening: at 7 a.m. next morning he had shot a wildgoose on a Scottish hillside!

The next problem was breakfast. We drove to the nearest town but the two hotels and the only cafe we could find seemed dead, dark and deserted. We pressed on to the next village, and there was a small grocer-cum-cafe whose "Open" sign told the truth. The proprietress gladly offered to give us breakfast — what would we like? There could be but one answer — bacon and eggs, toast and marmalade, and coffee. Under the regular routine of home life one can ring the changes with sausages, tomatoes, kidneys, kippers, fish cakes and all the rest, but when one has been out on a cold winter's morning for three hours, and comes in cold and famished, then nothing can compare with the traditional British breakfast. Under such conditions it is superb, and no other meal anywhere, anytime, can give such complete pleasure and satisfaction.

After this welcome interlude we took to the road again. I wanted to check on some geese I had seen on Monday feeding on a series of grass-fields. If they were there again, at this early hour, it meant they must have flighted in at dawn, and that it was an established "feed". Sure enough the geese were there in rather greater force, and so inviting us to deal with them on one of our two remaining mornings.

By now it was time to return to the Little Loch where Eric had arranged to meet us. He had nobly offered to show us some of the Capercaillie which live in his woods In fact, we were invited to shoot one each if we got the chance.

So Keith and I were each placed in a clearing in the largest wood on the shoot, while Eric went to the far end and started zig-zagging through the wood towards us, hoping to move the Capers from their perches in the tallest pine trees. I saw four of these majestic birds, but only one offered a possible shot, and I was not too greatly disappointed when I missed it completely. It was eerie the way they flew swiftly but quite noiselessly through the wood: none of the clatter or whirring that other game birds make when flushed.

Several roe deer also came forward, and one of them stood still within 25 yards of me and watched me intently, till it came to the conclusion I was not to be trusted, and made off at right angles.

The drive over we returned to our cars and ate our picnic lunches. Keith and I were tempted to have another final flight at the Little Loch, but thought we had already claimed enough of Eric's hospitality. But he solved our problem himself by saying we were welcome to come back again after the geese — morning or evening.

After lunch we went our respective ways, our own first call being to collect my car, now repaired and in good order. By then it was time to start thinking of the evening flight.

I had reserved "Peter's Post" in the Valley of Geese for this occasion. It was the surest place to provide some shooting for Keith. Robert and I had been a mile or more away on our own evening expeditions to the Valley, and were unlikely to have upset the regular flight higher up.

My own batteries still seemed rather run down, and I jibbed at the thought of struggling up the steep fields to the road after the flight, probably festooned with several geese. So I left Keith to take the flight alone, while I sat and rested in the car. I could not see him down below by the river, nor the flights of geese moving up and down the valley. With the window of the car open I could only imagine the progress of the distant encounter as a succession of shots began to reach me. In all I counted 18 shots, and I guessed Keith would have shot six geese! Eventually, when it was quite dark he arrived breathless at the car with seven geese, and had shot an eighth which he could not find.

Back then to Robert and Shelagh for supper, a re-packing of the car with all our luggage and gear, and then off to new quarters which we had booked at a small hotel where we had planned to finish the week. But we had to leave all our geese in Robert's outhouses, to be collected later.

Friday November 16th

Although we had moved to new quarters, three recent reconnaissances had shown that there were no geese on the farms where we had hoped to spend these last two days. So here we were, out on a limb, and still working the same old areas many miles away.

We had decided to take up Eric's offer, and as he was having a pheasant shoot on Saturday we went back to the Little Loch this morning, leaving the geese on the grass fields for Saturday morning.

It was a bitterly cold morning, and in the clear still air the geese flew high, but it was if anything a better flight than our previous ones. I saw Keith get a splendid right and left. I heard his first shot and turned to see a goose falling out of a high skein; then as I watched a second goose started to fall out of the sky, and in a split second the sound of his second shot reached me.

I only got one goose, and afterwards Keith complained that we were both shooting badly, but I was convinced the geese were much higher than earlier in the week, and that we were both probably trying shots at extreme range — or beyond. Anyway, we came back to the car with four geese — the same as yesterday.

We returned to our newfound cafe and fortified ourselves with another superlative breakfast. Then the usual midday recce, checking that the geese on the grass fields were again there in strength and ready for us tomorrow.

For evening flight we had no alternative but to return once again to the Valley of Geese. Robert had decided to join us, and to bring a friend who was anxious to see what all this goose-shooting was about. I also suggested he should bring his dog — a black and white springer spaniel. He had been left at home on previous outings, but my heart softened on this occasion. He would not be too conspicuous in the failing light of evening flight, and who knows — he might help us find a distant goose, or one that dropped in the river.

In due course Robert got a couple of geese, one of which fell in the river, but in a shallow patch where it lodged firmly. Here was a chance for "Bustle"; the goose might not be dead and would perhaps struggle into deeper water and be lost.

I watched and nothing happened. I moved along towards Robert and urged him to send his dog in to retrieve the goose. There was some reply to the effect that the dog could not or would not do it! However, he eventually sent the spaniel in, and it found the goose, mouthed it, picked it up, dropped it and in the end swam back to the bank without it. So I had to act as retriever myself. I found I could just wade out in my thigh waders, reached the shallows and recovered the goose.

Back at my post I had few opportunities except for a goose which I shot too late, and saw it fall in deep water and be carried away. It seemed I was going to finish with a blank outing at my last evening flight. And then at the very end of the flight, and in the last of the light, I saw a small bunch of geese gliding silently past me. Again I was a bit late with my shot and I saw a goose fall out of the skein and hit the river with a rather half-hearted splash. I rushed to the bank to see if there was any hope of retrieving it, but in the reflected glow of the dying sunset I could see no blob on the water, nor any ripples of a swimming goose. I flashed my torch across the water, and there out in the river, on a small shingle spit no larger than a hearthrug, the beam was reflected back from the pale breast of my goose! What an extraordinary piece of luck! I waded out again and duly recovered the bird. How lucky too that I had put on my long thigh waders, the first time I had done so this trip!

We collected together at the cars and found we had got four geese between us.

THE LITTLE LOCH

Saturday November 17th

And so we came to our last day and our final morning flight. Up at 5.30, into the car at 6 and on the site comfortably before 7. We set off across the grass fields and hoped we should not be faced with the same embarrassing confrontation with two rival gunners as we were the last time we shot on this farm, in January 1964. But this time we were left in undisputed possession.

The geese had been grazing in all three grass fields, and also on an adjoining stubble, so we decided to stage our ambush in the centre grass field. We knew where the geese would come from, and with a S.W. wind they would swing round and approach the decoys over the northern and eastern hedges.

The four decoys were placed well out in the field behind us, and we took cover behind the two hedges — straggling thorn affairs with a few hedgerow oaks along them.

The flight was late to start, and one began to wonder — as always — would they never come; had someone disturbed them yesterday evening. But at last they appeared. a few skeins at first, and then quite a steady procession at the height of the flight.

I had one right and left as a skein passed over my hedge, and later another as a skein swung round in front of me. Keith also had his share of the shooting, and at the end of it all we collected eight geese — all greylags.

By now it was 8 a.m. and we hastened to our cafe for a third perfect breakfast. We offered the lady of the establishment one of our geese, but she declined: "My family won't eat anything of that sort, not even pheasants — I think they're stupid". We said nothing, but silently agreed.

After that there was nothing left but to organise our departure. A call on Robert and Shelagh to collect our geese, a re-packing of the car, and then the road to the South, with a break at Newcastle for the night.

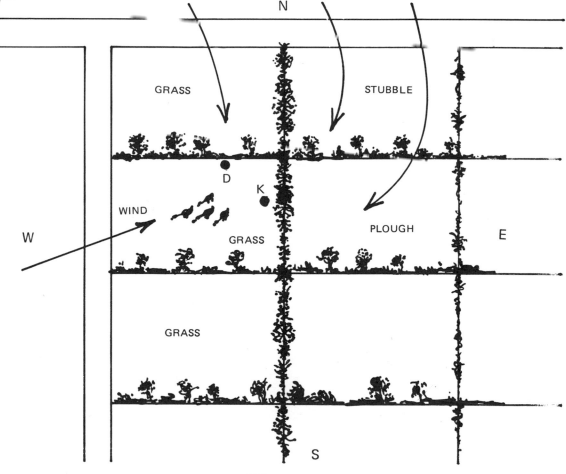

It had been a most interesting trip with opportunities for shooting on every occasion we ventured forth. In fact, I do not think we ever returned from morning or evening flight without some geese — except on those first two days. The total bag was 54 geese — all greys except for the three pinks, and though this looks a heavy bag by normal standards, it actually worked out at two geese per gun per flight.

The Sunday reconnaissances had paid off handsomely, largely in disclosing that two areas were devoid of geese and could therefore be ignored. In spite of this we seemed to have covered more ground than usual in our continual pursuit of the geese. On my arrival home the speedometer showed 1,700 miles since I set out twelve days ago.

The absence of the large armies of "pinks" puzzled us. there were none on the Laird's farms which at times hold 1,000 or more, and I only saw a few small lots of the Whiskey pinks. But on Friday we at last found a vast concentration during the course of our recce. They smothered several fields in an open stretch of country far off the beaten track, where the nearest roads were two miles apart in one direction and about three in the other — six square miles of secluded unobserved inaccessible territory! Wildgeese — and especially the pinkfeet — are well able to look after themselves!!

After all our plans we failed to manage a moonlight shoot. Although the moon was right the clouds were not; either too many or none at all. In any case, we never found a "strong feed" to which the geese were likely to return after moonrise. There had been too little frost to soften the potatoes on the "tattie bottoms", and very few potato fields held any geese. But perhaps most significant of all, at least one of the party was too exhausted at the end of a day (which usually started at 5.30 a.m.) to be dragged out again after supper.

The next most satisfying experience, after breakfast when you are cold and hungry, is bed when you are tired!

CHAPTER 37

LONG SHOTS

(A fresh look at an old problem)

It is a long established and well recognised principle in the shooting field that one should not take long shots at game when there is little chance of making a clean kill. One should not fire at targets beyond the Effective Range of one's weapon.

Effective Range has been defined as the range within which a correctly aimed shot will normally kill the quarry instantly, and this — in terms of shotguns — means that the target must be struck by a sufficient number of pellets to ensure that at least one will hit — and penetrate — a vital spot.

The basis of the principle of course is that shots taken beyond the Effective Range will only result in the bird or beast being wounded, and possibly suffering a lingering death later.

It is helpful to have a fairly clear idea as to the actual distances involved, and for this purpose one must start with a few basic ballistic facts. These facts will vary, of course, with the gun, the charge of shot, the size of pellet and the species of game.

For the great majority of all shooting at game birds in this country the equipment used will be a 12 bore shotgun, bored improved cylinder (in the right barrel at least), a 2½" cartridge, 1.1/16 oz. of shot and No. 6 pellets. And the target which I have little doubt accounts for the greatest expenditure of this ammunition is the popular and ubiquitous pheasant.

For such shooting there is an ample supply of statistics, graphs and tables available. Personally I can find almost anything I want in the *Shooters Year Book* published by the makers of Eley ammunition. From this handy little pocket book one learns that for the type of shooting I have described the maximum Effective Range of the 12 bore shotgun is 45 yards. This does not mean that you will kill every pheasant at 44 yards, and miss every one at 46; but it does mean that pattern fails at 45 yards, and beyond that distance the chance of a clean kill is at first appreciably reduced, and then with every successive yard fairly rapidly reduced.

For we must remember that the density of pattern does not deteriorate in simple proportion to the distance — it deteriorates with the square of the distance. The pellets that are spread over one square foot at say 100 feet will be spread over four square feet at 200 feet; and the bird that is hit by eight pellets at the shorter range will only stop two pellets (not four) at the doubled range.

But beyond the limit of Effective Range pellets will still retain sufficient energy to penetrate and kill for a further distance — *if* they should happen to strike a vital spot. This further distance I will call Extreme Range and it continues until the energy of a pellet falls below that required to kill. Expert opinion sets this figure of striking energy at from .8 to .85 foot-pounds for the usual range of game birds.

A pellet of No. 6 shot will have dropped to this level of energy at about 55 yards. So for normal game shooting using an improved cylinder barrel the further distance in which a kill is possible, but increasingly unlikely, is from 45 to 55 yards. Beyond 55 yards, when both pattern and penetration have failed, any

Diagram (not to scale) showing how the pattern of pellets spread over 1 unit of area at 100 ft spreads to cover 4 units at double the range (200 ft). At an increase of 40 per cent in range (140 ft) the pattern is already reduced to half its density

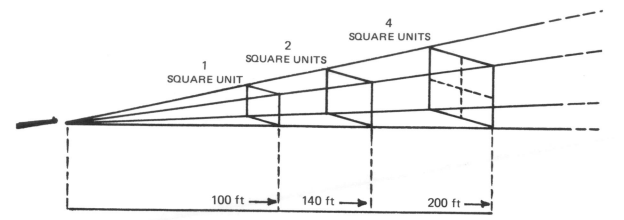

distance can only be described as "Out of Range" and anyone who wastes powder and shot in such circumstances is just plain stupid. But perhaps that is too harsh a criticism, as it is extremely difficult to estimate — in the few seconds available — the height of a bird flying straight overhead with nothing but a blank background of sky behind it. We can all make mistakes in this matter, and stupidity only arises if one knowingly fires a shot at a target out of range.

So much for game shooting. In wildfowling, and in goose shooting in particular, the picture is very different and also much harder to define with a standard set of statistics. There is much more variety in the type of gun used, the charge of shot fired and the size of pellet favoured. Ignoring punt-guns and other heavy artillery such as 4 and 8 bore shoulder guns, I think we can say that the best all round shoulder gun for the shoreshooter is the heavy 12 bore proved to fire the 3″ magnum cartridge loaded with 1.5/8 oz. of shot. As I have said elsewhere this should be fully choked in the left barrel, but if it is to be primarily chosen and used as a goose gun then let both barrels be full choke. As for shot, we will base our statistics on two shot sizes No. 3 and BB.

To start with, the Maximum Effective Range for such a gun (against geese) we find from the Eley tables to be 62 yards for No. 3 shot. When we come to try to ascertain what is the Extreme Range at which a No. 3 pellet will kill a goose the matter is not so easy. The answer depends on the striking energy required and various authorities quote different figures from the .85 ft.lb accepted for the usual game birds (pheasants etc.) to as much as 3 ft.lb for geese!

It seems indisputable to me that a pellet requires greater striking energy to kill a large tough bird such as a wild goose than a bird such as a pheasant. And as a goose will be twice as massive — in terms of weight — as a pheasant, I will arbitrarily suggest that the striking energy required will similarly be twice as much. To be on the safe side I take the higher figure of .85 ft.lb for game birds and double it to make it 1.7 ft.lb for wild geese.

This seems to match my own practical experience. It means an ordinary game cartridge with No. 6 shot should kill a goose at 35 yards — which I believe I have done, and that No. 3 shot will remain lethal up to 70 yards, which is a fact I proved with a greylag stalked and shot in December 1971.

When we come to make the same critical analysis of the results which we can expect from using BB shot instead of No. 3's the results of course are different — and extremely illuminating! The first point that stands out is that the Maximum Effective Range of BB shot is *less* than that for No. 3 shot. This is simply because the greatly reduced number of pellets produces an ineffective pattern much sooner than with No. 3 sized pellets. If we start with the Eley figure of 62 yards as the Effective Range for No. 3 shot, then with BB shot the range must be reduced to about 45 yards to produce the same density of pattern. This agrees closely with the pattern graphs published in the *New Wildfowler*.

These figures may be a little on the pessimistic side in actual practice. They provide for a goose being struck by five or six pellets, and this agrees with the general assumption that about 1/6 of the total target area of a flying bird represents the vulnerable areas of head, neck and heart. I should have thought that the massive energy carried by BB pellets (5 ft.lbs per pellet at 60 yards!) would render a larger area vulnerable and, together with the greater "shock" effect, incapacitate a goose from further flight even if it did not produce instant death.

So we can say that in theory the Maximum Effective Range of BB shot in a 3" Magnum cartridge is 45 yards, though in actual practice it may well be rather more. But in any case I am satisfied that it must be less than the range for No. 3 shot.

All this drives one to the inescapable conclusion that for any 12 bore shotgun BB pellets do not provide a suitable load and should not be used. Further confirmation of this conclusion arises — in my own case — from a dispassionate review of my practical experience in recent years, when so much of my goose shooting has been done with a 12 bore on inland fields and flight-lines. On many such occasions I have recorded how I killed a goose with my first barrel (No. 3 shot) but failed to complete a "right and left" with the second barrel (BB shot). This I have attributed to the evasive tactics of the geese as they reacted to the first shot, but I now believe that a second — and possibly more potent — reason has been the fact that my left barrel was charged with BB shot and the pattern was simply not adequate.

This shift in my attitude to pellet size of course only applies to 12 bore guns and cartridges; with 8 bores and their much heavier loads I still retain my faith in BB pellets for the left barrel. This also is confirmed by practical experience. In earlier years when so much of my shooting took place on the foreshore with my 8 bore, there was never any feeling of inadequacy with the second shot — on the contrary, many incidents occurred, and some recorded, when a miss with the first charge of No. 3 pellets was followed by a clean kill at a still greater distance with the second charge of BB pellets.

The Extreme Range of BB pellets I find more difficult to assess. There seems to be less material available in the form of well-established and accepted statistics so that there is a wide range of views expressed by those who venture to write on this aspect of wildfowling. The one firm figure which I rely on is the maximum range of 127 yards given by the cartridge manufacturers for the range at which BB pellets still retain a striking energy of .85 ft.lb. But this of course would be inadequate against geese, for which I have already assumed the necessity of 1.7 ft.lb. This figure is maintained at least up to 100 yards, and here again this seems to match practical experience. I have always understood that in punt-gunning (of which I have no first-hand experience) the fowler would not hesitate to discharge a pound of BB pellets at a bunch of geese at 100 yards — if he could not get any closer. My own experience is limited to a kill of 85 yards, as described in an earlier chapter. ("Old Haunts and a New Island")

So I would say that with our 3" magnum cartridge loaded with BB shot and fired from a fully choked 12 bore the Effective Range is 45-50 yards, and the Extreme Range 100 yards. But what a badly-balanced load! I can see no justifiable use for it, except perhaps as a last resort if one has a wounded goose that is going to get back to the open estuary, across a creek or river, or out to the open water of an inland loch. In such an event, if you have a few BB cartridges in reserve, you will have a slightly better chance of stopping the goose at extreme range with BB rather than with No. 3.

By contrast, what an excellent load is the same cartridge filled with No. 3 shot. Pattern holds out to 62 yards and penetration to only slightly more — 70 yards. If you use a heavier pellet pattern with fail before 60 yards; if you use smaller shot penetration will fail before this distance. No. 3 seems to strike the best possible balance within the choice available for 12 bore guns from the standard range of ammunition now manufactured.

The diagram that follows on page 187 attempts to show in simple visual form the capabilities — and limitations — of the various combinations of gun and cartridge under review. It emphasises the inadequacy of an ordinary game gun under the long range conditions of wildfowling. In fact, the normal rule of pattern failing before penetration is stood on its head; penetration gives out first. At the other extreme BB pellets in a 3" Magnum cartridge are seen to provide an equally unbalanced load with almost useless wastage of striking energy from about 50 yards to over 100.

We can perhaps now discuss the ethics and moral issues involved in taking long shots. The first point to realise is that the regrettable result of some such shots — wounded birds — is a common feature of all game shooting with scatter guns. There is no sudden change from clean kills to complete misses; there must always be a substantial "grey" area between the two, when pattern or penetration fails, or where the human element is unable to take advantage of the opportunity and fails to aim the gun correctly.

Wildfowlers certainly seem to come in for more criticism on this score than other shooting men, and I would not try to deny that this criticism is well founded in that wildfowlers are more likely to risk long shots at their quarry than are other men in other branches of shooting. But the pressure and temptation to do so is very great and calls for more understanding and toleration than is often displayed.

Consider the case of a wildfowl enthusiast who snatches a few days holiday in the middle of winter and repairs to his favourite bay or estuary in search of a goose. For two or three mornings he may go down to the coast at dawn and await the morning flight. But each time the geese flight in far to the left or right of his position and he never even fires a shot.

And then on his last morning his luck changes. He sees a skein lift from the distant mud and head straight for him. They are rising all the time, and our friend realises they will be very high indeed when they reach him — they will be beyond the range at which he could be reasonably sure of a successful shot, but yet within the maximum range at which a lucky pellet could produce a dead goose. What is he to do? Stand up and wave goodbye to the geese until next season? Not likely! He will keep down till the last moment, and then straighten up and let off both barrels in the desperate hope that a chance pellet will save the day and send him home in triumph with a goose for Christmas.

And which of us would not do the same! Now let us consider the case of the man who is invited to a "big" pheasant shoot. There will be an abundance of game; the bag for the day may well run into three figures, and our friend could easily fire 100 cartridges. Suppose he kills 50 pheasants: what happens to the other 50 shots? They will not all be clean misses. If he is a reasonably competent shot I would expect that a considerable proportion (perhaps 30?) will result in "pricked" birds; birds that have only been struck by two or three pellets for one of several reasons, e.g.:

1. The bird happened to meet a "thin" patch in the pattern of pellets.
2. The bird received its full quota of five or six pellets, but it so happened that none of them reached a vital spot.
3. The marksman's aim was at fault and the bird was only caught in the outer fringe of the shot pattern.
4. and finally — like our wildfowler — our pheasant shooter may have been tempted to risk a long shot beyond the Effective Range of his gun!

In fact a gun at a large pheasant shoot may well prick or wound more birds in a day than many wildfowlers will do in a whole season. And I would further hazard the opinion that in the midst of the season there is more lead flying round the countryside in the anatomy of pheasants, partridges and grouse than in all the geese and truly wild duck to be found around our coasts.

There is a particular branch of game shooting where long shots are frequently taken and where they are more vulnerable to criticism, and that is when the cult of the high pheasant is carried to extremes. One hears, from time to time, of pheasant shoots where the birds are driven out of hanging woods or woods on the very tops of hills and where many of them are quite clearly out of range of the guns placed in the bottom of the valley and perhaps a 100 yards or more back from the wood. The host or owner relates with glee how the most expert shots are quite unable to kill a bird at these stands — for the obvious reason that they are out of range.

And what do the guests do — expert or not? Do they sit on their shooting sticks and watch the pheasants fly overhead? Not on your life! Most men will be unable to resist the temptation of letting fly at these starlings in the clouds, hoping to bring off one of those spectacular shots which will fill the lucky marksman with a wonderful warm glow of self-satisfaction, and also provoke in due course murmurs of admiration and envy from his companions who have witnessed the near-miracle.

All this is only natural and normal human nature — the same that fills the wildfowler on the saltings. But if long shots beyond effective range are to be discouraged then the man who deliberately produces the temptation of them is surely much more to be criticised than those who succumb to the temptation.

So it seems that the whole issue is one of degree. The man on the coast can be forgiven if he is sometimes tempted to risk a long shot where his chance of success is slender; but there is surely little excuse for the man at a well-stocked inland shoot, who will be offered plenty of targets within the Effective Range of his gun, and who is under no pressure to take home a trophy for the larder.

DIAGRAM

To illustrate the range potential of various 12-bore cartridges

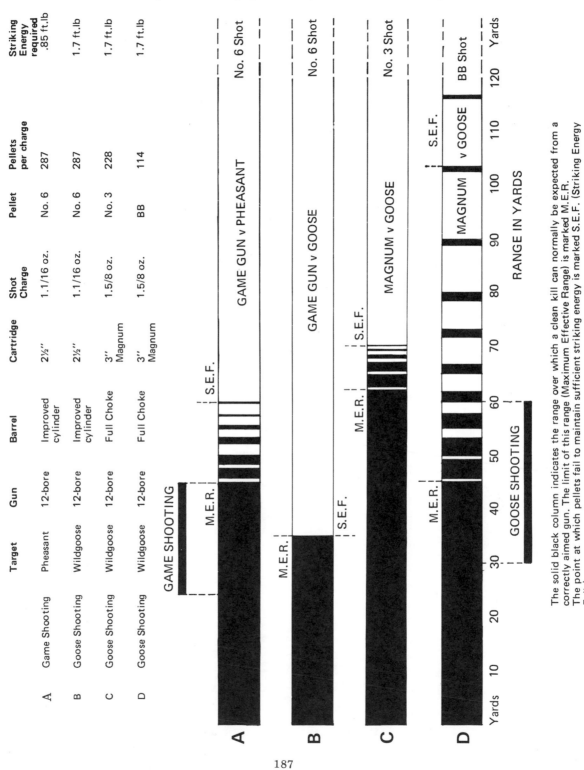

	Target	Gun	Barrel	Cartridge	Shot Charge	Pellet	Pellets per charge	Striking Energy required
A	Game Shooting	12-bore	Improved cylinder	2½"	1.1/16 oz.	No. 6	287	.85 ft.lb
B	Goose Shooting	12-bore	Improved cylinder	2½"	1.1/16 oz.	No. 6	287	1.7 ft.lb
C	Goose Shooting	12-bore	Full Choke	3" Magnum	1.5/8 oz.	No. 3	228	1.7 ft.lb
D	Goose Shooting	12-bore	Full Choke	3" Magnum	1.5/8 oz.	BB	114	1.7 ft.lb

RANGE IN YARDS

The solid black column indicates the range over which a clean kill can normally be expected from a correctly aimed gun. The limit of this range (Maximum Effective Range) is marked M.E.R. The point at which pellets fail to maintain sufficient striking energy is marked S.E.F. (Striking Energy Fails).

LONG SHOTS

There remains then the question of the damage and suffering caused to birds which are not killed outright, or at best within a short time of the shot so that they are retrieved and despatched with a minimum of delay. Of course there must be some cases of serious injury and lingering death, but my personal impression — both with game birds and wildfowl — is that in the great majority of cases it is either sudden death or recovery and survival. Otherwise our woods and fields would surely be littered with dead and dying birds after a big shoot, and the high-tide line round our wildfowl estuaries would be strewn with the corpses and skeletons of geese and ducks very early on in the season.

There is certainly evidence that geese can stand a lot of punishment and carry a tremendous amount of lead. Many wildfowlers must remember the results of examining over 1400 geese caught in one of the netting expeditions carried out about 20 years ago. Of the adult birds (i.e. excluding young birds of the year) 40 per cent carried shot! Even more significant was the statement that in most cases the birds suffered no great harm from the lead in their bodies, and the admission that the birds' weights indicated that there had been no loss of condition.

There remain two further questions arising from the tendency to risk long shots at wildfowl — the excessive disturbance of fowl generally, and the spoiling of sport for other wildfowlers.

I doubt whether the type of shooting has much effect on the disturbance of geese in an area. I suspect it is the overall shooting pressure and the continual invasion of their resting and sleeping quarters which soon reduce the numbers of fowl in an estuary and in particular will induce them to avoid a stretch of the coast where they will be met by a barrage of gunfire at every morning flight.

But the spoiling of other people's sport is a more definite hazard and one that we should all avoid. It is extremely frustrating to watch a skein of geese heading straight for you at reasonable height, and then to hear some over-keen but selfish gunner let off two barrels at another skein to your right which is quite obviously well out of range. Your own approaching bunch will change course and probably pass far to your left, or if they do cross the seawall overhead they will by now have climbed to a safe height and turned a reasonable chance into a forlorn one. So I would say that the most serious objection to the risking of long shots is the likelihood of spoiling sport for others.

However, when all is said and done I wouldn't like it to be thought that I am trying to encourage long shots — that is, shots taken at a range where it is unlikely that a clean kill will result. We should restrict ourselves to the Effective Range of our weapons, but with the heavier gun and shot charge available for goose shooting the Effective Range is very much greater than that to which the ordinary game shooter is accustomed. On top of all this it is much harder to estimate the longer distances involved. Who can assess with any degree of certainty the height of a goose flying overhead — against a blank background of sky — at 55, 60 or even 70 yards? Only the last would be beyond the fair range of a 12 bore Magnum 3" cartridge loaded with No. 3 shot, and even then it is within the extreme killing range of the pellets.

Many of us will at times take a chance with these long shots — either from sheer miscalculation of the range, or more simply from over-enthusiasm and the desperate urge to save a day's efforts — or even a whole expedition — from drawing blank.

So long as we do not make a nuisance of ourselves and spoil sport for our companions or others who are equally entitled to enjoy the freedom of the saltings, then an occasional shot at extreme range is not the heinous offence it is sometimes made out to be.

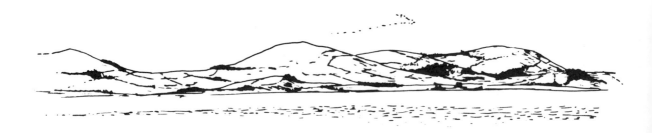

CHAPTER 38
THE END OF THE SEASON

(January 1974 — The Uninvited Guest)

Boxing Day came a little late this year: or rather it came late last year and overflowed into this year. It is traditional in our family to have a Boxing Day Shoot, when we collect as many able-bodied gun-bearing members of the family as we can, and set out to have a final round-up of the elusive cock-pheasant, a duck or two, and perhaps even a woodcock.

But this season it was January 12th before we were able to collect a suitable family party.

By 9.30 a.m. we were all present and correct — one son, three nephews, three grandsons and one friend on leave from Australia. A sprinkling of wives and younger children joined in at various stages of the day's proceedings, and made up a grand total of 17 for lunch.

A depleted farm staff nobly volunteered to help beat, and a couple of young men from the village also came along (with their invaluable dogs) to help beat, and at the same time indulge their own pleasure in a day's shooting.

The first set piece was to string out the guns in a reed marsh, whilst one of the party went and showed himself at the far side of the open stretch of water which we like to call our "Broad". We knew there would only be a few duck, but they responded as expected and flew off over the waiting guns — perhaps a dozen of them (ducks, not guns!) in twos and threes. A barrage of shots greeted them, but only one duck succumbed; a very high mallard brought down by Duncan and his 16-bore — quite the best shot of the day as it turned out.

The next drive was for pheasants, and the guns had only to re-align themselves at a fresh angle, and the beaters then proceeded to dislodge any pheasants they could find in a belt of alder carr lying between the farm fields and the marsh. As usual, several old cocks slipped away at right angles before the flank guns could get far enough forward to cut them off, and then only a handful came forward over the guns. Two or three were accounted for, but the only woodcock seen all day slipped through between two guns and passed unscathed.

After that, another drive was organised, with a couple of guns helping the beaters, and all the dogs pressed into service. There were four (or was it five?) spaniels, a retriever and the farm sheepdog, with only one retriever kept back with the guns. Thanks largely to the spaniels the drive — through a dense marsh — was more successful than usual, and for once I think everyone had some shooting.

And then when the drive was all over there appeared a large black labrador which nobody seemed to claim. He had come through the jungle with the others and was obviously enjoying himself hugely. He went off with the beaters to the next drive — the last before lunch — and went careering through Church Wood in full enjoyment of the day's sport, though it was obvious he was not trained to the finer qualities required in a gundog. In fact when he appeared in front of the guns a good hundred yards ahead of the beaters and spaniels behind him, it became clear that something must be done to restrain him.

He came back with us all to the house for lunch, and fraternised freely with the other dogs left outside in the yard, obviously a nice friendly type. We held him by his collar — no name or address on the plate — and decided that he must be excluded from the afternoon's operations, which would involve a good deal of walking-up in the marshes. So he was shut up in the stables and we set about trying to trace his home and ownership.

Someone had suggested a family in the village who were known to own a black labrador. We phoned them up: "Have you a large black labrador?" "Yes". "Well, have you in fact got him?" "Yes — he's here in the house". Explanations and apologies followed but at least another possible owner was suggested. Another phone call and another similar conversation. More explanations and apologies, and again another suggestion. Third time lucky! "Yes, my dog went streaking across the fields this morning — that sounds like him".

And so dog and master were reunited, with no hard feelings between them and the shooting party, though it was made plain that it would be better if such liberties could be discouraged, and preferably prevented, in future.

And so we came to the end of another Boxing Day Shoot, and for all practical purposes the end of another shooting season. The reward for our efforts? Sixteen pheasants, a couple of rabbits, one hare — and Duncan's duck.

Everyone seemed to have enjoyed themselves; not least our four-legged uninvited guest.

CHAPTER 39
THE TWELVE DAYS OF CHRISTMAS
(1974-1975 — Arthur's Year)

This year I had been offered two days shooting on an estate in the far north which I knew held great wildfowling possibilities. The dates in question were December 20th and 21st — perilously close to Christmas as it turned out — and this meant that the rest of my shooting holiday had to be fitted in during the middle of December. So I planned to spend a week in my usual well-proved haunts, with Peter joining me for a couple of days; and then Keith would arrive at the end of the week and join with me in the two days at our new centre, and also provide company and relief driving for me on the long haul home for Christmas. This would leave me with twelve days on the trail of the grey geese — December 10th to 21st.

Tuesday December 10th

As usual I soon found geese on arrival in goose country, but sleet showers swept the countryside and covered the roads in slush so that visual reconnaissance was difficult and at times impossible. However, by the time I reached the Valley of Geese the skies had cleared, but a careful inspection proved most disappointing. I could only find two small lots of geese sitting out in the centre of grass fields, though one of them looked possible for a morning ambush if I could find nothing better.

Pressing on I made an equally thorough inspection of the Laird's estate, and this was even more depressing. Not a single goose could I see on any of his three most likely goose farms. A call on Eric, however, was more hopeful: he assured me there were plenty of geese in his neck of the woods, but he was having a shooting party himself on the Saturday — including a dawn rendezvous with the geese before breakfast — and therefore I would have to leave the geese undisturbed till after the weekend.

Eventually I reached Robert and Shelagh in the late afternoon, and found that they had also been unsuccessful in their enquiries. I had sent Robert a list of farms and farmers further north, and he had promised to check with them and see if anything promising was available for Wednesday morning. But he too had drawn blank and found no geese on their usual haunts.

So I was left with little option but to try the grass field in the Valley of Geese next morning.

Wednesday December 11th

Robert was not free to join me at morning flight, so I had to set off by myself at 6.30 a.m. for the distant grass field. It was frosty with a light covering of overnight snow, but there was a good track down to a set of farm buildings where I left the car, and then I only had a few hundred yards walk to the field. There were a few scattered thorn bushes along the down-wind fence, so I placed my two decoys a good 50 yards out in the field behind me, where they stood out clear and sharp against the white ground, even before there was any appreciable light from the dawn. I stumped up and down to keep myself warm and waited for a sign of movement, but there seemed to be little passage of geese along the valley that morning, and it was nearly full daylight before a few skeins appeared from the east and flew straight over me, high and unfaltering. Later a small skein did circle round and have a look at the decoys, but never came near enough to offer me a shot.

So in the end I gave it up in disgust, cold and gooseless, and spent the rest of the morning in further fruitless reconnaissance.

I had no plans for the evening flight: the only promising places I knew of I wanted to keep till I had Peter or Keith with me to share the fun. So I called it a day and retired to bed after lunch to prepare myself for what I hoped would be more strenuous days ahead.

That evening Peter arrived to spend the next two days with me.

Thursday December 12th

As I looked out of my window I could see that more snow had fallen during the night, and it seemed prudent to limit our outing to something near at hand. The nearby coast was the obvious answer so we set out thither — Robert and I — collecting Peter from his quarters in the village on the way. There was some goosetalk out on the water but Robert and I had neither the enthusiasm nor the energy to struggle out through the reedbeds to the edge of the mud. Peter was more enterprising, and I showed him my favourite track out to the edge of Goose's Graveyard and watched him disappear into the jungle of reeds and the darkness of a dull overcast dawn. There was no sign of any flight along our stretch of the sea wall, but in due course we heard a double shot from Peter's direction, followed quickly by a single shot. That sounded like a third shot to finish off a wounded goose on the mud.

Robert and I soon made our way back to the car and breakfast, leaving Peter to follow from his further outpost. We subsequently heard that he had in fact got his goose, and had seen several hundred flight in further beyond him. Some of these geese had dropped into fields close behind the seawall, so perhaps the Home Beat is not yet a complete write-off. At any rate we had started to score, though we still had nothing lined up for the morrow.

So after breakfast Robert and I set out to find and recce a farm in a completely new direction where we heard there were geese. We found the farmer, and he confirmed that geese had been feeding on his farm. He indicated several fields up on the hillside to the east of us. But there were no geese there — they would be clearly visible against the white covering of snow. But while we chatted I noticed that there were a lot of geese — in exactly the opposite direction — three fields away to the west! In fact the geese were over his boundary on a neighbouring farm. It looked as if we might be able to deal with them by lying up in the boundary burn and setting our decoys out in our new friend's field. At any rate it would be worth a try in the morning.

In the meantime there was an evening flight to deal with, and after lunch Peter and I set out for the distant Valley of Geese, and hoped to repeat the success we had three years ago. But conditions were very different; the ground was still covered with snow, the little flashes of fresh water which the geese liked to visit at dusk were all frozen over, and above all we lacked the wild stormy conditions which always help to make a good flight.

I managed to get a single and then a right and left, but only found one of them. Peter also had a couple but similarly lost one; so we trudged back to the car with our three geese.

Friday December 13th

Off to our new farm for the dawn flight. In the meantime Robert had traced the owner of the neighbouring farm, and obtained his permission to shoot there. I assumed the geese must come from the estuary, some six miles to the south; so we lined the southern boundary — a solid stone wall — and set out our decoys in the field behind us. How wrong I was. After a few small skeins had appeared from nowhere, a steady flight developed from the opposite point of the compass; from the hills inland to the north! We were helpless — a couple of hundred yards away, on the wrong side of the field and the wall. We tried moving the geese, and an early small lot did swing round the field and give Peter a chance — which he took. So we were lucky to add just that one goose to our score.

After lunch we went back to the Valley of Geese, but to a stretch of fields a mile or more from yesterday's encounter. In surprising contrast to Tuesday's recce the valley now seemed full of geese, with large gaggles sitting out in various fields up and down the valley, and on both sides of it. But they all seemed reluctant to start flighting while it was still light, and one began to wonder "will they never come?"

THE TWELVE DAYS OF CHRISTMAS

And then, at about 5 p.m., when it was nearly dark a typical evening flight developed with skeins swinging along the floor of the valley and giving us both some shooting. I could hardly see the geese till they were right on top of me, but at last I saw a skein in time, and saw the goose crumple to my shot. As I swung on to a second bird I was aware of a celestial body hurtling past my head and hitting the ground just behind me with an almighty thump. It was, of course, the shot goose, and it very nearly felled me on its plunge to earth (what poetic justice if it had!) Peter fared better and came along with three geese.

Saturday December 14th

It was now time to try the Laird's fields. Although there had been no geese on them at the beginning of the week, I had kept the fields under observation and had been pleasantly surprised to find flocks of geese building up on them again. The last check had shown 3-400 geese, so a dawn expedition looked hopeful.

Peter had returned home but Robert came with me this morning, and we made our way to the plantation of young conifers which lay in the well-known flight path of the geese. Sure enough a good flight of pinks developed, but unfortunately they mostly came in two large mobs, and they carefully avoided both our own plantation and also Patrick's Wood on the far side of the fields.

Eventually a few small skeins came wandering back towards us, seeking a suitable grazing area. At last one lot cut the corner of our plantation and I got a nice high goose which fell far out in the field behind me. But that was all for the morning.

I made no plans for the evening as Jimmy was having a pheasant shoot that day, and had asked me to leave the ground undisturbed — not so much for the sake of his pheasants but because he thought some of the party might themselves like to try an evening flight with the geese after the main shoot. I was invited to join them at the end of operations, so I made my way to the bothy where they were due to foregather before dispersing. I found someone from the farm had lit a roaring fire to welcome them, and in due course they all straggled in. What a pleasant cheerful party! Clustering round the fire with a glass in everyone's hand I could hardly see anyone of them venturing out again for a chance shot at a goose! I do not know if they considered that they had had a good, bad or indifferent day; they all seemed well content with the day's exercise and sport, and I didn't hear a single boring anecdote or post mortem on what might have been. By our own standards at Catfield the bag was large — 92 pheasants plus several "various": by the standards of many big pheasant shoots it was puny. But what matter! It had obviously been a grand day.

Sunday December 15th

A long lie-in; breakfast at 10 and then a somewhat perfunctory tour of reconnaissance with lunch out in the country.

Monday December 16th

Another of those early morning panics. I slept through my alarm clock and when I awoke the clock seemed to say 7.45 — and geese would already be flighting. I might as well turn over and have another lie-in. But a second glance — through clearer eyes — showed that it was 6.45, and I could still meet the geese if I didn't have too far to go. So it was a case of tumbling into my clothes and off in the car to the Laird's again. We had not had much shooting on Saturday morning and I was hopeful there would still be a fair flight.

As I was on my own I decided to try two experiments. Firstly, as the geese were obviously (and rightly) suspicious of the plantation I would stay out in the open fields on the main flight line, and rely on a simple improvised screen to hide me from their searching eyes. Secondly, I would test my latest convictions about pellet sizes and take nothing but cartridges loaded with BB shot. The results were illuminating. The geese were deceived by my simple camouflage, and several skeins passed directly over me, no doubt encouraged by the two decoys I set out 50 yards behind me.

On the other hand, my shooting performance was disastrous. Several easy shots I seemed to miss completely. Only three geese were eventually secured, and none of these was killed outright in the air but fluttered to earth 100-200 yards away, though they were dead when I went out to collect them. At least three others were clearly hit and lagged behind their skeins, but quickly recovered and rejoined their formation. One almost reached the ground and I felt sure it was in the bag, but a few feet from the field it recovered control, resumed flying and then proceeded to accelerate and rise, so that before the skein had left the field the laggard had rejoined its companions and was flying as strongly as the rest. What guts! What amazing powers of recovery!

Although a single flight and the firing of perhaps a score of cartridges prove nothing, I am all the more convinced that with BB shot in a 12-bore one simply has not got an adequate pattern at the usual 40-50 yard range at which so many shots are taken.

I was probably hitting my targets with only three or four pellets, and none of them happened to reach a vital spot. Some, with their massive striking energy, would probably rake through the bird and cause havoc in the less vital organs, causing death in a short time (the three birds I collected): in the other cases the pellets probably merely shocked the geese and lodged in their dense muscles. Ballistic calculations lend support for these views. I was firing 1.3/8 oz. of BB shot, and my right barrel which is half-choke should put 39 of these pellets in the 30 inch circle at 50 yards. The target area of a pinkfoot goose, ignoring the wing structures, is about 60 square inches as far as I can measure from the outline of a plucked goose traced on to squared paper. So a correctly aimed shot would only place three or four pellets in the bird, and this I do not believe is sufficient to be reasonably certain of a clean kill. The vulnerable area of a pinkfoot (as far as I can similarly measure it — head, neck and heart) is about 12 square inches: not more than one fifth of the total target, so in theory a strike of at least five pellets is called for.

By contrast, if one uses No. 3 shot then the inescapable fact is that one discharges exactly twice as many pellets (140 per oz. as against 70 per oz. for BB), and the pattern is just twice as dense. And as No. 3 size pellets hold sufficient striking energy up to 70 yards I can no longer see much justification for the use of BB pellets in *12 bore guns.*

In the middle of the day I set out to replenish my stock of cartridges. There is a great shortage this season of any unusual loads, and the only gunsmith I could trace who had a stock of 3″ magnums was 20 miles away. So off I went, doing a recce of several likely places on the way, but to no avail. Snow started to fall on my way back so it seemed prudent to call off any plans for an evening flight and take the opportunity to rest and recuperate.

Tuesday December 17th

I had planned to try the Little Loch this morning. Eric — like Jimmy — had had his own shooting party on Saturday and had asked me to leave the ground undisturbed till after the weekend as his own party started the day with the dawn flight of geese before breakfast. But now the coast was clear. Robert had other engagements and couldn't come with me so I set out alone and found the snow and ice nearly all gone, though still lying on the road over the hills. I didn't dare take the car across the fields so had a long walk to a thornbush I had in mind from last year, which seemed to be on the flight path of many geese. There sounded a lot of goose chatter out in front of me, and before long an early skein of pinks loomed overhead. I dropped a goose with the first shot, missed with the second and then a quick concentrated flight developed. Several skeins gave me fair chances but I only got two more geese, and one of these I never found though it appeared to fall like a stone to the bare field behind me. It was all over by 8 a.m., and I was back for breakfast at 10. At any rate there were still plenty of geese using the old flight lines, and I planned to return again to this attractive spot for a final flight with Keith on Thursday morning.

For the present there was an evening flight to deal with. Robert was free to join me and we decided to return to the Valley of Geese and take our stand by the reach of the river which I had discovered three years ago, and where Robert had shot five geese to my three last year.

The thaw had continued and the grass on the Long Meadow was now all clear, while all along the valley we could see concentrations of geese in the fields awaiting the moment to embark on their evening flight to the valley and their night-time roosts. The Long Meadow is a grassfield which borders the river for perhaps a quarter of a mile, but is hardly more than 100 yards wide. It never contains any stock when we invade it in winter; probably because it is liable to be flooded when the river rises in spate. After rain it usually contains several flashes of shallow water which the geese like to visit for a drink and preen, and often in the daytime it will hold several hundred geese, resting or grazing on the grass.

But it is at dusk that the place becomes alive with wildfowl: packs of duck sweep to and fro, and then the geese start flighting. Some come from further up the valley, some come down from higher ground on either side of the valley, but mostly they stream in from the east, following the course of the river, but many flying over the open stretch of the Long Meadow. This evening the first sign of activity was the sudden appearance of a group of six greylags who swept in and actually landed on the grass right in front of me. They could not have been more than about 50 yards out, so I bobbed up and let them have both barrels — one on the ground and the second as they lifted. I got my goose with each and hurried out to retrieve them. Soon after, as the light began to fail, I moved out into the centre of the field so that I could shoot in any direction and not lose birds by dropping them in the river. And thus for about half an hour, I found myself in the midst of a thrilling flight. The western sunset was blacked out by a thick bank of storm clouds, but the eastern sky was clear and comparatively light so that I had a good background. A fairly strong wind in these stormy conditions kept the geese down to a reasonable height, and the air was all the time full of the clamour of the approaching skeins. Before long I had shot my self-imposed quota of six, but in view of the very modest bags of the past week I felt that this was an occasion when I could grant myself some dispensation. So I continued for as long as I could see — and shot two more.

Robert now came along to see how I had fared and confessed to no success for himself, but on struggling back to the car across the Long Meadow we came across a freshly-shot goose which could only have been his. So out total score was nine — a wonderful evening for me; quite one of the best I have ever had.

Wednesday December 18th

With such a splendid day behind me, a fresh companion shortly to join me, and the unknown rigours of the next few days ahead, it seemed an appropriate opportunity to have what is described as a "rest-period". So I slept on late, breakfasted at leisure and lazed in the house all morning. Keith duly arrived about midday, having flown up from Norwich and continued his journey by hired car.

We set out again after lunch, firstly to turn in the hired car at the nearest depot, and then on to the estate where I had first shot last season thanks to Robert's introduction. Robert was unable to come with us, so Keith and I took our stands in much the same positions as had proved so successful last year. But this time the sky was clear and the wind slight. The geese came late and high, and not in such numbers as previously. I had a few ineffective shots but Keith, further along the river wall, seemed to be having better luck. Twice I distinctly heard the dull thud of a fallen goose a second or two after his shot. When I could no longer see I rejoined him and found he had collected three, but lost another two which he had dropped in the river.

On the way back we called at the Big House where the Lady of the Estate had asked us to call in for a drink and a chat. We relaxed and thawed out, and left her with the friendly warning that we should almost certainly come back and ask for more next year.

Thursday December 19th

A quick visit to the Little Loch and then we would be away to our last two days shooting further north. It was a dull late dawn with thick cloud and nearly 8 a.m. before I heard Keith's first shots from the distant thorn bush. I stayed at the Loch itself and waited behind a bush of broom, whence I could see any approaching skeins through the network of bare branches of the trees surrounding the Loch.

Several skeins followed their usual flight path over the Loch, and others were streaming over Keith far to my right. I collected four greylags, all clean killed and falling on the open field behind me; Keith came in with only one, though he had shot two more which he never found.

And so, back to base, a quick breakfast and packing of the car, and off again heading north. After a couple of hours driving the navigator decided to take a "short cut" over the range of mountains on our port bow. Before long we found ourselves slithering along third class mountain roads where the recent snow had been beaten down into solid ice. This slowed progress and frayed tempers, and there were some caustic remarks about people who tried short cuts over Scottish mountains in the depth of winter. The navigator was instructed to direct the expedition as quickly and directly as possible back on to the main road on lower ground. Harmony was restored as we neared our destination, and we were in time to watch the evening flight of hundreds of geese returning from their feeding grounds to the safety of the Loch for the night.

The next two days were to be spent on an estate whose land bordered this large fresh-water loch which held several thousand geese (and many duck) throughout the season.

I had imagined that it would be somewhat similar to Loch Leven, which must surely be one of the most attractive wildfowl shoots in the British Isles. I have shot there on three occasions and never pass through Kinross without reviving nostalgic memories. The setting of the loch with the town clustered at one end of it, the hills on two sides of it, and the islands with their romantic associations: St. Serfs with the ruins of its ancient Priory, and the smaller wooded island where Mary Queen of Scots languished for nearly a year — and then made her daring escape; all this the home and sanctuary for thousands of wild geese. What a combination of beauty, history, romance and sport!

Our new centre is also — like Loch Leven — a happy example of the fact that shooting and conservation can exist side by side with mutual respect for each other's interests. For while the local landowners retain their sporting rights but exercise them in a strictly limited and controlled manner, the two lochs are at the same time under the supervision and protection of Conservation interests.

On arrival at our hotel we found Arthur already there, also a fourth member of our party — a German doctor who had come over, with his wife, to shoot his first wildgoose. The fifth gun was to be recruited from more local sources and would join us in the morning.

Friday December 20th

A call at 6.00, a cup of coffee in the hotel kitchen at 6.15 and into the Landrovers at 6.30. A rough ride over some of the worst farm tracks I have ever known took us across the fields to within a few hundred yards of the loch. Then there was a belt of marshy ground which reminded me much of our own Norfolk marshes — reed, marshgrass and sallow bushes. We crept quietly into position, the doctor first on the left of the line, then myself, then Sandy, and finally Keith and Arthur far along on our right. All now depended on whether Arthur, who was in charge of operations, had correctly forecast the areas of the loch where the geese were roosting, and also their likely flight path as they set out at dawn for their feeding grounds.

I was hardly in position before three geese sailed past me. But it was still too dark to start shooting, and anyhow the other guns were probably not yet in position. So I held my fire and let several more small lots pass by unmolested.

Then after a while, as the light improved, a bunch of six passed overhead at a fair height, and I was just able to get in one shot which dropped a goose in the marsh behind me. At the report there was a roar of wings and a large mob of geese lifted from the loch out in front of me. I could just make out a large dark cloud of them as they appeared against the sky and faded into the distance.

So much for the morning flight I thought: there won't be much more now. I could hardly have been more wrong! After a while a steady stream of skeins appeared from far away on our left. They came flying along the belt of marsh and started crossing the line of guns diagonally, from left front to right rear, so that most skeins offered chances to at least two guns. I and my two neighbours seemed to be in the best positions, and before long I had exceeded my normal ration of six geese. At this point I had a slight argument with my conscience, which went something like this:

Conscience: Are you not on record as saying you do not like to shoot a large number of geese at a single flight?

Myself: Yes, but conditions are rather different today.

Conscience: How come? That sounds a very feeble excuse.

Myself: Not at all. When I am out by myself or in charge of a party I can make and observe my own rules, but on this occasion I am one of a party for whom others have gone to some trouble to provide good sport. It would simply be churlish in the extreme not to respond and take advantage of the sport provided.

Conscience: Even so, could you not have quietly stopped shooting when you had achieved your usual quota?

Myself:	And how, pray, would I explain my action — or rather inaction — to the others? My neighbours would notice it, and probably conclude I had dropped down in a dead-faint, or just plain dead, or was struggling with a jammed gun.
Conscience:	Well then, why not continue shooting, but take care not to hit any more geese?
Myself:	That would be the worst solution of all. I should be written off as a fraud. "Here's this bloke who has the nerve to write about wildfowling, and goose shooting, and he can't even perform competently in the field; his yarns about goose shooting must be sheer fantasy, or at least gross exaggerations".
Conscience:	So you're quite unrepentant?
Myself:	Yes, as I have written of a similar occasion 19 years ago "It was wonderful while it lasted, and I have no regrets".

The flight continued till 9 o'clock and the final pick-up was 39 geese, all greys except one pink.

As a matter of special interest to me, in view of my performance with BB shot last Monday, I was now using only No. 3 shot in 3″ magnum cartridges, and the difference in results was very impressive: nearly every goose I shot was clean killed, and I don't think I lost a single runner.

Moreover in terms of ammunition expenditure the results were also more satisfactory. I am not one of those who keep meticulous records of the number of cartridges fired and the resultant score of game killed, but of course we are all vaguely conscious of this ratio and are appropriately impressed — or depressed — by the number of cartridges we have to fire to put a bird in the bag.

In wildfowling, with its comparatively limited amount of actual shooting, one is very conscious of this ratio of "cartridges-to-kills", as on many occasions one can recall and count every shot fired, without having to collect empty cartridge cases at the time.

In this present case I know that my expenditure of cartridges was something better than 3 to 1. By contrast, but under very similar flighting conditions, the score last Monday with BB cartridges had been somewhere around 6 to 1.

We all set out again soon after lunch to deal with the evening flight.

This time we hoped to intercept the pinks as they returned at dusk to the other end of the loch. But the main skeins all flew high and held on till they were safety over the water before dropping down; There was very little shooting and between us we only collected three geese and two duck.

Saturday December 21st

We went back to the same positions for morning flight as we took yesterday. One could hardly hope for a repetition of the same exceptional spectacle: far fewer skeins came our way and the main body of geese left the loch far away to the left of our line. I got an early grey out of one of the first skeins, and then a tremendously high one with the last shot of the morning. I had brought my 8-bore with me — anticipating high skeins at morning flight — and risked a charge of BB shot at a single bird. It was clearly hard hit and turned back as only such birds do. After a few hundred yards it collapsed and fell like a stone.

All the others had only limited shooting and the total bag was eight. It could have been more if one of the party had not persisted in firing at every skein that passed over him, whether 50 or 150 yards high — an irritating and stupid performance by one who should have known better.

After breakfast the other four set out with a packed lunch to walk the fields for snipe and any other game. They came across geese coming into a potato field, and by lying up for them collected another eight, one of which to everyone's surprise proved to be a bean goose; only the second one I have ever had the opportunity to examine and handle. Here again, the bag should have been greater but for the activities of the anti-aircraft enthusiast.

For the evening flight we went to a different stretch of the loch-side. But again the weather was too calm and the geese returned late and high. I had several lots over me, but too high to shoot. Only at the very end did a single pink slip past me close and low, and I just saw it in time to drop it with the 8-bore.

What a pleasant finish to a most interesting and varied trip. It had been fun to give the old 8-bore an airing as I had not used it for several years, but it is still surrounded by an aura of happy memories. It was good of it to get me a pinkfoot with the last shot of the trip, and I thought how appropriately it bore the family motto of some previous owner on its butt-plate — *Semper Felix*.

Between us all we only collected another three geese that evening, but the total score for the two days was — 50 greylags, 10 pinks, 1 bean goose and 10 various.

The long drive home is usually a dull sedentary anti-climax to the activity and exhilaration of our holiday, but this year the monotony was broken by two incidents, one of which threatened to land us in dire trouble, the other merely providing some light relief.

We had hardly been an hour on the homeward road when the car faltered and then came to a stop on a lonely country road miles from anywhere! It was clearly fuel trouble and as both tanks held petrol it seemed that the petrol pump must have broken down. The prospects looked grim in the extreme. Heaven knows how many miles it was to the nearest telephone — let alone garage, and in any case there was slender hope of anyone tackling repairs on the Sabbath, even if we got towed in to a garage. And if a new pump or spare part was required it might take a day or two to get it from the nearest stockist. And if we couldn't wait for the car to be repaired there was the problem of our own persons, and also the vast collection of gear packed loose in the back of the car and in the boot. So while I feverishly searched the service manual (in vain) for details of the fuel system, Keith started to unpack the boot, as I knew the pump was somewhere behind the lining of the boot.

It was while surveying the growing medley of luggage strewn along the road-side that it struck me that it all seemed to represent the modern fowler's version of the old Christmas carol —

2 whistling wigeon
3 pairs of rubber boots
4 precious shotguns
5 yards of tow rope
6 stuffed decoy geese
7 sundry packages
8 or 9 Pinkfeet
10 or 12 Greylags . . .

It seemed that all we lacked to complete the Christmas inventory was the traditional 'Partridge in a Pear Tree'.

But my gloom deepened as I contemplated all this impedimenta and the predicament we were in. The reception that would await us if we were late home for Christmas was too painful to contemplate (and it was now Dec. 22nd). Perhaps, after all, the best way out of all our afflictions would be to "do a Stonehouse". Australia was clearly beyond our resources and our ingenuity, but perhaps we could sneak away to the Orkneys and there get lost in the vast complex of the North Sea oil industry. Jobs on a drilling platform would give us the protection of isolation and immunity far out in the North Sea.

Meanwhile Keith had been fiddling around the car trying to trace petrol pipes and filters, and happened to open the filling cap on one of the tanks. There was a "woosh" of in-rushing air, and our troubles vanished like a bad dream at dawn. Somehow the vent pipes on both tanks had got bunged up, and a vacuum built up which the pump was unable to overcome.

We went on our way rejoicing — until we reached the Forth Road Bridge. I had not realised there was such a long stretch of motorway on the north side of it, nor that there was no petrol station on all the length of it. As I neared the bridge both tanks registered "nil" petrol, and I feared I might not get across. So we pulled up in the lay-by on the northern approach, where there is an office of one of the national motoring organisations. On such a site surely I should find an emergency supply of the three essential fluids — petrol, oil and water. But not a hope: the superior gentleman in the box could no doubt sell one some life assurance, a set of cutglass goblets, a floral encyclopaedia or some other irrelevant fringe service, but to help a near-stranded motorist across the Forth Bridge with a quart of petrol — that was too much to ask.

While I mused on this curious and irritating craze for diversification in the place of concentration on the main function of an organisation, a damsel drew up in front of us in a flurry, and rushed over to enquire if we would buy her last packet of cigarettes for 10p, as she was short of cash to pay the toll! I pointed out that we had our own problem, but if she carried any spare petrol, I would gladly pay her a king's ransom for a quart of the precious fluid. She in turn replied that she only had a gallon left in her own tank, but that I was welcome to extract a quart — if I could. Unfortunately a piece of tubing for sucking petrol out of other people's tanks is not part of the emergency kit I carry on my car (but it certainly will be in future — one lives and learns). But I do carry a length of tow rope. Would she tow us across? In the end we decided to leave the tow as a last resort. We would go across the bridge in convoy, myself leading, and if we stalled she would nip smartly in front, we would fix a tow, and she would pull us across the bridge, through the toll-gate and along to the nearest petrol pump. In the end all this was unnecessary: we got across under our own steam — or rather petrol. I should add that the damsel had meanwhile flogged her cigarettes to the superior gentleman in the box for 10p, so we were relieved of any financial complications. And perhaps I shouldn't be too critical of the motoring organisation: it helped one damsel in distress, though it was a dead loss to two other travellers.

And so back home on schedule, with untarnished reputations and with memories of another splendid wildfowling trip.

The first ten days had been hard work, with moderate bags, though there was that one outstanding evening flight on the Long Meadow. But the highlight of the trip consisted of the last two days in a completely new area, with that remarkable flight on Friday morning. For that experience and for the company of the man who organised our sorties I shall always associate those twelve days of Christmas with Arthur, who like myself seems to suffer from (or should I say enjoy) the same incurable symptoms of chronic Goose Fever.

CHAPTER 40
THE SPICE OF LIFE

One of the most attractive features of shooting as a recreational sport is the remarkable variety it offers in almost all aspects of the sport. In choice of game, in type of countryside, in cost, and in the final result of a day's shooting I suppose no country can offer such a wide range as Great Britain, and no other country can offer so much in such a limited over-populated area. From red deer and ptarmigan in the high tops of Scotland, through grouse on the moors to partridge and pheasant in the farmlands and woods we can find every type of game and every type of shoot, from the large heavily stocked estates to the small rough shoot of perhaps 100 acres or even less. And then beyond the limits of the land and of private rights of ownership, we find the real wild game of these islands — the wild geese, which belong to no-one, which recognise no boundaries, and which spend much of their time off the land altogether — on the mudflats and sandbanks of the various bays and estuaries round the coast. There they are — free for all — and a worthy quarry for anyone who has the luck and skill to get within range of them.

I often think that wildfowling — in pursuit of geese — has much in common with deerstalking. The man who sets out to shoot a stag may spend the whole day tramping the hills, searching and spying, and perhaps starting on one or two abortive approaches. Eventually he may find a shootable stag in a stalkable position, and if his luck and skill hold out he may bring the day to a successful climax. And so he returns to the lodge with a single trophy for the day's efforts; perhaps having fired his rifle only once in the whole day.

A wildfowler can have a very similar experience. He will be up and out before dawn to make his way out across the saltmarsh, and perhaps beyond, in the hope of meeting the morning flight. But the geese may all pass inland far out of shot to right or left. Perhaps he hangs about for an hour or two after the main flight is over, hoping to snatch a chance at some of the little parties of geese that sometimes move to and from the bay during the day. Or he may turn his back on the coast and set out on a search of the inland fields to find where the geese are feeding. A chance of an "instant" stalk or drive may present itself, but in any case he will be back at the seawall by sunset pinning the last hope of the day on a shot at evening flight, as the skeins leave the land and return to the safety of the estuary for the night. Somewhere and sometime in this long day of searching and waiting, he may have had the opportunity he was seeking, and like the deer-stalker he will return to his base with a single trophy to set the seal of success on the day's operations; and also like the deerstalker he may only have had the one occasion to use his gun.

THE SPICE OF LIFE

When we first started wildfowling, before the war, the two or three of us would be well content if we returned with one goose between us after a weekend on the Wash. Later, as we got more expert and ventured further afield, we would set our sights a little higher and would hope to come home with a goose each. And finally, when the long apprenticeship was served and we considered ourselves reasonably proficient, we adopted a sort of "par score" of one goose per gun per day. So that if three of us set out for a week's wildfowling, we would expect to return with 18 geese between us. If we got less the expedition had not been quite as successful as one had hoped — though none the less enjoyable and interesting. If we got more then we came home in high spirits and with memories of one or two outstanding encounters.

One is always thinking and dreaming of the really "big day" when everything goes right, the geese stream in from the bay or into the field where you are waiting, and you are there right in the thick of it, and of course shooting superbly! It is good to have these dreams and still better for them to come true — but only once in a while.

My dream came true one morning in December 1955; a morning which is described in the chapter on "The Laird's Flight". I shot 17 geese that morning within the space of about 3 hours, and when it was all over I realised that I never wanted to do it again. It was wonderful while it lasted, and I have no regrets, but it made me realise as nothing else could, that wildfowling is not a sport of large bags where geese are concerned. I'm sure others have found the same reaction.

There is on record the story of a party of fowlers who shot 80 pinkfeet under the moon one night. They realised it was excessive and unnecessary, and set themselves a modest limit for future occasions. And I have a friend — a keen shooting man — who was once invited to one of those massive gooseshoots that take place on certain large estates in Scotland. The day's slaughter runs well into three figures and on this occasion my friend himself killed an astronomical number of geese. He found the whole performance so distasteful that it put him off goose shooting altogether, and I believe he has never shot a goose since that day though his own estate often holds plenty of geese. Elsewhere I have mentioned the shooting of over 100 guns at morning flight on another of these large estates, and I have no doubt there are quite a number of places where this sort of shooting can happen — and does occasionally happen. But it is alien to the true spirit and enjoyment of wildfowling.

For myself, I have come to the conclusion that for any single flight — morning, evening or under the moon — half a dozen geese to one's own gun is quite a large enough bag to make the occasion a resounding success. That is about the measure of our most enjoyable outings throughout the years — something between 10 and 20 geese to our three guns. I keep this self-denying ordinance in mind on every expedition now, and have several times been restrained by it, but I do not treat it as a rigid rule that can never be relaxed. If I were to spend a week in search of geese without success, and then found myself in the thick of a wonderful flight on my last morning, I have little doubt I would allow myself a bigger limit; after all, there would be blank days to make up for and a week's score to level up!

In recent years a new factor has cropped up which ought to have a restraining effect on the shooting of large numbers of geese and that of course is the embargo on the sale of dead geese. Whatever excuse or even justification the sale of surplus geese may have given to large bags in the past, it is surely completely indefensible now for any party of guns to shoot more geese than they can consume themselves. To shoot for the mere pleasure of shooting and to discard as useless the resultant bag, is surely to deny the main foundation on which all game shooting rests; the hunting of wild birds and beasts for food.

This shooting of geese for the market certainly used to take place. I knew a man who used to claim that he shot about 400 geese a year. Living in good "goose country" and having plenty of local contacts with farmers, he could wait till a strong "feed" had developed in a certain field, and then by choosing the right morning or moonlight night, he was assured of a massive bag. On such occasions he would collect 30 to 40 geese to his own gun. At several shillings per bird this must have been a useful supplement to his income.

All this was fair enough; it was a semi-professional approach similar to that of the professional fowlers round the coasts in bygone days, and the only danger lay in too many men indulging in this form of shooting and taking too great a toll of the goose population. I hope this enthusiast still enjoys his goose shooting, but now limits himself to what he and his family and friends can consume.

Another factor which certainly exercises some effect on the size of bags is the use of decoys, and one sometimes comes across criticism of this practice. Certainly decoys can help a lot; they can produce chances of a few shots where but for their aid the geese would never pass within range of the hidden guns. They will similarly turn a small bag into a larger one, and on rare occasions they may make possible an exceptional killing — as two decoys did for me on that memorable morning in the winter of 1955. But even decoys have their limitations; there are occasions when they will have no effect at all, and certainly they do not by themselves turn wildfowling into an easy sport with assured large bags. Just how much they help it is difficult to say; one can only express an opinion based on one's own experience. Looking back over the years and recalling all the many wildgoose chases we have embarked upon, with all the variety of place and time and type of shooting that these expeditions have involved, I would say that with the help of decoys we have probably shot twice as many geese as we would have done without them.

But I can see no reason why the use of decoys should be considered unfair or unsporting. Decoys are surely a legitimate aid in persuading the quarry to come within range of the shooter, in exactly the same way as a line of beaters is used to drive partridges over a line of guns standing waiting and unseen behind a hedge. In fact, on a well managed partridge-drive every bird will have to run the gauntlet of passing within range of one or two guns, whereas when geese are flighting to their feeding grounds it is only a proportion of the skeins which will offer a chance to the hidden fowlers. Many will sheer off as they see and hear what is happening to those in front of them, and the bag of geese after a whole morning in the fields will usually be less than the pick-up after a single partridge drive.

There is another practice in wildfowling which emphasises its difference from orthodox game shooting, and that is the taking of "sitting shots". This, at first sight, might seem unsporting, but it must be realised that a sitting shot is almost always the climax to a stalk, and stalking geese on the fields, or even on the marshes, can be as difficult, as exciting, and as satisfying as stalking red deer on the hills. It is also comparable on land to the challenge of getting within range of geese on the water by means of a gunning punt. In all these cases the stalk is almost everything, the eventual shot — whether from gun or rifle — being merely the final act that brings the whole operation to its exciting conclusion. And even if the shot is bungled and the geese fly away unscathed or the stag gallops off untouched, there is still much to enjoy and to recall with pleasure in the problems and tactics of the stalk. No — anyone who can bring himself within range of feeding geese deserves his trophy and is entitled to a sitting shot with his first barrel. Even so, he will probably have had to approach to within about 50 yards to be reasonably sure of success, and this is a good deal closer than the range at which many deer are shot. And he may have had several hundred pairs of alert eyes and ears to contend with rather than those of a comparatively small group of animals.

And so, wildfowling — and particularly goose shooting — though it may seem at first sight a rather narrow and limited branch of shooting, probably provides greater variety than any other form of the sport. Apart from the traditional methods of intercepting geese on their morning and evening flights across the coastline, one can wait for them in the fields as they flight in to feed, and there are occasions — as I have described — when one can outwit them by driving or stalking. For myself, I prefer above all else those rare and special occasions when conditions happen to be just right for a sortie under the moon. There have not been many of them; a few on the Wash, one I remember on the Severn at Slimbridge (with five Whitefronts flying slap across the huge orange orb of a November full moon), a memorable one at Flanders Moss, the best one of all with Colin on Mitchell's farm by the Dark Estuary, and the last one on New Year's Day 1964 when with Colin, Keith and Chun we waited for the geese on a potato stubble just over the burn from Mongi's farm.

There is a fascination about waiting for geese under the moon which for me exceeds that of all other forms of goose shooting.

This fascination seems to be compounded of several elements. The mere fact of being out in the open countryside in the middle of a winter's night brings a special zest to such expeditions, and seems to sharpen one's senses. The rest of the human community are mostly safe and warm in their houses, and even the thin trickle of traffic along the country roads gradually dies to nothing. The whole world seems to belong to you alone — to you and the wild geese that you will soon be hearing.

THE SPICE OF LIFE

There will probably be one or two companions out with you; that adds a welcome touch of companionship — almost of conspiracy — to the loneliness of the vast expanse of flat fields and domed sky. And then there is, as always on such occasions, the sense of excitement and anticipation as the climax draws near in this battle of wits, and one hears the first distant calls of approaching geese.

At last there come those fleeting chances that your quarry offers you — a few seconds at most — when a bunch of dim shapes loom into view and into range; and only your own sharpness of sight and hearing, and your competence with a gun, will decide whether the encounter ends in success or not.

Those who have experienced such occasions must surely sense something of the fascination of these nocturnal sorties — and not only wildfowlers. Was there not a legendary character in Lincolnshire who expressed more simply the fascination and excitement which I have been trying to describe when he joyfully proclaimed:

"— 'tis my delight on a shiny night in the season of the year"

EPILOGUE

Myself when young did eagerly frequent
Solway and Wash and heard great Argument
About Pinkfooted Geese: but evermore
Came Home as empty-handed as I went.

Think, in this scattered Caravanserai
Of Fowl who flight at Dawn and Dusk each Day,
How Fowler after Fowler full of Hope
Waited an Hour or two, then went away.

I sometimes think that never glows so red
The Dawn as when the Geese flight overhead;
That every Shot the eager Fowler fires
Spreads o'er the Marsh an ounce or two of Lead.

Here with a Crust of Bread beside the Pow,
A Flask of Scotch, a Cigarette — and Thou
Beside me waiting for the Morning Flight —
And Morning Flight is Paradise enow.

Behold this Bush of Gorse whose sombre Green
Fledges the River's Bank on which we lean —
Come, crouch behind it quietly! for who knows
By what approaching Skein we might be seen!

Ah, Moon of my Delight that's on the wane
With fleecy Clouds to frame each flighting Skein;
How oft hereafter shall I have to wait
For such a perfect Night as this — in vain!

The Flight of Flights men set their Hearts upon
So seldom comes, but when it does — anon,
Like Snow upon the Saltings' muddy Face,
It lasts a little Hour and then is gone.

One Morning Flight upon some coastal Waste,
One Moment of the Spice of Life to taste —
The Stars are setting, and the restless Geese
Start for their distant Pastures — Oh, make haste!

Wild Geese that can with Magic absolute
Both Young and Old inflame with their Pursuit:
Those subtle Alchemists that in a Trice
Life's leaden Metal into Gold transmute.